BY
EASTERN
WINDOWS

BY EASTERN WINDOWS

THE STORY OF A BATTLE OF SOULS AND MINDS IN THE PRISON CAMPS OF SUMATRA

BY

WILLIAM H. McDOUGALL, Jr.

NEW YORK

CHARLES SCRIBNER'S SONS

1949

TO MY SISTER
JEAN

CONTENTS

BY

EASTERN

WINDOWS

Locale of Author's Prison Years in Indonesia

Palembang Jail — April 5, 1942–January 1943
Barracks Camp (in city of Palembang) January 1943–September 1943
Muntok Prison — September 1943–March 1945
Belalau — March 1945–September 19, 1945

1

The Other Side of the Door

OLD Brinker rolled his head on the slab-like concrete platform where he lay dying in Muntok Prison hospital Christmas Eve, 1944, and asked, "When does the music begin?"

"Pretty soon now," I said, stepping from the floor up onto the platform beside him. "The choir is being counted through the gate."

"Good," said old Brinker, cracking his last joke, "then I'll be able to compare them with the angels."

His face was a grey blur in the feeble light which barely reached this corner of the room from the distant kerosene lamp.

"Afraid the angels won't sing as well," I said, "because they won't have Father Bakker to lead them."

Despite his exhaustion and the pain it cost him, Brinker chuckled. Father Bakker, a soft-voiced little Hollander with a Vandyke beard, was the choir director.

When Japan had invaded the Netherlands East Indies in February, 1942, Father Bakker had been pastor of the Catholic church in the harbor town of Muntok on Bangka Island, some 250 miles south of Singapore—just below the equator and off the east coast of Sumatra. Muntok Prison was an old pile of stone and iron built by the Dutch in a previous century to house life-term native prisoners and, after many years, abandoned and converted to a warehouse for Bangka's foremost crop, white pepper. The Japanese had reconverted the prison to its original use and interned there hundreds of Allied nationals including Father Bakker; Brinker, a rubber plantation inspector, and me, an American war correspondent who now worked in the prison hospital. Death rapidly was thinning our population.

The dying Brinker, whose mother tongue was Dutch and for whom English was difficult, gathered his strength to speak again.

"Ask Father Bakker to come and see me . . . afterwards."

I evaded a direct answer. Father Bakker wouldn't be leading the choir tonight. He was ill himself, lying in his cell shivering with malaria.

"I'll ask him to dedicate a song to you," I said, feeling Brinker's pulse. "Got any special request?"

"Silent Night."

"Okay," I said, stepping down off the bench, "I'll tell him."

The dysentery ward where Brinker lay, like the other six wards in Muntok Prison hospital, was a long, narrow room. Two cement platforms, or benches as we called them, eight feet wide and sloping from head to foot, ran its entire length on either side of a central aisle. Men lay shoulder to shoulder, fifteen and sixteen to a bench, their feet toward the aisle. Patients tended to slip downward because of the slope. Attendants were busy readjusting sick men on the benches and answering pleas for bedpans.

I walked outside to catch a breath of fresh air and to watch the choir. Eleven emaciated singers, tottering remnants of a once splendid twenty-six voice a capella chorus, had just filed through the gate which barred the hospital from the main prison. A Japanese guard had counted them through. Now he waited, bayoneted rifle at rest, in the shadows of the tropic night.

The singers stood in a semi-circle of light halfway along the covered cement walk onto which all the wards opened.

At the rear of the middle ward a Dutchman and an Englishman stood on a platform erected on one of the benches so that their heads would be higher than the tops of the partitions separating the wards and their voices thus could carry through the entire hospital. A wire mesh extended from the top of each partition to the ceiling. They were to read, in their respective languages and a verse at a time, the gospel story of the birth of Christ. Three years before, Father Bakker had set St. Luke's words to music of his own composition and his choir had sung it each Christmas Eve since. The same two announcers also had done the reading: Beissel von Gymnich, who once had been our chief cook; and huge-barrelled, black-bearded W. Probyn Allen, of the ringing voice and Gargantuan laughter, who once had helped me edit the prison "newspaper."

The substitute choir director sounded key of C on his pitch-pipe and pointed his baton. Singers hummed their respective notes. The humming grew in volume, reflecting off walls which acted as sounding boards and lent their singing the deep, sustained quality of organ tones. The buzzing of voices in the hospital ceased. Beissel's voice, then Allen's, rang through the wards.

And it came to pass that in those days there went out a decree from Caesar Augustus, that the whole world should be enrolled. This enrolling was first made by Cyrinus, the governor of Syria. And all went to be enrolled, every one into his own city.

Allen stopped speaking, the director's baton pointed upward, swept down and the sacred cantata began.

The delirious mutterings of a malaria patient sounded from a bench nearby. This was the fever ward. From the next ward came bubbly groans of beri-beri victims whose lungs were filling with serum as they literally drowned in their own juice. Beri-beri is a malnutritional disease that takes one of two courses, depending on what complications accompany it. The victim either swells with liquid or shrivels to skin and bones. From the dysentery ward came sounds of bedpans banging on concrete, reminding us that dysentery patients, although they were trying to be quiet, could not wait.

The story continued, Beissel speaking first, then Allen.

And Joseph also went up from Galilee, out of the city of Nazareth into Judea, to the city of David, which is called Bethlehem: because he was of the house and family of David, to be enrolled with Mary his espoused wife, who was with child.

Allen stopped speaking and the choir took up the words. I knew Father Bakker could hear them where he lay in a cell across the yard in the opposite wing of the building which held the hospital. After he was interned Father Bakker had organized the choir from among his fellow prisoners, transforming their heterogeneous and mediocre voices into one superb instrument of song. Many pieces, like the Christmas cantata, were his own compositions. Everything the choir sang was his own arrangement. It had to be because when he was thrust into jail he went with only the clothing he wore. His beloved music was left behind. He wrote his music on whatever scraps of paper he could find and composed without instruments in the babel of a place so crowded that men lived and died, elbow to elbow, cheek to jowl. Father Bakker's mind was instrument enough.

And it came to pass, that when they were there, her days were accomplished, that she should be delivered. And she brought forth her first-born son, and wrapped him up in swaddling clothes, and laid him in a manger; because there was no room for them in the inn.

Directly at Allen's feet lay a dying man who had been a police official in Sumatra before the war. I first met Officer

Francken in a hill station of western Sumatra, April 2, 1942, the night after I was captured for the second time.

With other shipwreck survivors cast up from the Indian Ocean I had been added to a cortege of Dutch civilian residents of southwestern Sumatra who were being rounded up for internment on the other side of the island. Glumly we were trying to find space on the floor to sleep when Francken was added to our numbers. He was loaded down with luggage which had not yet been searched. As soon as the guard left the room Francken opened his luggage, laughed and pulled out a bottle, and another bottle, and another.

"Drink up," he shouted. "Drink up! Tonight we must laugh because it may be a long time until we can laugh again."

Later he asked me,

"Mr. American,"—I was the only American in a crowd of Hollanders—"you are a correspondent?"

"That's right. United Press."

"Someday you will write a story about this?"

"Perhaps."

"If you do, write that Francken gave you your last drink of cognac on your last night outside of jail."

He handed me a bottle containing just enough for a final drink. I held it aloft in salute, then drained it and returned the empty bottle, saying,

"Okay, pal, you will be immortalized in print." *

And there were in the same country shepherds watching, and keeping the night-watches over their flock. And behold an angel of the Lord stood by them, and the brightness of God shone round about them, and they feared with a great fear.

---

* Francken is not his real name, nor is Brinker the real name of the other dying man. Because of their families I have used fictitious names for certain men whose stories appear here. Wherever a pseudonym is used it will be indicated. My fellow prisoners who read this book will easily recognize the men described.

I thought of the fears that plagued these men around me as they lay, many knowing that this was their last Christmas. What do men think of when they are about to die? I knew what I thought when I myself was about to die because I had waited one whole afternoon—conscious and with a clear mind—for certain death, only to be saved by my own private miracle. And I had nursed and watched die of starvation and disease more than two hundred men in this chamber of horrors for prisoners of war.

I came to believe that, although every individual has thoughts peculiar to his own conscience, there are certain basic thoughts shared by most men when they, irrevocably, face their Great Common Denominator, Death: What and Who await them on the Other Side of the Door?

Take old Brinker, who wasn't really old in years, only 55, but was physically old with the premature age of a lifetime in the tropics.

As a youth fresh out of school he had come from Holland to the Indies in search of fortune. Now he was lying there totaling up the score, balancing the *is* with the *might have been*. During his early years there had been lonely periods of exile in jungle outposts; and later, easier, more convivial years in the restricted white colonial society of little Sumatra towns that were trading centers and clearing houses for rubber or tea or coffee or tobacco. Hard work there had been on plantations, yes, but work wherein he moved on a higher plane than the brown-skinned natives around him. And, at the club in town, there was companionship and harmonizing over schnapps and beer. He had been so busy with the day-by-day things of life that he had lost track of time until suddenly thirty-five years had gone down the calendar and it was time for retirement. But a prison camp had interrupted his pension plans and accelerated his physical decline.

First had come fever. Malaria was not new to an old jungle hand like Brinker but malaria without quinine was.

Meanwhile, hunger sapped his vitals. His protein-and-vitamin-starved body broke out with blisters, then sores which deepened into ulcers on his hands, arms, feet and legs. So he progressed from the fever ward to the septic ward, and was grateful that he had been able to skip the beri-beri ward. However, when a few weeks ago he had been carried into the dysentery ward, he knew instinctively it was the end and he began to think about God.

Brinker was a Catholic but it had been so easy to forget God during the pleasantly busy years away from Holland in the outposts of Sumatra. Sunday was the one morning of the week he could rise late, dawdle over breakfast and coffee and read the accumulated newspapers from Batavia. And when he did go to Mass the priest's sermon too often included something which uncomfortably reminded Brinker of sin. He didn't want to be reminded of sin. Damn such reminders. So he stayed away. Life was too short not to have a little fun.

How short they had been . . . the years . . . and the fun shorter still. Here in prison he couldn't sleep sometimes, for thinking about the fun and the wasted Sunday mornings piled up on the red ink side of his bank account with God. He sent for Father Bakker and told him,

"I've been away thirty years."

Then to Father Bakker he whispered his confession.

Every morning after that a priest brought communion to Brinker in the dysentery ward. And, when I made my rounds of the wards, changing bandages and swabbing sores, and stopped at Brinker's place, he had a smile for me instead of a sour look. That was quite a transformation for a man who had been one of my grouchiest patients. He could smile because his heart was calm. He was at peace inside. He figured that Father Bakker had turned for him the key to the kingdom of heaven.

The music stopped again and Allen's voice carried to the dysentery ward.

And the angel said to them: Fear not; for, behold, I bring you good tidings of great joy, that shall be to all the people; for, this day is born to you a Saviour, who is Christ the Lord, in the city of David.

The hospital was singularly quiet now. Patients able to sit up might have been statues sculptured with bent heads as their minds projected them away from the prison, across the seas to home. Next after death, fears concerning their families dogged men most. For nearly three years their names had been on the lists of missing. Had they long ago been given up for dead? More than anything else, except food, men wanted their families to know they were alive.

I felt sure, as the music filled my heart, that somehow my family must know I was alive. That prisoner of war postcard the Japanese had allowed each man to send two years ago must have gotten home.

Please, God, let them know I'm alive.

Again the music ceased and Allen's voice narrated the angel's words to the shepherds near Bethlehem:

And this shall be a sign unto you: You shall find the infant wrapped in swaddling clothes, and laid in a manger. And suddenly there was with the angel a multitude of the heavenly army, praising God, and saying: Glory to God in the highest; and on earth peace to men of good will.

Choral voices swelled. Climactic Hosannas rolled through the wards and resounded off concrete walls, then died. I told the director of old Brinker's request for Silent Night. The choir sang it, alternating the verses in English and Dutch.

Silent Night, Holy Night,
All is calm, all is bright
Round yon Virgin, Mother and Child,
Holy Infant so tender and mild,
Sleep in heavenly peace, sleep in heavenly peace.

That ended the concert. Singers were marched back to the main prison. Gates were slammed and locked. I started for my own bunk in the hospital staff quarters.

An attendant stopped me, saying,

"Brinker wants a priest."

At first I thought Brinker merely was requesting Father Bakker to visit him but the attendant said no, any priest.

"He says he's nearly finished."

Walking across the court to one of the cells in the wing opposite the hospital I called a priest, Father Van Thiel, and accompanied him back to the dysentery ward. We stepped up on the bench and squatted on either side of the dying man. I held the kerosene lamp so Father Van Thiel could see. Yesterday old Brinker had declined to receive the last sacraments of his church, explaining, with a gesture indicating his fellow patients:

"They'll all say old Brinker is dying and I don't want that."

Now it did not matter what they said because it was the end. Father Van Thiel unscrewed the cap of a small silver vial containing blessed olive oil and smeared a tiny amount on his right thumb. He told Brinker to close his eyes while he anointed the lids and said a prayer in Latin that translates, "Through this holy unction and His most tender mercy, may the Lord pardon thee whatsoever faults thou hast committed by sight." Then, repeating the same prayer but changing the last word to suit the senses of hearing, smell, taste and touch the priest rubbed oil, in a brief sign of the cross, on Brinker's ears, nostrils, lips and the palms of his hands.

When the last prayer of the rite, known as Extreme Unction, had been said Father Van Thiel thanked me for holding the lamp. As I stepped down from the bench and replaced the lamp in its customary wall holder I could hear him whispering prayers, in Dutch, to Brinker.

Straightening my aching back I took a deep breath. Immediately I wished I had not. Every cubic inch of the ward's foul air seemed to rush into my lungs—the odors of dysentery, the sickly sweet smell of beri-beri, the heavy stench of necrotic flesh on ulcerated limbs. If we who were used to it sometimes are nauseated, I thought, to a stranger the smell would be appalling. I hurried outside to breathe clean air, look up at the stars and pick out the Southern Cross. I could not see it and figured it must be too far down in the western heavens. So I tried to pick out Argo, the old sailing ship. I found the stars that are Vela, the sails; but I could not discern those that are the keel and hull. Either they, too, were below my horizon or Argo was too complicated for my simple astronomy. Sometimes I could find them and other times I could not.

The scrape and clatter of wooden sandals—our prison footgear—along the covered walk aroused me from my star-gazing reverie and signaled that a new shift of ward attendants was going on duty, replacing those whose turn ended at midnight.

I walked into the staff room, identical in construction with the wards. Each of us had a space twenty-seven inches wide on the long, concrete platforms. Some of us had built wooden frames in order to sleep level. Others, preferring the natural slope even though they did slide downward, spread their straw mats on the slabs. Mosquito nets were grey blurs in the darkness. I started to crawl into mine when a whisper from across the aisle halted me.

"Mac."

Eric Germann, the only other American prisoner and my partner and fellow worker, was calling. I stepped over to his bunk and sat on the edge of the bench.

"Hold out your hand," he said.

We fumbled for each other's hands. In mine he placed a "tailor made" cigaret. Months before there had been a Red Cross issue—the first and last—of American cigarets. He had saved one for this occasion.

"Merry Christmas," Eric said.

We shook hands. I started up, to go after a light at the dysentery ward lamp, when an idea struck me.

"We'll really celebrate," I said. "We'll use a match."

One of my most precious possessions was a box of matches preserved, in a water proof tin, for emergency use. Opening the tin I struck a match for the first time in nearly three years. Its flare was blindingly welcome. Ceremoniously I lit the cigaret Eric had rolled for himself of nipa palm leaf wrapped around raw, native tobacco, then lit my own. We smoked in silence.

I thought of another Christmas, the one that had started the series of adventures which landed me in Muntok Prison. On Christmas night, 1941, Pepper Martin and I put a Japanese floor guard to bed and a few hours later escaped from Shanghai. Pepper was United Press bureau manager and I was his assistant. With all other enemy nationals of Japan we became prisoners in China's busiest city when the Japanese took over, the day of Pearl Harbor.

To begin at the beginning: I resigned my newspaper job in Salt Lake City in 1939 and headed for the Orient where I figured there was going to be a war I might cover as a correspondent. My first stop was for ten months in Tokyo and a job on an English language daily newspaper. Next came Shanghai, where I landed in October, 1940, to join United Press. When war appeared imminent Pepper and I and Francis Lee, a former United Press man, began casting around for means of escape should the Japanese occupy Shanghai. Chinese guerrillas agreed to send a man into the city for us.

During the first week of Shanghai's occupation the Japanese military police, called *Kempeitai*, did not arrest newspaper correspondents. Like other American, British or Dutch nationals, we moved around at will inside the barricaded International Settlement. During the second week a few correspondents disappeared. All would be arrested eventually. We were getting jittery lest our turn should come before the guerrilla guide arrived. Our jitters increased when a Japanese civilian guard was placed on our hotel floor to check on movements of Americans. Although he was an old friend and did little checking we knew our time was coming. Christmas night Pepper and I took the guard to dinner, filled him with Tom-and-Jerries, brought him back to his hotel post at midnight, saw him to bed and retired to our own room. The guide arrived a few hours later.

That was splendid except for one hitch. We were broke and couldn't get the money we needed for the journey until daylight. There was one man who might have a large sum at four o'clock in the morning and be friend enough to lend it to us. We rode by ricksha to a church, awakened the priest and borrowed part of his Christmas collection.

The guide told us we would have to pass the first set of barricades on our own and meet him at a village outside the city. Our plan involved play-acting three drunken Germans staggering home from an all night party. Germans, being Japanese allies, had passes permitting them to cross the first barricades if they lived in suburbs outside the Settlement proper. We weaved up to a sentry box and went through a long, futile search of our pockets for the necessary identity cards. The bluff worked. Grinning, the guards waved us on.

Our guerrilla guide was waiting in the village. The Shanghai barricade was only a minor hurdle in our journey to freedom. From the village where we met the guide to Free China was several hundred miles of Japanese-occupied territory and two strongly guarded "lines." We were inside an iron triangle, formed by three railroads, of which Shanghai was the apex. We had to cross the base. The railroads were solidly barricaded their entire length and patrolled by soldiers and dogs. Beyond the triangle's base was a well-held highway between Hangchow and Nanking. Behind us, we knew, a search would begin as soon as we were missed.

We traveled westward in freezing weather, by foot and sampan, until ten days after Christmas when, to the tune of gunfire and barking dogs, we crossed the highway and stumbled, dirty, hungry, and vermin-ridden, into Free China. Another twenty-four days travel brought us to Chungking and our next assignments from United Press. Mine was to fly immediately to Java and cover the battle for the Netherlands East Indies.

The battle was brief. As Java fell I fled in a ship which was sunk in the Indian Ocean. I reached Sumatra, the nearest land, after a long swim and six days in a lifeboat. Three weeks of hiking barefoot along Sumatra's jungle-fringed west coast brought me to a little harbor town where I had planned to obtain a native sailboat and, with some companions, escape and sail across the Indian Ocean to Ceylon.

But the Japanese got me again, transported me across Sumatra to the oil port of Palembang, and put me in Palembang Jail the night of Easter Sunday, April 5, 1942.

As I walked through the jail gates I glanced up, half expecting to see something written above them. There was an inscription in Dutch I could not read and a date, A.D. 1883. An alarm kept ringing in my brain, "I'm a prisoner! I'm a prisoner!"

I did not conceal my identity, hoping that news of my recapture would reach Tokyo and that I might be returned to Shanghai, or at least the Asiatic mainland, either for punishment or—wild expectation—repatriation when American correspondents and diplomatic officials would be exchanged for their Japanese counterparts. Once on the Asiatic mainland I hoped I could escape * again because I knew the ropes. Naturally, I said nothing in Palembang

* The full story of my Shanghai escape, sinking and recapture is told in *Six Bells Off Java*, Charles Scribner's Sons, New York, 1948.

Jail about the Shanghai escape, merely gave my correct name and occupation, believing that the Japanese Foreign Office eventually would be informed of the capture of a correspondent. (How wrong I was!)

After interrogation and registration on prison rolls, I was added to the tangle of men trying to sleep amid a welter of junk in a peculiarly smelly room. Without space on the concrete floor to lie down, I sat in the doorway and dozed off while dreaming of escaping again.

Now it was Christmas, 1944. All the dreams and plans of escape that had helped sustain my spirits through two years and nine months of imprisonment had every one been foiled. But I still schemed. Men without hope die.

The cigaret Eric had given me for a Christmas present long since had been consumed as I sat on the bench in the dark staff room. Eric had lain down. By his silence I judged him either asleep or also reminiscing. Stiffly I rose from the bench, fumbled at my bunk until I found my tobacco and started for the dysentery ward and the lamp. I couldn't afford another match. The attendant on duty was standing in the ward entrance.

"How's Brinker?" I asked.

"I think he's dead. I was just going to call someone to check."

I stepped up on the bench and felt Brinker's pulse. No pulse. The attendant handed me the lamp and I looked into Brinker's half-open eyes. Sightless. I touched the lids. Not a flutter. Listened for his heart. Not a beat. Squeezed hard with my fingers on the flesh of his upper arm. My fingerprints remained. Held a small hand mirror to his open mouth. Not a breath fogged it.

"He's dead all right," I said, and stepped down to the floor. "Better call the doctor."

Sleepy-eyed, the doctor came, listened with his stethoscope and told us we could carry Brinker out. We lifted the body onto a stretcher, carried it into the bamboo shed which served as a mortuary and put it into one of four plank coffins. One coffin already held the body of a man who had died just before the concert. The other two would soon be occupied, perhaps before the day was out. Officer Francken and two others were very low.

Back in the staff room, lying on my bunk, I filled the time until sleep came by mentally constructing the framework of a book that would tell the story of this prison life.

Today would be an appropriate place to begin, I thought, because it would be a kind of key to this other world far behind enemy lines, in a tropic backwash of war where men long believed dead were fighting a battle of souls and minds instead of bullets and bombs.

But, before narrating how they won or lost in their struggles with their greatest adversaries—themselves—it would be necessary to explain how they got here and what they did. This would require switching back to the first morning of imprisonment when I awakened after dozing off in the cell doorway, dreaming of escape.

And so I have . . .

2
Roll Call

DAWN stirred the trees which made a dark horizon beyond Palembang Jail. The desultory voices of awakening birds sounded an ornithological overture to the day—my first day of internment, April 6, 1942. Soon the sun peered over the east wall. Men emerged grumpily from their cells to stand in its early rays, hoping to melt from their flesh the imprint and from their joints the stiffness of hours on damp cement bunks and concrete floors.

Night had washed the sky nearly clean of clouds, giving the sun full scope to kindle the day with brilliance. The impact of light, glaring off cell block roofs, walls and pavement walks threw every detail of the jail into sharp, painful relief. What had been concealed by darkness last night when I entered stood out this morning in harsh reality.

Peaked tile roofs of buildings inside the prison were higher than the surrounding wall, so that its somber grey stretch was visible only in sections between the cell blocks. The wall looked about fifteen feet high and was surmounted by another six feet or so of barbed wire curving inward at the top like the fences around animal pits at the zoo. I was standing inside still another barbed wire fence, perhaps twelve feet high, which divided the hollow square of jail yard from cell blocks around it on three sides. The fourth side housed guardrooms, storerooms and the double iron gates to the outside world.

The cell where I had spent the night was one half of a two-compartmented building set in a corner of the main wall. Also, it stood apart from the long cell blocks on my side of the yard and was isolated from the nearest one by yet another private fence of its own. Between the building and the wall was an open-air bath tank where two men, their skin glistening wetly in the sun, were washing. Standing outside the tank they dipped water with small hand buckets and splashed it over themselves. I stripped and joined them. The first bucketful was a cold shock; the second pleasantly cool; and the third a delight. We dried ourselves as swimmers do when they climb from a pool, skinning water from our flesh with the palms of our hands and letting the sun do the rest.

Donning my scanty clothing—a pair of shorts and a shirt —I stood with other men looking through the fence into the yard where a square of grass made an oasis in this desert of barbed wire, stone and iron. A shaggy hedge grew along the narrow section of fence directly in front of our building. I wondered aloud who had planted it and tended it during the years it must have struggled to survive in such inhospitable surroundings.

"Women," said a scrawny, sarong-clad individual who had just emerged from the other half of the two-room building.

"That's exactly what I said," he continued in reply to my look of incredulity. "Native women planted it. Female prisoners."

My informant introduced himself as an English merchant seaman and a veteran of Palembang Jail, having been there a week. He said he had been told this isolated cell block used to serve the dual purpose of jail clinic and women's quarters. Female prisoners lived in the cell from which he had just come. The place where I had spent the night was the clinic. That explained a peculiar odor I had been wondering about.

The hedge was high enough to have screened small statured Malay women from the gaze of men in the yard. A tiny patch of grass sheltered in its shadow. I stepped onto it, savoring its tensile crispness between my toes. Directly across the yard was the highest building inside the walls. Smoke rose from behind its steeply pitched roof and through its doors could be seen flames in open hearths. The kitchen.

The sailor touched me on the shoulder, cleared his throat apologetically and in a half whisper, perhaps so other men standing around wouldn't hear, asked,

"I say, mate, have you any tobacco?"

"A little."

"In that room are some sick men who haven't smoked for days."

I followed him into the room from which he had come. Its interior was nearly filled by a knee-high cement platform, the width of the room and seven or eight feet deep, ending against the back wall. Six men lay shoulder to shoulder on it, their feet toward the door. Two other men lay on straw mats in the narrow floor space between the platform, or bench, and the front wall. The former women's quarters now had been converted into the jail hospital. The sailor proudly announced his good news.

"Here's a gentleman will share his tobacco."

A chorus of appreciation filled the room. Three patients sat up immediately. One of them, a huge-barrelled fat man with a beard which recalled pictures of King Henry VIII, smiled and said,

"Luckily for you, not all of us smoke."

A thin man with a doleful face and a "let-me-tell-you-about-my-operation" voice asked if by any chance I had some milk.

"My ulcer must have milk," he whined, "or my days are really numbered."

"Sorry," I told him. "Tojo confiscated my cow."

"Well, then, I will appreciate a bit of your tobacco."

While distributing what remained of my tobacco and rolling a cigaret for myself I asked how it happened that all the patients were Englishmen. They said they were from ships sunk or captured off Sumatra's east coast while fleeing Singapore. The fat man, who looked to be in his early thirties and must have weighed 240 pounds, introduced himself as W. Probyn Allen, Far Eastern representative of an English drug firm.

"I don't smoke," he said, declining tobacco, "but you may bring me a drink of water if you will."

I fetched my water bottle from next door.

The sailor went outside to get a light, returned and lighted our cigarets. The first inhalation of smoke went down my throat like a rasp, searched out the empty crevices of my stomach where food should have been and dispersed comfortingly until it seemed to touch and bless every sensate fiber of my being. Thoughts of no more tobacco disturbed me, so I took only a few drags then sniped the cigaret for a final smoke after breakfast.

At that moment a sudden clanging burst on my ears. Sound waves filled the jail with metallic racket, richocheting from wall to wall, bouncing off iron doors, battling with the sun's glare for violent attention. When my neck unshrank, my shoulders sank back to normal posture and my eyes opened, I stepped to the doorway and looked toward the front gate whence the clamor came. A Japanese soldier was rattling a metal bar around the inside of an iron triangle of the type familiar to American ranchers who for generations have been summoned to meals by similar dinner bells. But, though the instruments were similar, the effects differed. When the dinner bell rings outside an American ranch kitchen, the results are music in the mountain air because trees and open country soften the strident notes. In Palembang Jail every blow on the triangle hurled percussion waves onto hostile surfaces which magnified the sound's intensity. When the last ear-shattering note splintered into silence, my jumbled thoughts assorted themselves and asked why such clamor to announce breakfast. I learned it was not breakfast but the signal summoning prisoners to morning roll call.

Men stood in double lines on the walks outside their respective cell blocks. The sergeant guard commander, flanked by two tin-helmeted soldiers carrying bayoneted rifles at ready and followed by a fat, sad-faced Dutch interpreter, took the roll call. Counting began at the kitchen across the yard and proceeded counterclockwise around the jail toward the hospital which thus would be the last to be counted. Roll call followed a fixed ritual. As guards arrived in front of each cell block, prisoners bowed to them and the soldiers saluted in return. A leader for each block reported the number in his lines. Guards then verified the report by counting, after which captives again bowed and captors saluted.

As we stood silently waiting our turn I studied the men within vision. About half wore only shorts. Some were barefooted, others shod. Their skins varied in hue from the deep coffee of the darkest Indo-Europeans up through many shades to the flat whiteness of sedentary business men whose chests had not felt an unobstructed sunbeam since they were children. Between those extremes were dark browns, light browns, yellow browns; tans from saddle to atabrine; whites from the healthy glow of youth to the tired, large-pored flaccidness of age. Since all were newcomers and thus only recently had taken to living shirtless, there were many assorted stages of sunburn, ranging from the delicate pink of a first blush to painful crimson. Nearly all necks and wrists had well defined rings marking collar and cuff lines. Physically the men ranged from thin to very fat; from short to tall; from runty, round-shouldered, pot-bellied torsos to the strong, virile proportions of a men's underwear ad.

One physical characteristic predominated. They were well nourished. Even the thin ones were thin in a natural

way. Until interned, the thin ones had missed no more
meals than the fattest man in line. I wondered how long
they would continue to be well nourished. My misgivings
concerning the future were deep and black. I thought it was
going to be a long war and that many prisoners captured in
the early stages would not be living at the end. For this was
tropical Sumatra where fever and disease would thrive
unless checked by constant medical care and proper nourishment. There was little likelihood of either in a Japanese
prison.

Rainswept Sumatra straddles the equator and with other
islands of the Malay archipelago divides the Indian Ocean
from the South China and Java seas. A jungle-clad mountain chain sprawls along its thousand-mile west coast, on
the southern tip of which my lifeboat landed; while the
east coast is a vast, steaming plain of swamps and turgid
water courses. Palembang lies at the inner edge of the
swamps and fifty-four miles up the crocodile-infested Moesi
river. Two great refineries of Shell and Standard Oil are
near the city's outskirts, at the termini of pipe lines from
interior oil fields. Palembang also is a trading center through
which move tobacco, tea, coffee, rubber, coal, palm oil and
other bounties of nature that make Sumatra rich.

Palembang was a city centuries before the Dutch arrived.
Historians have pushed back the curtain of its antiquity
to the Sriwidjayan Empire that flourished for nearly a thousand years until it was conquered in the fourteenth century
A.D. by the Hindu Madjapahit Empire of Java. But the Mad-
japahits crumbled and most of Java and Sumatra was converted to the religion of Mohammed. The Dutch arrived in
the seventeenth century, obtained a concession in Palembang and converted it to colonial capitalism. In the last
quarter of the nineteenth century the Dutch built high-
walled Palembang Jail to hold native malefactors. The Japanese arrived in February, 1942, and in March they removed

the native prisoners and replaced them with Dutch and British.

Another notation was added to Palembang's long history when the jail received its first American prisoner, me. Now I was being counted in my first roll call line.

From that morning of April 6, 1942, when a crowd of well fleshed men answered its first summons, to an August afternoon in 1945 when a group of shambling skeletons obeyed its last command, the roll call bell dominated my existence. It rang in the dawn of morning, at high noon and in the dark of night. It summoned men to stand in line for water, for food, for tobacco; for announcements, for meetings and for funerals . . . especially for funerals.

The bell rang so frequently for so many different purposes in the various jails and camps where I lived until freedom came, that a bell code was necessary . . . a certain number of rings for this, another number for that. First there would be an admonitory rattling as the metal ringer was twirled around the triangle . . . clangety-clang-clang-clang. Clangety-clang-clang-clang. A pause. Then the measured strokes—one, two, three; or one, two, three, four; or one, two, three, four, five, six; or maybe only one.

Quickly we came to anticipate, even to pray for, the routine calls—to collect food, to line up for boiled water, or tea, or a handful of peanuts, or a teaspoon of palm oil. Sometimes there were phenomenal, red letter, hallelujah days when we lined up for 100 grams (3½ ounces) of sugar and 25 grams (less than an ounce) of salt per man. Such were the rings which regulated our lives down to the last detail. The unexpected rings were the ones which threw chills into us—the roll calls which rang in the night, summoning us from sleep to stand in the damp air during the long, exacting process of counting to determine who was missing, who had gotten out in a desperate smuggling endeavor to find food and get back in again undetected. I was one of those who engaged in food-smuggling, but I managed always to get back in before roll call. Some did not.

Sometimes the bell chattered angrily to announce an infraction of prison rules and sometimes it tolled slowly, signaling the grave gang to carry away another body.

Roll calls had a sequence in avoirdupois and number as well as time, while the once well nourished men slowly changed from overweight to underweight, from underweight to emaciation, from emaciation to skin over bones, eyes in skulls, caricatures, corpses.

Cell block by cell block the guards counted their way until they came finally to the line in which I stood. The interpreter relayed the sergeant's command.

"Attention."

We came to attention.

"Bow."

We bowed. The guards saluted.

"How many?" asked the interpreter.

"Twenty-three," said a man on the end of the line. "Eight inside and fifteen outside."

The sergeant counted us outside then walked to the barred window of the hospital cell and peered at the eight men lying inside. Then he counted us again, calling the numbers aloud in Japanese and stabbing his finger at us with each count:

"*Ichi, ni, san, shi, go . . .*"

Then the interpreter spoke again.

"Attention."

The command was superfluous because we had been at attention all the time, but he had to say something. Obligingly we straightened our shoulders even more and the interpreter said:

"Bow."

We bowed again. Guards saluted, about-faced and

marched to the front gate. One of them picked up the bell ringer and struck the triangle, then whirled the ringer around in a long, jangling rattle that bounced off walls and iron doors, violated my ear drums, convulsed hands into fists, propelled a shiver up to my scalp and prickled there until the ringing stopped.

My first roll call was over.

3

Ode to Phoebus

I TURNED hopeful eyes toward the kitchen when roll call ended. Breakfast should be soon. Instead, however, there was a reshuffling of men to make room for more prisoners. My companions were removed from the room in which I had spent the night, leaving me alone with two chairs and a table covered with dusty, gummy bottles and tins of ointment—remains of the pre-war clinic. Claiming they had established prior rights, my erstwhile roommates took with them most of the junk which had littered the place. One thing they left, however, was a piece of jute sacking about ten feet long and half as wide. It would serve as a mattress until something better came along. I laid it out in the sun while I explored the area surrounding the bath tank. In a heap of rubbish I found a chipped, blue enamel dish with a small hole in the bottom, a handleless spoon and a half of a coconut shell someone had started to polish, then discarded when a triangular section broke off the edge. Poor as they were I now had eating utensils. The next thing was something to eat.

Gates in the barbed wire fence were opened after roll call and men circulated at will inside the jail. I crossed the yard to the kitchen. It looked more like a foundry. Instead of stoves or ovens there was a row of round, open hearths on top of which sat huge, iron kettles or smoke-blackened containers which were large oil drums with the tops cut off.

Long metal tongs and pokers and axes and saws hung on the walls. Smoke rose to the ceiling and theoretically escaped through wide roof vents. The volunteer kitchen workers were nearly as smoke-blackened as the pots over which they labored.

Tops of the steaming cauldrons were too high to look into, so I asked one of the cooks what was boiling.

"Water," he said.

"For coffee?"

"We haven't seen coffee since we came here."

"Then why boil so much water?"

"Tea. We're having tea for breakfast."

"And what else?"

"Nothing."

"Nothing?"

"Absolutely nothing else. Rice and vegetables haven't arrived yet. Only the Japs know when they will and I doubt if they really know."

I left the kitchen, thinking how comforting it would be if, at times like this, we had cuds to chew on between meals.

A group of white-robed men sitting on a wooden bench in front of a cell block attracted my attention. Walking over I introduced myself to the first man on the bench and met the Catholic Bishop of Palembang.

"Pleased to know you," he said. "Have you any tobacco?"

"Not a shred," I replied, thinking 'this fellow is surely a fast operator.'

"Good," smiled Bishop H. M. Mekkelholt, "then I can make you a present."

Fishing in his cassock he brought out the remains of a *lempeng,* the Malay name for a quantity of native tobacco fiber about the size and consistency of a shredded wheat biscuit. Pulling it apart he gave me half. I declined to take so much but he insisted, explaining,

"Americans were most kind to me when I was in your country last year. This is a token of appreciation."

At that moment the Japanese sergeant guard commander strode up shouting angrily. He delivered a long harangue most of it unintelligible; but the general idea was plain. I was an American and therefore in a special category of wickedness. My cell had been cleared so I could be kept in solitary confinement. I was to remain there and not mingle with other men. He seized my shoulder, turned me around and marched me back to my cell. It wasn't really a cell in the same sense of others in the jail because it had no sleeping platform and the door was an ordinary wooden one instead of a barred iron gate.

He closed the door but did not lock it. After a while I walked to the barred window beside the door and looked out. Two guards were sitting at a table on the covered walk near the main gate but the sergeant was not in sight. I opened the door and walked out into the small area behind the hospital fence. A man was at the bath tank cleaning his teeth with a large, black stiff brush of a type not generally associated with teeth.

"How does it taste?" I asked.

"Inky," he replied.

"Where's the typewriter it came with?"

"In my cell. Fellow brought it in with him."

The brush wielder, a sunburned man clad only in a pair of black shorts held up with a drawstring, introduced himself.

"Burt," he said. "Gordon Burt. Late of His Majesty's Engineers, Malaya."

Burt was a gaunt but wiry New Zealander with little knots of muscle where they would do the most good. Thick black eyebrows and a hawk nose frowned over a stubby black beard. He finished his tooth-cleaning operations, removed his shorts and started splashing water over himself.

"My third bath this morning," he shouted. "I can't get too much of this water."

Burt said he was the only survivor of a group of British engineers who, on the last leg of a run from Singapore to Palembang, were chugging up the Moesi river in a launch when they ran smack into a Japanese gunboat. That was their first intimation that Palembang had been captured. The launch was blown out of the water. Uninjured, Burt swam to shore, pulled himself up in the weeds and lay there until sundown. He hid for ten days in the jungle but hunger and mosquitoes finally drove him out. He waved down another Japanese river craft and was taken to Palembang, stripped naked and left for two weeks in a guardhouse cell. Finally, he was given the pair of black shorts he was wearing and brought to the jail.

The clangety-clang-clang of roll call bell interrupted our conversation.

"Food," said Burt, "have to grab my dish and get in line."

He jumped into his shorts without bothering to dry himself, dashed through the fence gate which was left open so men could use the bath tank, and ran toward his cell. But Burt's food guess had been wrong. The bell did not signal dinner but rang to summon prisoners who had arrived the night before to claim their luggage.

On arriving in Palembang we had been compelled to leave our luggage in the street where we had disembarked from a river ferry. The Japanese had promised it would be delivered to us later. We had not believed them but here it was. My luggage, acquired during three weeks of wandering on the west coast before the Japanese patrol found me, consisted of:

One bicycle tire inner tube picked up on a hunch it would prove handy.

Two bottles of beer.

A small quantity of quinine.

A bottle of iodine.

Half a dozen paper-backed books found in the house where I met the Dutch policeman Francken who had the cognac.

One mosquito net and two white bed sheets found in another house where I had spent a night.

The mosquito net was wrapped around the beer bottles. The sheets, folded and knotted, enclosed the entire bundle.

As each man claimed his luggage it was searched by a Japanese officer. Knives and razors were confiscated. The officer and guards offered to buy any wrist watches prisoners were willing to sell. That surprised me. I thought they would simply take them. When the officer came to my beer bottles he held them up to the light, laughed and passed them to me.

Enroute back to my cell I noticed that the door to a storeroom just outside the fence gate from the bath tank was slightly ajar. After depositing my bundle I returned to the gate, stepped through when guards were not looking, pushed open the storeroom door and slipped inside, leaving the door slightly ajar. The sliver of light through the door crack disclosed a pile of metal chains and leg irons and a small tin trunk.

The trunk lid opened easily. Inside was clothing of the type peculiarly half eastern, half western, affected by many Malays who wear trousers on the street and sarongs in their homes. All the articles were too small for me, but a pair of white trousers offered the possibility of being cut down to shorts. Another garment, which looked like the upper half of a Mother Hubbard, would serve as a shirt. The next articles selected were a yellow Malay waist sash, two ordinary neckties and a tiny wooden container holding a stick of menthol.

Closing the trunk I explored the room further and picked up a dirt-stiffened blanket and a bath water dipper. The trousers, shirt, sash and neckties I stuffed inside the dipper. Then I opened the door quickly, closed it behind me and stepped through the fence gate. A few days later I again visited the room, found the tin trunk empty and so appropriated it to use for my growing possessions.

Breakfast, lunch and dinner were served simultaneously in midafternoon. I joined the food queue of two hundred-odd men and after a seemingly interminable time held out my chipped enamel dish for the ration of rice and soggy vegetables. To my horror the dish was too small. The servers told me to return later for the remainder of my share. Precious liquid off the vegetables leaked out the hole in the bottom of the dish. I reproached myself for not having brought the broken coconut shell as well as the dish. Quickly I ate the meal and hurried back for more, but food servers only shrugged sympathetically and pointed to the empty food drums.

That night, as I was lying on my sheets and gunny sacking, the door creaked open and a white robed figure slipped inside.

"Good evening," said a voice plainly in difficulties with the English tongue. "I am Father Elling."

I rose from the sack and we shook hands.

"How did you get here?" I asked.

"They do not lock the fence gates until ten o'clock."

"What about the guards? You took a chance on coming in here."

"Took a chance?" he repeated. "What is that meaning?"

I explained. He listened carefully, repeated the words, laughed, and said,

"Thank you. What is life without taking chances?"

We were friends from that moment. I decided it was a good time to drink the beer and Father Elling agreed. A heavy nail solidly impacted in the door frame solved the bottle opening problem. I filled the coconut shell nearly up to the break in the side and handed it to him. He raised it and said,

"Your health."

I drank from the bottle. The beer was warm but had a pleasant bite. I asked if there were any Chinese in Palembang.

"Many," Father Elling said.

"Do you know any who would help a foreigner?"

"If it is possible."

I had unlimited confidence in Chinese courage and in-genuity. The right Chinese, I felt sure, could help me escape to the sea and a sailboat.

Father Elling drank quickly, almost as if it were a draft of medicine. Months later I learned he disliked beer. I asked why he had drunk mine if he disliked it.

"Because I was afraid you would be offended if I did not," he said. "You were so proud of the bottles."

Next morning after roll call prisoners were ordered to line up in the yard, fully clothed, for inspection. Fully clothed meant shirts, shorts or long trousers and footgear of what-ever description we possessed. New Zealander Burt stood in line wearing only his brief, black shorts. A guard, through the interpreter, ordered him to go and get dressed.

"I have nothing to put on," Burt said. "The blighters threw me in here just like this. Tell them I have no shirt or pants or even shoes."

The guard commander swelled up and chattered angrily. A fellow prisoner offered to lend a shirt.

"No," said Burt, "I want one of my own. They can give me a shirt if they will."

The commander ordered Burt to borrow the necessary garment or be beaten on the spot. Burt capitulated but, because he was still barefooted, was ordered to change places with a man in a back row.

During the verbal exchange we gathered that a high Japa-nese officer was coming to inspect us and we must put on a good appearance. After carefully scrutinizing the lines to see that all were properly clothed the commander ordered us to stand at rigid attention. We stood.

Standing attention for prolonged periods can be torment. The sun climbed higher in the sky, probing our flesh with burning fingers as one hour passed, then two. Occasionally a man would faint, causing a small, welcome flurry of commotion as he was dragged from line and placed in the shade. A tall, lean, red-faced Dutch planter named Dyken began retching and vomiting with strained, painful noises that made us flinch. Conspicuous by the red trimming on his cassock and by the impassive dignity of his carriage, Bishop Mekkelholt stood among his priests. He seemed impervious to the sun, the jail and the Japanese.

Toward noon the high officer arrived. Then I heard for the first time another sound which was to become part of the routine noises of prison life. The sound was a command, *"kiotsuke!"* meaning "attention!" and was bellowed by the gate guards whenever an officer appeared. While shrieking, they would present arms. The cry they uttered doing it sounded like a combination yell, snarl and vomit. When I first heard it, standing in line waiting for inspection, I thought Dyken was expiring with one long, horrid death rattle. Then I realized the officer had arrived.

He came through the gate with a swagger that might have befitted Napoleon on a triumphant entry into Paris. His collar bore the single gold star of a major-general.

"Kiotsuke!" shouted the guard commander at us.

We stiffened our shoulders.

"Bow," commanded the interpreter.

We bowed.

The general surveyed us, slowly turning his head as his eyes traveled around the three sided square we had formed in the yard. One hand rested on his sword, the other hung straight down at his side. His polished leather boots clumped heavily as he walked leisurely around the inside of our lines. Aides hovered behind him. He paused in front of Bishop Mekkelholt, looked him over, asked the guard commander a few questions and walked on. Returning to the gate he stood for a moment watching us while we bowed again. He returned the bow with a salute, about-faced, clumped out the gate and the inspection ended. It had lasted perhaps five minutes. We had waited for it hours in the sun.

Back in my solitary cell I lay down to rest my aching back and legs and clear my head of sun dancing vertigo. Neither the aches nor the vertigo would leave. Presently the room became too cool and, shivering, I returned to the sun to get warm but instead I grew colder and the shivering increased. Someone had said there were two doctors in jail. I asked a passerby to fetch one and returned to my room and lay down. The dinner bell rang and I could hear the rattle and bang of tin dishes as men queued up for their rations. Food no longer interested me. At last a voice said,

"You sent for me?"

Opening my eyes I looked at a pair of legs encased in white, knee-high stockings and white shorts. Turning my throbbing head slightly on the sack so that I could look higher I saw the legs supported a fat, tight paunch. Rolling over on my back so that I looked above the melon-like bulge I saw a sharp face with a grey goatee. I sat up.

"Lie down," said the man, "I am Dr. Hollweg."

"Have any trouble with the guards?" I asked, thinking that was why it had taken him so long to come. He snorted.

"Pigs," he said, "nothing but pigs."

He thrust a thermometer into my mouth and launched into a long, excited recital of how the Japanese came to Palembang. Eventually he removed the thermometer, frowned at it and shook his head.

"How high?" I asked.

"Nearly forty."

That puzzled me, so I asked again.

"Forty," he repeated.

I thought he was making some kind of Dutch joke so I replied in kind, saying,

"Only eight above freezing, eh? Soon I will congeal."

He looked at me sharply, without replying, opened a small bottle and shook out two white pills.

"Take these," he said. "I will return after roll call."

"No kidding, Doc," I insisted, "what was my temperature?"

"I said nearly forty," he snapped, and walked out.

That was my introduction to Centigrade, and to Dr. Hollweg who, I later learned, was a nephew of ill-famed Theobald von Bethmann-Hollweg, German Chancellor in World War I. Von Bethmann-Hollweg, after German troops invaded Belgium, termed a "mere scrap of paper" the treaty guaranteeing inviolate Belgium's frontiers.

I once asked Dr. Hollweg, who said he himself served with the medical corps of the French army in World War I, if he had ever spoken to his uncle about those historically notorious words.

"Yes," said the doctor, "when he was visiting my family after the war, in 1920; but he only smiled and said there would be another war in about twenty-five years, when Germany had rearmed. And then can you guess what he said?"

"No," I replied. "What did he say?"

" 'Germany will fight again,' he told me, 'but you need not worry because Germany never, never, never will invade Holland.' "

The chills and fever had gone when Dr. Hollweg returned after roll call. He said my illness was malaria.

"You must have been exposed before you came here," he said. "There is no malaria in Palembang."

I asked him how long the attack would last.

"Until you recover."

"How long will that be?"

"My dear, the Japanese pigs took my crystal ball. Perhaps one week. Perhaps two."

Changing the subject I asked how many Dutchmen were in jail and how many English.

"Do not call us Dutchmen. We are Hollanders."

I corrected myself.

"How many Hollanders?"

"My dear, go to sleep. Tomorrow I will come again."

Next morning two Hollanders, as fat as they were cheerful, came in carrying a heavy wooden door between them.

"Your bed," they said. "It is better than the cement floor."

One of them, Holscher, had been an officer on the ship which was sunk under me in the Indian Ocean. I asked him how he obtained the door for it obviously had been removed from a cell. Holscher laughed and said,

"It spoiled the view from our club house."

I wondered again about the guards. Actually they proved indifferent to what we did inside so long as we were quiet and answered roll calls promptly. Within a few days the guards forgot me completely and visitors came and went at will.

One morning an Englishman walked in bearing a cup of coffee, the first I had tasted since capture. He introduced himself as Curran-Sharp, a planter from Malaya. Because the patients in the hospital were all English, he said, he had volunteered to fetch their food daily.

"Have you met Paddy West?" he asked.

"No, who is he?"

"The Irish doctor here," said Curran-Sharp, enunciating with the slow, precise diction of a schoolmaster lecturing to a class. "He was my estate doctor. Excellent fellow."

"What is an estate doctor?"

"Excuse me, please," he said, "while I light my pipe."

He started for the door. I told him to wait, that I would reward his cup of coffee with a match.

"Save it for the night when there is no sun," he said. "Matches are precious things. Watch."

Standing just outside the door he took from his shirt pocket a monocle which he used as a sun-glass, holding it so that the captured sunbeams were focussed on a tiny scrap of paper placed over the bowl of his pipe. After a considerable wait he was rewarded by a curl of smoke rising from the paper. The curl became an infinitesimal flame and he began puffing on the pipe stem. The tobacco lit. He puffed furiously until smoke finally was sucked through the stem and blown with impatient blue-grey spurts, out of the side of his mouth. Triumphantly he returned inside and sat down.

"Wonderful thing, the sun," he said. "I have composed a poem to it."

"Yes?"

"I call it Ode to Phoebus."

"How does it go?"

He needed no more encouragement, but began,

> *"Hear my cry, Phoebus, strongly defend me,*
> *All my needs comfort, all thy aid lend me.*
> *Always through daytime generously send me*
> *Sunshine quite cloudless."*

Rising to his feet and puffing vigorously on the pipe between lines in order to keep the tobacco burning, Curran-Sharp declaimed five more stanzas, describing how Phoebus' rays, through the instrumentality of spectacle lenses, kept his pipe burning. The ode ended in a paean about burnt offerings and a plea for "quintals of good 'backey, lit by thy splendour."

I asked him what kind of tobacco he used, because it smelled so strange.

"It is not tobacco," he said. "It is dried hedge leaves."

4

Dysentery and Palembang Bottom—No Relation

RAIN clouds, rolling with the west monsoon, piled up mighty battlements in the mid-afternoon sky over Palembang. Like a searching dog snuffling on a scent, exploratory puffs of wind blew over the jail wall, whirled dust in the yard, stirred clothes drying on lines and fences and the little plot of grass. Soon the rain would come, drumming violently on tile roofs, splattering like ricocheting machine gun bullets from cement walks and walls, slanting through barred cell windows and doors. Except for the wind's huffing and desultory clattering from the kitchen where workers cleaned up after the noon meal, the jail was quiet. It was the siesta hour.

Straightening to ease the crimp in my back I removed my hands from the reeking waters in which I was washing scarce and precious rags used to clean dysentery patients, and studied the clouds. Boiling masses, the color of angry surf, advanced across the sky ahead of the darker storm center and had reached a point almost directly overhead, so that the heavens were divided. It was as though towering cliffs at the edge of a mountain lake were trembling from some mighty, inner upheaval and at any moment would collapse and fall. Rain would hit when grey spilled into blue—in about half an hour, I estimated. There was just time to finish the few rags left in the tin.

Beside me where I sat on the concrete walk in front of the jail hospital was a pile ready for rinsing in a disinfectant which smelled like creosote. Disinfectant was one of the few things our Japanese captors gave us for the jam-packed cell block we had transformed into a sick bay. The rags had been carefully cut from clothing donated by prisoners from their own backs. Consequently, they had to be used over and over again. Washing dysentery rags at first had been a revolting task but we soon lost our squeamishness. They were washed during the siesta hour—the only daylight period when necessary receptacles were not being used for other purposes.

I finished the last rag, emptied the wash tin's slimy contents into a slop bucket, scrubbed the tin, refilled it with fresh water, replaced the rags and put the bucket on a fire. The cloths would be sterilized by boiling and afterward spiked to dry on the barbed wire fence separating the hospital cell block from the jail yard proper.

Glancing at the sky I saw the battlemented clouds were spilling into the blue. Rain was almost upon us but I calculated there was still time for a quick bath. Wrapping what passed for a towel around my waist I walked over to the low concrete water tank between the hospital and the wall, dipped a bucket of water and, holding it aloft, let the liquid cascade over me. Delicious. At that moment the wind stopped playing around and surged over the high wall in a steady flow bearing scattered rain drops.

"Rain!" I shouted. "Rain! Rain!"

The cry was taken up by men who swarmed from cells to rescue drying garments. I laughed until, remembering my mosquito net, I deserted the bath tank, dashed into the yard, still clad only in my birthday suit, gathered up the net and fled into the hospital clinic where I lived and worked dressing wounds and ulcers on the skins of fellow prisoners. Seconds later struck the kind of cloudburst known in the Indies as a "Sumatran." For thirty minutes it punished us, beating with a steady thunder which obliterated all but shouted conversation. Men who, because of overcrowding, had to live out on the covered walks, retreated into neighboring cells with their possessions and, with the cell occupants, withdrew as far as possible from doors and windows to avoid flying spray. Soon water was pouring through roof leaks and those with bedding underneath cursed and tried to find dry spots. Almost as quickly as it began, the rain diminished to a drizzle, to scattered drops, to nothing. Clouds moved eastward, unveiling the sun. Soon the rain was returning to heaven in the form of steam. Sumatra was as notorious for steaming humidity as for violent rains. Long ago, on first landing there, I had decided that if the humidity were a few degrees higher birds would need fins instead of wings.

During the six months that had passed since the morning of my first roll call, over two hundred new prisoners had been crammed into the jail. The storerooms next to the guardhouse had been cleaned of their chains, leg irons and the junk of years to make room. Those for whom no additional space could be found spilled over onto the outside walks. Most newcomers were from Malaya, shipwrecked Englishmen or Australians who had swum or floated ashore on Sumatra's east coast and adjacent islands. They had come to Palembang after two months of forced labor on little food and no medical care. I was just recovering from the malaria attack when they arrived. A special roll call rang in midafternoon of April 15th to announce them.

When the bell rang the yard was cleared, fence gates were closed and locked and, while we watched through the barbed wire, they straggled through the front gate. I wondered if we looked as disreputable when we arrived as did these ragged, sun-blistered newcomers. Some hobbled, hanging to men on either side. Others limped on canes or crutches. Some were carried on homemade stretchers. As the stretchers passed through the gates, a whisper, like a little wind, blew from the still forms, ran along the lines of incoming men until it reached us behind the fence. The whisper said, "DYSENTERY!"

Dysentery was a dreadful word and a mortal enemy. We feared it like the plague. We had been thankful that dysentery had not visited Palembang Jail. We had taken every possible precaution, in our confined and crowded circumstances, to avoid it. Now it was coming in on stretchers through the gate. The stretchers were laid in the middle of the yard. Guards gave them a wide berth as they counted the men, who lined up along the fences for inspection, and searched their bundles. The Japanese feared dysentery as intensely as did we.

Inspecting the 162 men took so long I returned to my bunk but was summoned from it by a man who called to me,

"There's an American out here."

I hurried out. My informer indicated a man standing in line with his back to me. He was a big, well built fellow in fantastically patched shorts and shirt which did not conceal his powerful neck, broad shoulders and slim hips. Below the shorts was a pair of well muscled legs. Heavy Australian army shoes shod his feet and on his head was a small, tight fitting, black stocking cap which caused me to tag him in my mind as a merchant seaman.

Reaching through the fence I tapped his shoulder. He turned and I was looking into a pair of harsh, blue-grey eyes. A scraggly, sandy colored beard covered his face but not enough to hide a prominent jaw and a wide, but thin-lipped mouth. My first impression was that I wouldn't want to meet him in a dark alley.

"I'm the other American here," I said.

His hard eyes lighted, the wide mouth grinned and his whole face was transformed into the rugged features of a good guy as he thrust his hand through the wire and we shook. A guard bellowed at us and we did not speak further.

Later, after the newcomers had been officially added to our midst, he came into my cell and handed me a nipa leaf cigaret. I was about to light it when I noticed he had none.

"What about you?"

"Just finished one," he replied.

Some time later I learned he hadn't had a smoke for days but had scrounged the one he gave me with a plea that "there's a sick American in there who looks like he needs a cigaret."

He proved to be a 30-year-old brewmaster, not a seaman, named Eric Germann. New York was his home. He had been called to Singapore shortly before the war's outbreak to help step-up production of beer for troops brought in to strengthen Malaya's defenses. We became close friends and, eventually, partners in a food smuggling enterprise to which Eric's muscles heavily contributed. Food smuggling was accomplished by getting out at night, trading goods for food with native Indonesians and getting back in again. It was a dangerous means of avoiding starvation but it worked —except for those who were caught. Eric and I became members of a little band of food smugglers whose adventures appear later in this story.

The new prisoners, with their wounds and dysentery, urgently required some kind of hospitalization. G. F. West, a 38-year-old, six-foot-three-inch Dublin Irishman, whom Poet Curran-Sharp had referred to as "my estate doctor," took charge of the hospital. Although this was Dr. Hollweg's home ground, the sick men were all Britishers and West naturally, and by means of his innate qualities of leadership, became the senior doctor. He was a lieutenant-colonel in the British medical corps and a casualty of the battle for Malaya, suffering machine gun bullet wounds which clipped off one finger and part of another of his right hand and pierced both his legs.

He turned the sick bay next to my solitary cell into a dysentery ward and moved the patients there into my quarters which henceforth were called the clinic. Together, the two cells became Palembang Jail Hospital. As men in the clinic recovered they moved into other cells in the jail. However, W. Probyn Allen and I stayed as assistants to the doctors. I became a "dresser," swabbing and bandaging wounds and ever increasing tropic skin sores.

The universal treatment for skin sores, no matter on what part of the anatomy, was soaking in hot water, followed by removal of dead tissue and bandaging. Ingenious handicraft workers had fashioned metal receptacles in which a man could sit and soak his festered bottom, if that was where the sores were; or dunk his hands, feet or elbows in smaller containers. While it lasted, we put potassium permanganate in the water and after that a solution of caustic soda. The solution was extracted from wood ashes by soaking twenty-four hours in water then draining off the liquid and straining it through a cloth. When our soap supply ended, the solution also was used to wash clothes.

Half an hour's soaking prepared a patient for "dressing." With surgical scissors and forceps I removed dead flesh from live tissue and treated the wounds with salves we made ourselves from coconut oil, rock sulphur or salicylic acid crystals. We were able to obtain the compounds and a few other ointments and medicines from sources outside the jail.

Sores and ulcers were not our only skin troubles. Various itches and a variety of impetigo the Dutch called monkey-pox was common. Herbert Smallwood, a broad, thick-set cockney seaman with a black handlebar moustache, sharply pointed on the ends, barrel chest, the arms and legs of a gorilla and hammer-toed feet, was our most monkey-pox afflicted customer. In bulk Smallwood was only a few pounds lighter than Allen. He perspired so copiously he always reminded me of a sea lion just emerging from the deep. When monkey-pox got him there was not an inch of his body free from blisters. He was my special job.

Every other day Smallwood appeared at the clinic, trumpeted a tune, and offered his bulk for treatment. His voice was a hoarse, tenor rasp and because he couldn't sing he trumpeted with lips and tongue in remarkable simulation of the real thing. When Smallwood first cut loose—in another prison camp—Japanese guards ransacked it trying to find the hidden bugle they insisted was blowing secret signals. They remained skeptical even after Smallwood staged a demonstration. After that he performed only in subdued tones.

Smallwood's working life had begun as a London grocery boy. Then he went to sea, spent several years in Canadian lumber camps and finally, when the war broke out, signed on a Canadian Pacific steamship as a kitchen flunky. The boat was bombed and burned in Singapore harbor. Fellow sailors said Smallwood risked his life to save others in his section of the blazing ship. Penniless and cheerful, he worked like a horse around the jail and did the hospital washing until monkey-pox claimed him.

While I worked on him he quivered like a dish of jelly and alternately laughed and cried but he always insisted that I continue until the job was done. Beginning at the top and working down I broke every blister on his hide, then bathed him with a mild solution of potassium permanganate. It took just an hour, while he trembled and winced and the spiked points of his moustache wiggled like the noses of twin rabbits about to sneeze. He sometimes fainted by the time I reached his feet and for that reason I made him sit on a stool so he wouldn't have far to fall if he passed out.

When it was all over I would roll him a cigaret and give him a drink of tea we brewed for dysentery patients.

Another steady customer was the New Zealander, Burt, who developed our first colossal case of "Palembang Bottom." Burt was the case history on which we based our subsequent treatment of that ailment and by which we proved the efficacy of hot water, the sun and Gentian Violet, in the order named.

Palembang Bottom usually started with small blisters which developed into running sores where one sits down. We experimented on Burt for a long time before we finally hit the curing combination. In the beginning nothing worked. Sulphur, salicylate, coconut oil, poultices of various kinds and descriptions were of no avail.

"What am I going to do, Doc?" I asked West in despair one morning when Burt presented his bottom for another treatment.

"You've got to do something," Burt chimed in. "My wife will never believe me if I tell her I got these just sitting in a jail."

Doc had an idea.

"Burt," he said, "go sit in a bucket of hot water."

Faithfully, Burt followed instructions. Since we had only two kinds of receptacles for holding water, five gallon kerosene tins and ordinary pails, neither of which had the necessary staunchness or circumference, Burt's gymnastics dunking his backside each morning were something to behold. Audience reaction was terrific. Within a week Burt's backside had improved remarkably, but it reached a certain stage of cure and there remained. Something else was needed.

Doc's next idea was sunshine.

"Do your soaking early," he told Burt, "and then take a sunbath for about fifteen minutes."

The hospital was on the side of the jail which received the first rays of sunlight. Every morning for several weeks Burt stood there, posed at such an angle that when the sun peered over the east wall the first thing it saw was Burt's backside. Hot water and sunshine almost but not quite cured him.

I can say, with pardonable professional pride, that the final touch was my idea. In our meager medicine chest was a tube of ointment labeled Gentian Violet. What it was for I didn't know but experimenting on my own skin had shown that it was a mildly astringent indelible dye. Once applied it had to wear off. One morning after his sunbath I painted Burt's bottom gentian violet. The effect was startling especially when, due to some chemical cause unknown to me, Burt's bottom turned from gentian violet to a certain shade of vermilion I had seen many times before in the zoo at home on the bare posterior of a Hamadryas baboon.

Needless to say, many other sufferers from Palembang Bottom were following the experiment on Burt with an interest approaching the breathless. No class of medical students ever assembled with more eagerness in their lecture ampitheater to watch a professor stage a demonstration than gathered each morning outside the hospital of Palembang Jail to study the ups and downs of Burt's case as he progressed from bucket to sunbath to painting.

As I delicately traced gentian violet lines on Burt's anatomy I reflected, sadly, that probably this was the nearest I would ever come to knowing the inner thrill an artist feels while students follow his brush strokes. The greatest thrill, of course, came the morning Doc pronounced Burt cured. Cheering spectators shook Burt's hand and the beaming patient said, "Now I can fearlessly face my wife."

Second in command to Doc West in the other half of the hospital—the dysentery ward—was Old Pop, 58-year-old English ex-planter whom we called "The Matron."

Matron Pop was one of the happiest men in jail, probably because for the first time in years he found himself in charge of something and indispensable. His adult life had been spent in Sumatra and Malaya as a planter but he had never attained full managership of a plantation. In fact, he had considered himself fortunate to land a job in the government rubber restriction office. He was a humble man who joked about his failures and whose reminiscences were never sour. He told my favorite Malay baby story.

First you must remember the Malay words for "Hello Mister," which are "tabe tuan" and pronounced tah-bay too-ahn. Got it? Hello Mister—Tabe Tuan.

Pop was walking a jungle path between plantations and came to a flimsy suspension bridge of bamboo over a deep stream. Pop always came to that bridge with trepidation because its swaying and swinging required a nice sense of balance and a firm grip on the rope handrail. This particular morning he approached it on one side just as a Malay woman carrying a child started across from the other. The baby was having his morning breakfast at his mother's breast. To Pop's experienced eye the child looked about two years old, an uncommon age for breast nursing but not infrequent in the Orient. The nursing continued as the mother catwalked across the swinging bridge without using the handrail because one hand steadied the baby astraddle her hip and the other held a basket balanced on her head. She was chewing betel nut and casually spat into the stream.

What startled Pop was the child. In one hand the infant held a lighted cigaret and was alternately mouthing his mother's breast and puffing on the nipa straw. When the mother had crossed and the astonished Pop stepped aside to let her step off the bridge, the child removed the cigaret from his mouth, exhaled a gust of smoke, looked brightly at Pop and said,

"Tabe tuan."

Pop had taken charge of nursing the dysentery patients before they arrived in Palembang Jail and he continued in the job afterward. He slept on the floor of the clinic, or, if he took a notion, curled up on the floor of the dysentery ward. He could have had a door for a bed and even a mattress when a patient died who owned one, but he preferred only an empty rice bag.

"Less trouble," he explained. "All I have to do is hang it on the fence in the morning."

The most nauseating jobs never fazed Pop. He always ate in the ward without a stomach flutter. He reveled in adversity and was happy to be on his bare feet, moving all day except during the siesta hour immediately after the midday meal. Then he slept for an hour while the dysentery rags were being washed and boiled.

We heated water for sterilizing and hot baths on an open fire in front of the hospital. The fireplace was a small thing of tin, loose bricks and a grill fashioned from cell door bars. We also used the fire to boil rice down to a thick soup for dysentery patients. That was an uncomfortable job because the bubbling stuff frequently popped with little explosions which splashed scalding liquid on our bare skin. I've still got little brown scars on my belly which mark soft rice blisters.

The hospital staff kept occupied during daylight hours, nursing, dressing, cleaning, boiling, and cutting into firewood the logs supplied by the Japanese. We were too busy to mope, so time passed quickly. I had always imagined that the worst punishment of being imprisoned would be waiting for time to pass . . . the slow drag of hours and days, months and years. But I was kept so busy in the hospital that time never dragged. As I spiked the last rag on the fence after the rainstorm and looked back to the first time I had done so, it seemed that only a few weeks, instead of six months, had passed since the shipwrecked Englishmen joined us and brought dysentery.

An admonitory jangle sounded from the roll call bell, followed by one stroke and a shouted, "Tea!" Prisoners queued up to receive their afternoon cupful each from the big iron tong which had been simmering in the kitchen. Cups in hand, men returned to their respective quarters, squatted around the yard to enlarge the latest rumor or formed a line at the clinic for opening of afternoon business. When the rush of dressings had ended Doc, Allen and I discussed what always was the biggest news of the week. Who would be sent out next day to Charitas?

5
Charitas

IN the city of Palembang were three hospitals—New Charitas, Old Charitas and Dr. Gani's. New Charitas had been opened by Bishop Mekkelholt and the Dutch Sisters of Charity in 1940. When the Japanese arrived they took over the new hospital and gave the nuns five hours to return to their former building, which had been turned into a school, and open a hospital there for war prisoners and Dutch oil technicians forcefully transported from Java to help put the refineries outside Palembang back into operation. The sisters were forbidden to take any equipment except beds and one operating table. The nuns, two doctors, and patients who could walk, moved the beds and patients who couldn't walk across the street to Old Charitas.

Native patients were ordered moved to the clinic of an Indonesian doctor named A. K. Gani, who after the war became a minister in the Indonesian Republic. Under Japanese direction the clinic was expanded into a hospital for natives with Dr. Gani in charge, assisted by Dr. Hollweg, who was taken from jail for that purpose along with another fellow prisoner, a British dentist named H. Harley-Clark. Old Charitas—known henceforth as simply Charitas—for eighteen months served the civilian prisoners in Palembang Jail and the Women's Camp, Australian, British and Dutch soldiers in two military camps, and the oil workers who were interned at Pladjoe and Soengei Gerong, sites of the Shell and Standard refineries.

Despite vigilance of Japanese guards, who supervised the moving from New to Old Charitas, the nuns managed to spirit out some surgical instruments, drugs and medicines. Half of their supplies they had already removed and hidden before the invaders reached the hospital.

For several months the Japanese paid no attention to our sick prisoners unless one died; then there would be a bustle of activity and a few critically ill persons would be taken to Charitas. Bishop Mekkelholt became seriously ill and was among those who thus were removed from jail to Charitas. Due in part to his influence—when he recovered sufficiently to negotiate—and in part to Japanese civil officials taking over administration of Palembang from the military, there was arranged a system of weekly "exchanges" of recuperated patients from Charitas for sick patients in the jail, the Women's Camp, the two military camps and the refineries.

Charitas thus was a godsend, not only to the sick but to the well, for the "exchanges" enabled it to function as a clearing house of information between the otherwise completely isolated prisoner groups. Men and women returning from Charitas brought smuggled letters from husbands and wives and relayed news of the war picked up by radios hidden in Charitas, one military camp and the oil camp. Charitas served as a money exchange depot, cash traveling both ways, depending on whether husband or wife was carrying the family purse when they were separated. We also got medicine and bandages from Charitas via the smuggling route.

Two Japanese doctors alternated in visiting the jail to inspect patients destined for Charitas. One allowed only critically ill men to be sent. The other let any one go whom Doc West recommended. When the lenient doctor was on duty, West usually included among the legitimately sick someone who had a wife or child in Charitas. West's choices were never questioned by the lenient doctor, a friendly man who spoke English. Occasionally he would visit our clinic and talk about medical matters. On one such visit he announced he was returning soon to Tokyo. I asked him if he knew the Japanese government spokesman, Tomokazu Hori, whom I had known in both Shanghai and Tokyo. It chanced that he did.

"Will you give him a message for me?" I asked.

The doctor nodded assent. I handed him a note, previously written for such an opportunity, asking Hori to notify the Red Cross that I was interned in Palembang, Sumatra. Whether or not Hori received it I never learned. If he did, the message was never relayed to the International Red Cross.

Meanwhile I had other irons in the fire. Before Dr. Hollweg was taken to the Indonesian hospital he told me he had Chinese friends in Palembang who he thought would help me escape. The problem was not so much escaping from jail as hiding afterward and getting aboard one of the native sailboats which, I learned, were being allowed to operate in inter-island trade. Such boats had arrived at Palembang from Makassar, 1,000 miles eastward in the Celebes. I had visions of thus reaching the Celebes and then New Guinea and Allied-held Port Moresby. The radio frequently mentioned Port Moresby.

Hollweg was allowed to move at will in Palembang and was a frequent caller at Charitas. I determined to go there. Doc West sent me as a sick patient . . . not to escape, for escaping from Charitas would be disastrous to the hospital, but to make a contact with Chinese and to get some news. News was nearly as important to jail morale as food and for two months we had been starved for news. Returning patients said the secret Charitas radio had been dismantled because Japanese were suspicious. That was not surprising because many prisoners were so indiscreet they would shout for joy when they heard good news and moan loudly if it was bad. However, I had a hunch Bishop Mekkelholt was only playing safe and had not dismantled the radio.

Eight of us, including two stretcher cases, arrived at the stone-flagged entrance of Charitas and were searched by Japanese guards who went through our pockets and looked inside our shirts but did not strip us. During the search I noticed a tall, slender nun standing just inside the entrance, watching. One of the patients, a Hollander who had been there before, was carrying letters inside his shirt. He stood so he would be the last man searched. A guard had just gone through his pockets and was about to look in his shirt when the patient, feigning sudden weakness, moaned and staggered back against the wall. Quick as a flash, the nun emerged from the door and seized him by the shoulders as though to prevent him from falling. Behind her came another nun. Supporting him between them the two nuns half carried the pretender past the guards into the hospital. The frustrated searcher followed to finish his job but the nuns brushed him off by saying their patient was "very sick."

That was my first sample of the stratagems of Charitas. The nun who had first appeared was Mother Alacoque, hospital superintendent. She was a slender, middle-aged woman with disarming brown eyes and a shy, nervous manner. Beneath that deceptive exterior, however, was inflexible courage and purpose. She completely fooled the Japanese— until someone betrayed her.

She knew the idiosyncrasies of every guard—who was tough and who was not. If a tough one was on duty no smuggling attempts were made by patients leaving the hospital. But Mother Alacoque or another nun would be busy at the front steps as outgoing patients, having been searched, walked to the waiting truck. If the moment was judged opportune the nuns would "accidentally" bump into a man and slip him some small object. When "good" guards were on duty they would allow patients to leave without being searched. In those and other ways we got limited amounts of medical supplies into the jail. The nuns were not direct parties to letter smuggling. They simply assisted patients in and out of hospital and looked the other way when necessary.

Charitas hospital was a rambling, one-story structure divided into three parts, one for male civilians, the second for military personnel, and the third for women. Communications between the groups were forbidden by the Japanese, who were constantly patrolling inside and outside, but Mother Alacoque arranged evasions of the rules when good reasons arose to evade them. Whenever a wife arrived in Charitas, word was sent to the jail and her husband would be in the next batch of patients if Doc West could arrange it. She even had an ally in one of the Japanese guard commanders who revealed to her he was a Catholic. When he was on duty, the hospital garden was never patrolled during certain hours and there husbands and wives could meet. A husband once arrived at the hospital just as his wife was being returned to the Women's Camp. Mother Alacoque told the friendly commander. He brought the couple into the guardroom and left them while he stood at the entrance so they could visit undisturbed.

Guards were changed frequently and the friendly commander's group was replaced by Japanese field police while I was at the hospital. They were uncouth, ugly men who made life as disagreeable as possible for prisoners. But Mother Alacoque and her nuns, smiling all the while, continued to fool them.

Three nuns were midwives who long before the war had made themselves indispensable to Palembang's native community. The Japanese had acquiesced to a petition from natives that the nuns be allowed to continue assisting at births in the city. They were on call day or night. When-

ever we saw a nun bicycling out of the hospital grounds
we knew that Palembang's population was about to be
increased.

Sister Paula, a little woman with smiling blue eyes and
a voice constantly on the verge of laughter, was one of the
midwives. Although she may have been up all night assisting at a childbirth she put in the same day shift as the other
sisters, beginning at 4:30 A.M. when they rose to pray. In
the evening, after a day of scrubbing, cleaning and nursing
that should have exhausted her, she sat in the ward where
I stayed, sewing and practicing English, or cheering some
lonely Hollander who wanted to hear a woman's voice. I
never saw an idle nun or a gloomy one. Despite their toil
and their daily hazards they were the happiest persons I
met.

The hazards were both internal and external: internal in
that the law of averages eventually would trip a letter
smuggler, and external in relations with temperamental and
frequently changing Japanese officials. Sooner or later,
Mother Alacoque feared, the hospital would be closed entirely. She planned, therefore, for the war's end when she
would need medical supplies to reopen her hospital.

How safeguard the supplies? The midwives took care of
that. Under the folds of their habits when they pedaled
away on a natal case would be some article to be given a
faithful native for hiding until the war ended. So well did
Mother Alacoque plan that when the day she feared finally
did come, the Japanese were astonished to find that Charitas was down nearly to its last bottle of alcohol, its last
ampule of morphine and its last package of roller bandages.

Three doctors functioned at Charitas: Surgeon Peter
Tekelenburg, a rock of a man, big, steady, quiet, and re-
sourceful; Dr. Ziesel, a small, slender Indo-European with
a stout heart; and a German woman physician named
Goldberg-Curth who had fled from Hitler Germany to
Singapore.

Tekelenburg had been a well known athlete in his youth and a member of Holland's national soccer team. He came to the Indies as a young army doctor and, after a few years, began private practice in Palembang. He once called me into his surgery and said with a smile, "Today someone told me they heard the Chungking radio."

Tracing with his finger an imaginary map on the operating table he outlined the military situation in China as broadcast by the radio. Next he sketched the Russo-German front and the situation there.

I had a hunch who "someone" was. Bishop Mekkelholt later confirmed it. Dr. Tekelenburg lived in a house across the street from the hospital. There was hidden the Charitas radio. Once a week he listened to news broadcasts and relayed them to the Bishop whose task it was to get the news to the jail without the source being known. This the Bishop did whenever patients he could trust left Charitas. The secret was never discovered by the Japanese, who frequently made routine searches of Dr. Tekelenburg's house.

Because of his brown skin Dr. Ziesel was allowed to live away from the hospital. He used his freedom and his friends among the Ambonese colony in Palembang to aid war prisoners. The Ambonese were native to the island of Amboina, in the Moluccas near New Guinea. They were extremely loyal to the Dutch and strongly anti-Japanese. Through them Dr. Ziesel managed to obtain many things for prisoners, especially for the penniless British women. Although hospital patients continually importuned him for news, because they thought his Ambonese friends had hidden radios, Dr. Ziesel refused to be pumped. He was taking grave risks already and he did not wish to increase them by talk which could be traced to him.

He brought me copies of an English language newspaper published in Singapore under Japanese auspices. How they reached him in Palembang, Dr. Ziesel did not say. One of them devoted columns to an exchange of nationals between Japan and the United States. Japanese news dispatches quoted the American repatriates on their good treatment and gave long lists of names, among them those of correspondents from Tokyo, Shanghai and Peiping. I knew them all. Now they were going home while I, who had congratulated myself for having escaped, was again a prisoner. Had I remained in Shanghai I would have been with them. The stories traced the route of the two exchange ships. They skirted Bangka Island, less than one hundred miles from Palembang, and passed through the Sunda Straits between Java and Sumatra. I daydreamed fantastic schemes of rowing out to intercept them.

The story killed my repatriation hopes. Now there was only one way out—escape; and my reliance on Dr. Hollweg and his promises was rapidly weakening. I was beginning to question his judgment and his discretion. Twice he had visited Charitas and assured me that his Chinese friends were willing to help and wanted to speak with me. A wall about five feet high surrounded Charitas. Hollweg told me to stand at a certain place along the wall so a Chinese friend, in passing by, could loiter within talking distance. I followed instructions but the Chinese did not appear. The third time Dr. Hollweg visited Charitas he had no sooner passed the guardroom than he began shouting,

"The Americans have landed in Java! The Americans have landed in Java!"

That was in late 1942.

When he was finally shushed and pinned down as to the source of his information it proved to be a rumor in the Palembang market place. After that I placed no more hopes in Dr. Hollweg.

Just before I returned to Palembang Jail both Bishop Mekkelholt and Dr. Tekelenburg asked me to tell Dr. West they feared serious trouble if prisoners continued to smuggle letters through Charitas in such volume. They asked that the number and frequency of letters be drastically reduced. I relayed the message and Dr. West tried vainly to halt the smuggling. He made an issue of it before our elected "Camp Committee" but his efforts were bitterly opposed by men who insisted on continuing to write frequently to their women folk and who declared it was "brave to fool the enemy" by smuggling as many letters as possible. They derided warnings of possible dire results.

When the reckoning finally came it cost the lives of Doctors Tekelenburg and Ziesel, sent Mother Alacoque to military prison and closed Charitas.

6

We Keep Holy the Sabbath Day

AFTER escaping to Sumatra's west coast I was just shoving off for India in a native sailboat when a hand prodded me awake, ending my dream of freedom.

"Okay," I whispered through the mosquito net and watched the white blur that was Father Elling glide silently through the clinic's darkness. For a moment his figure was outlined in the doorway, then it disappeared.

Sleepy eyed, I wriggled through the net, shuffled outside, looked up at the star spangled sky and wished the dream had finished before I was awakened. It was always thus. My dreams of escape, real and imaginary, always evaporated just before fulfillment. Drawing a bucket of water from the bath tank I washed, brushed my teeth, returned to the clinic, discarded the sarong in which I slept, pulled on shorts and a shirt and started across the yard to Sunday Mass, which was said early so as to be finished by daylight and pre-roll-call activities.

White robed clerics were moving quietly from the darkness of their cell block to the concrete walk outside where Mass was celebrated. The altar was a wooden door laid across two boxes and covered with a white linen cloth. Behind it a red sarong hung from a barbed wire fence. A single candle furnished light for reading the missal. The narrow walk was bounded by a cell wall on one side and a deep gutter on the other. Three Australians slept on the walk about fifteen feet from the altar. The congregation stood or knelt within those boundaries while the Australians slumbered. As Mass ended, dawn chased away the shadows and suddenly it was day.

As if awakened by an alarm the jail stirred to life. Men hurried out of their cells, racing for the water tanks or space on drying lines or the grass to sun their bedding. Sunning was imperative to rid bedding and clothing of the night's dampness and bedbugs. Bedbugs would scuttle for cover as soon as they felt the sun. That was the moment to catch and squash them between the fingers with a pop and squirt of their pirated human blood. Crushed bedbugs filled the jail with a repulsive scent. There was no other way of de-bugging and even such measures meant only temporary relief and the possibility of getting to sleep at night before another wave swarmed from cracks and crevices. What I hated most was having them fall off the mosquito net into my face.

The welcome shout of "coffee" sounded at half past five. That was a Sunday morning custom when coffee was available. We queued up with cups, coconut shells or tin cans to which handles had been soldered. Back at our cells with the steaming brew we squatted in the sun and sipped and smoked. The sun was still only comfortably warm. The air carried a hint of night. We were fresh from sleep and not yet tired. No bells had rung to remind us of our status. This was the best hour of the day.

After roll call church-goers "dressed up" to attend services in the Dutch Protestant, Church of England or Catholic faiths. Catholics had two services on Sunday, Low Mass before roll call and High Mass with a full choir afterward.

Since they had no regular minister, Dutch Protestants alternated among themselves in conducting services. Most frequent speakers were two oil executives who had shared shipwreck and other adventures with me, W. H. Oosten, director general of Shell's vast East Indies holdings, and Anton H. Colijn, manager of the installations at Tarakan, near Borneo.

Like myself, Colijn had once before been a prisoner of the Japanese and escaped. He was a slender, wiry, highly strung man in his late forties, well known for his explorations and mountaineering in New Guinea. His father for many years was Prime Minister of Holland.

Oosten was a big, heavy-set, purposeful man and a life-long friend of Colijn's. The three of us had first met just before sailing from Java. After our ship was sunk we were reunited on a Sumatra beach and, along with Colijn's three daughters and two other men, banded together in an effort to escape before the Japanese found us. Our effort failed but the friendship cemented by our common vicissitudes was a lasting one.

Until his death, Church of England services were conducted by a minister who had been in charge of a seamen's mission in Singapore, and afterward by a British government officer from Malaya. Reverend A. V. Wardle, the minister, and H. G. Hammet, the officer, read from the Book of Common Prayer and led in the singing of hymns.

Both Dutch and British Protestants held their services outdoors and on rainy days skipped them. The Catholic clergy who occupied nearly all of one cell block transformed it into a church for High Mass on Sunday mornings after roll call. It was a large, square room with small barred windows high in the walls. Worshippers sat on the cement bench which ran around three sides of the room, or on wooden stools in the central floor space. Sermons alternated in English and Dutch, with Fathers Elling and Bakker giving the English talks. In the beginning neither of them could speak better than awkward English but by study and practice they gradually attained fluency. Father Bakker and I traded language lessons—his Malay for my English; while

Bard Curran-Sharp, who was a Mason, tutored Father Elling and coached his Sunday sermons.

An English friend I will call Wembley-Smythe dropped into the clinic after Church of England services to debate whether he should have his finger freshly bandaged before going on shift in the kitchen.

"I hate to have it bandaged at all," he said, sucking on an empty pipe, "but I suppose it is the thing to do. An ounce of precaution and all that sort of thing, you know."

"If you fill that pipe and light it, so we won't have to listen to that dreadful sucking noise," Allen told him, "we might settle your dilemma."

Wembley-Smythe was an Oxford man while W. Probyn Allen had gone to Cambridge. Years afterward and half a world away from the halls of both hoary old English universities, these alumni reflected their schools' traditional rivalry by continually exchanging gentlemanly badinage with a bite in it.

The Oxford man, like many before him, had taken government examinations and gone into colonial service while the Cambridge man had gone into business. From remarks of both, I gathered those two careers were traditionally typical of alumni from the respective universities.

"But, as is common knowledge," Allen once sniffed, "the Malayan civil service definitely is second rate. India gets the top career men."

"And the poorest business types," retorted Wembley-Smythe.

Allen's Far Eastern headquarters was Calcutta where, he said, club life was more sophisticated and business life more British than in Malaya.

However, to Wembley-Smythe, the most empire-conscious Briton in jail, his position as magistrate in an obscure corner of Malaya was infinitely more important—even though it paid less—than Allen's club or business life, because it stood for that indefinable something that was "forever England."

I used to wonder what kind of magistrate was Wembley-Smythe, who is well described by the cliché "a scholar and a gentleman." Although he was an exceptionally well read man, and could converse informatively on almost any subject, he was completely inept at the practical business of living. He could do nothing with his hands, nor think of any idea whereby he might make even tobacco money. He was a willing, earnest, hard worker but bungled every job so badly his friends were always trying to find easier things for him to do. Hollanders liked him so much he was for a long time the only non-Dutchman on the regular kitchen staff but he was both their joy and despair.

"Believe it or not," Chief Cook Beissel sighed one day, "I think he even burns the water."

And he was always hurting himself. Hardly a day passed that Wembley-Smythe did not come in for first aid, although he dreaded the clinic as a small boy dreads the dentist's chair. Working on him was, I imagined, like doctoring a skittish horse. He shied away when I reached for the iodine, or scissors, or even an ointment swab. We might be standing in the center of the room but when we finished I would have pursued him into a corner.

As he sucked on his pipe this Sunday morning after church and debated whether to have his finger redressed now or later, he complained of a headache.

"If you had an aspirin for this beastly headache," he said, "I would settle for that. And it would be much more convenient all around than fixing my finger."

I suggested that since we had no aspirin he might be interested in a headache remedy I learned in Japan.

"Another fellow and I shared a cottage in Kamakura," I began, and got no further.

"Did you really live in Kamakura?" interrupted Wembley-Smythe.

"Yes, right on the beach. Have you been there?"

"No, but I read a bit of a poem about it once that endears Kamakura to me and I've seen pictures of the great bronze Buddha that sits in a tree-shaded glade near the sea. I suppose you visited it often."

"Yes, often," I said. "Do you remember the poem?"

He recited Kipling's lines, of which I remember two:

> *Be gentle when the "heathen" pray*
> *To Buddha at Kamakura!*

That set us to discussing religion. Wembley-Smythe attended Anglican services every Sunday but he apparently had no very deep personal convictions about his faith.

"Religion is all right for the masses," said Wembley-Smythe, echoing trite and familiar words, "but I think an educated man grows away from the need of it. The masses do need it, however, or there's no telling what they'll do."

Allen interrupted him.

"Caught you in the act," he said. "You're cribbing from Napoleon."

He picked up a book of quotations he had been perusing and read aloud,

" 'Religion,' says Napoleon, 'is the vaccine of the imagination; she preserves it from all dangerous and absurd beliefs. . . .' "

Wembley-Smythe stopped him, saying,

"I'll finish it from memory.

" 'If you take faith away from the people you will end by producing nothing but highway robbers.' End of Napoleon quotation."

"You must have been just ahead of me on the library list for this book," Allen said.

"I agree with Napoleon that the masses need some kind of religion," said Wembley-Smythe, "but I'm not so sure about my own need for it."

"Did God create you differently from other people?" I asked him.

"The question is whether or not God created me at all," said Wembley-Smythe. "If we all evolved from apes and the apes from reptiles and the reptiles from fish and the fish from amoeba and the amoeba from primordial ooze, where does God come in?"

I asked, "Who made the ooze?"

"It all goes back to a gaseous nebulae," said Wembley-Smythe, "or so my science teacher said, although I suppose he, too, was only theorizing."

"Let's take the nebulae, then," I said, "will you grant it had to begin?"

"For the sake of establishing a basis for argument," said Wembley-Smythe, "I'll grant it had to begin. I'll even grant that some Intelligence might have begun it. But that such a vast Intelligence should bother with creating individual creatures is too great a miracle for my imagination to swallow. He started things spinning and after that let them run their course."

"Seems to me the kind of evolution you refer to would be an even greater miracle and proof of God's omnipotence than if He created you as you are right here, on the spot."

"How?"

"If you were a sculptor and molded a lump of clay into the figure of a man that was so real people thought it was alive, they would credit you with wonderful powers. But if you took the lump of clay and threw it into the air and said, 'Presto! I endow this with special qualities that will change it, in time, and of itself, into a beautiful statue,' and it happened, wouldn't that be a greater miracle?"

The bell summoning kitchen workers rang just then.

"Damn," said Wembley-Smythe, "we'll continue this later. I've got to run. You haven't fixed either my finger or my headache. Just as well, you'd probably make them worse."

He laughed and ducked out the door. I watched him cross the yard, with his peculiar gait, shoulders stooped but swaggering as he bobbed, rather than walked, along.

Allen laid aside the book of quotations, yawned and said it was about time for language class.

Language lessons, private and en masse, began in the first days of internment. Classes were conducted in Dutch, English, Malay, Spanish, French, German, Japanese and Russian. Languages were only part of our scholastic curriculum. Fully half of the prisoners were technicians of various kinds. They organized the Palembang Jail Engineering Association and held weekly symposiums on technical subjects, and smaller, twice weekly classes in various branches of engineering.

New Zealander Burt was the most dogged student in jail. He put in five hours a day for a year on Spanish and when he had reached a certain stage of proficiency reduced the Spanish studies to one hour daily and took up lessons on a jail-made guitar, strumming four hours a day for another year. He did it all to surprise his wife, explaining,

"She won't believe it's me when I walk in singing Spanish and strumming a guitar."

"How about organizing a poker game?" I suggested to Eric, my fellow American, one Sunday night when restlessness was making my nerves crawl.

"Good idea," he said, "but I couldn't last long with my present capital."

"How much have you?"

"Eight cents."

"We'll play for mills and use beans for chips. Ten beans to a cent."

The jail's lone Canadian, a young fellow from Vancouver named Christie, enthusiastically seconded the idea but added a restriction.

"Three bean raise limit and not more than two raises. I've got only six cents."

Planter-bard Curran-Sharp signified his eagerness to participate by quoting from Shakespeare and stipulating that some one else had to furnish the beans.

Bill Attenborough, a Eurasian sailor from Singapore, became the banker by supplying the beans.

The game proved such an antidote to jail nerves that it grew into a Sunday night custom, with shrewd Curran-Sharp usually quitting a little ahead and Christie a little behind. Eric, Attenborough and I fluctuated violently in our wins and losses. We played as though the beans were dollar chips and the night I made my biggest killing—36.6 cents, and the other night I took my worst loss—17.8 cents, were just as notable as if that many dollars had been involved.

Occasionally we ended the game early enough to join in Sunday night singsongs in the yard. Although most of the singers were Hollanders, the tunes which predominated were American—from Stephen Foster to Irving Berlin. Sometimes the song fests changed into story telling bees. My favorites were told by two Dutch *contrôleurs*, as the civil service officers are called who have charge of areas which would correspond to a county in America. Each *contrôleur* is the supreme authority in his district, responsible, of course, to the Resident who would correspond to a governor of one of our states.

Controleur De Mey told how, in the course of administering justice, he used an old fashioned hand-crank telephone as a "lie detector." The idea was born one day when he suffered a slight shock on cranking the phone. Thereafter he laid two wires from the telephone into another room where he questioned native malefactors.

He would have the suspect hold the wires and tell him,

"Those are truth wires. If you do not tell the truth the wires will betray you."

Then he would begin questioning.

"Name?"

"Amat, Tuan."

"Age?"

"Thirty, Tuan."

"Married?"

"Yes, Tuan."

"Were you at home last night?"

"Yes, Tuan."

De Mey knew Amat had not been at home, so he signaled his assistant who was standing at the telephone in the other room, then repeated the question.

"You say you were at home last night?"

"Yes, Tu . . ." Amat jumped and with a yell dropped the wires.

"What is the matter, Amat?"

"The wires, Tuan. They bit like many ants."

"That is how the wires talk when you do not tell the truth. Were you at home last night?"

"No, Tuan."

Thereafter Amat told the truth.

Controleur De Raat's story illustrated how the Malays looked upon the primitive people of a jungle tribe known as Kubu. They roam the jungle without habitation, living more like animals than men. A Malay taxidermist, envisaging the financial possibilities of exhibiting such a strange creature, sought from De Raat the necessary permission.

"Long have I wished for the opportunity of mounting an Orang-Utan," the taxidermist wistfully explained to De Raat, "but alas, that man of the forest [orang-utan literally means 'man of the forest'] lives far north of here."

De Raat sympathized with the taxidermist's unfulfilled desire.

"But now I have thought of an even better animal on which to practice my art," the taxidermist said. "With your permission I would like to kill and stuff a Kubu."

Another story that amused me was told by a Shell technician named Nick Koot who joined us in 1943. It concerned the Dutch foreman of a machine shop and how he succeeded in keeping his Javanese workmen busy while he was absent from the shop. He had a glass eye. Whenever he left the building he would remove the eye and place it on a special shelf so it could "look" at the room. Then he would tell his native workmen,

"Don't loaf while I'm gone. I have my eye on you!"

As I returned to my clinic quarters one Sunday night after a singsong and story telling bee I heard the sound of music playing outside the jail. Palembang natives were having a singsong too, in a nearby public park. An orchestra alternated between native tunes, known as krontjon music, in which stringed instruments predominated, and American popular airs in which piano, saxophone, drum and cymbal were loudest.

Despite Japan's New Order in East Asia, Sumatra natives still preferred American jazz when they gathered to sing and play on nights when there was a full moon. The orchestra whammed away at "The Sheik of Araby," "Roll Out the Barrel" and "Hold That Tiger." Then it switched to one song that was compulsory at all gatherings and had been ever since the sons of Nippon arrived. The song was the wild, lilting sea chanty, Tai Hei Yo—O Great Pacific— which I had heard morning, noon and night from the first day I set foot in Japan to the day I left. It is one of the few truly Japanese songs with a western style, and is martial, stirring music in any language. Dorothy G. Wayman of the Boston Globe, whose Japanese is so fluent she can even compose Japanese poetry, once told me that the popularity of Tai Hei Yo convinced her—in 1939—there was going to be war in the Pacific. Every foreigner from 1937 onward in Japan heard Tai Hei Yo several times a day but few bothered to learn the words and fewer still to ponder their significance. Here they are as translated by Dorothy Wayman into a ballad form westerners can understand.

O Great Pacific

I

Come all you seamen and hark to my lay,
The sea is our pathway, our faring forth gay.

Chorus: *O great Pacific! Gather us in,*
Friends, strangers, all brothers in kin;
One world turned to peace let us win.

II

Now rings out the call for enthronement on high
Of our glorious homeland, ordained from the sky.

Chorus: *O great Pacific! Your bidding is clear,*
We shall, on our voyage, still tireless steer
Till the globe has been bound in one rope
centered here.

III

Chrysthemum crest on our warships shall show
Who can rule the blue furrows of sea here below.

Chorus: *O great Pacific! Shine, Rising Sun!*
Let thy crimson illumine the lands we have
won
To hold for our country years thousand and
one.

IV

Long ages ago, our ancestors dear
From ocean a foothold carved out for us here.

CHORUS: *O great Pacific! Your treasure of space*
Spread out anew for the heroic race
West-reaching for bounds to be added apace.

V

Tide favors us now,—for the bold and the brave!
Sing praise to our life-blood, the ocean's blue wave.

CHORUS: *O great Pacific! We come, we come!*
Fearless and dauntless, the sons of your
foam;
Ready to die for the sake of our home.

O Great Pacific ended on one of those peculiarly Oriental dissonances which to a westerner seem merely a pause in the music. He waits for the next note but there is none. That is the end. I never got used to it and was irritated anew every time it happened. As Tai Hei Yo died discordantly I damned it again, and then almost immediately was mollified when the orchestra suddenly began playing my favorite of all Japanese tunes, Ai Koku Koshin Kyoku— the Air Corps Patriotic March. It is a stirring, zestful, foot-lifting melody strangely combining the oomph of a Sousa march with the sigh of a bleeding heart. (I never heard the word Kamikaze until after the war, but the Air Corps March well expresses the sentiments that must have motivated those suicidal pilots.)

As Dorothy Wayman translates the march its words paint the picture an aviator would see taking off just before dawn and reaching an altitude where the sun comes over the horizon to blaze a path of light over grey waves and tip with rose and gold the wraiths of cloud above the dead volcanic cone of Mt. Fuji. It suggests to the aviator how brief is a human life compared with the centuries of ancient Nippon. Ardently he desires that his short life might burn for one glorious, dedicated instant, dyed with his lifeblood but adding a touch of beauty to his country's future—just as the crimson-hued cloud adds to Mt. Fuji's beauty.

O Great Pacific and the Air Corps March were the songs to which Japan's soldier millions sailed and flew and marched to war—first in China and then down the Pacific— all the way down, over the Philippines, Malaya, the Indies, to the Coral Sea.

Neither of these two songs is heard in Japan today, I am told, having been banned by Occupation authorities as unsuitable to Japan's new life.

The Air Corps March shrilled through the night, over the jail wall and into the clinic where I sat reading. Allen snored behind his mosquito net. The orchestra blew out the last note of Ai Koku Koshin Kyoku, paused to catch its breath, then swung into their other favorite, "The Sheik of Araby." The music was not so loud it drowned the nearer sounds of night . . . the creaking of cicadas and buzzing of heavy, flying insects hypnotized by the light which we could burn all night because this was the hospital clinic. Suddenly a gecko lizard erupted into the hoarse, guttural squawks on which Malays lay bets, wagering how many times in succession the lizard will make his peculiar, double-squawk which sounds something like his name—gecko, gecko, gecko. After one initial squawk the lizard may subside and wait for answer from another lizard or he may signal any number of times up to nine. The highest I ever counted was seven. Consequently, whenever a gecko started squawking I listened, hoping he would make it nine.

While listening and counting I tried to locate him. He sounded as though he was on the top outside ledge of the window, but lizards are ventriloquists. He might be anywhere. My eyes roamed around the clinic, probing cob-webbed corners, peering under, then over, the table whereon lay bottles, bandages and a tin holding palm sugar. A moving black line on the table caught my eye. Ants. Damn ants. They worked nights as well as days and they always bridged our ant traps.

Ant traps were water-filled tins in which stood whatever the ants were not supposed to reach. A tin had to be sufficiently large in circumference so that a space of water intervened between the edge of the tin and the side of the object inside it. The object might be a smaller tin container or it might be a table leg. In our case all four legs of the table stood in such traps, as did the palm sugar on top of the table. Unless the water was changed at least every other day a film formed on the surface permitting one particularly agile species of ant to walk across it. This species was a reddish-grey variety of infinitesimal size and legs of such fragility as to be nearly invisible. Larger black ants broke through the film. We suspected, but could not prove, that the ants carried their own dust to cast into the water and form the film. Once I caught a black ant ferrying across on a straw he must have carried there especially for that purpose. Intensely interested fellow ants were watching his experiment.

Palm sugar was an especial delight to the ant sweet tooth. Despite the tin's supposed air tightness, ant proofness and its location in a water-filled ant trap, I knew that ants were swarming inside it because I had neglected to change the water for twenty-four hours.

Ants and flies were supposed to be lizard meat, therefore Malays believed it good luck to have a gecko in the house, but our lizards scorned ants and only occasionally caught flies. They were more interested in signalling to each other. The lizard squawked again.

Gecko, gecko, gecko, gecko, gecko, gecko, gecko . . . seven times. Would he make it eight?

"Make it eight," I said aloud. "Make it eight."

The lizard did not answer.

"Nuts to you," I said, and went outside for water to

replenish the traps. Returning, I poured fresh water into the tins, breaking the stagnant film and throwing ant ranks into confusion. Signals flashed up and down the table leg, starting a wild retreat. Those above the trap were cut off. Members of the first rush already were struggling in the water. Wiser heads behind were searching for another route of escape. I chortled fiendishly and crawled into my mosquito net. But my chortle was without real satisfaction. By morning they would have another bridge operating, or at least a ferry, and our sugar would be disappearing like snow in the June sun.

Ants, I reflected, were like Japanese. They got into all kinds of mixups and stumbled around making a big fuss among themselves as to procedure but their persistence usually won. As Correspondent Percy Whiteing once told me while we sat in the lobby of Tokyo's Imperial Hotel:

"The Japanese are like a bunch of ants trying to get a dead fly into their hole. You watch them milling around the fly, pulling in opposite directions, working at cross purposes, seemingly without any coordination or plan of action, and you go away contemptuous of the foolish things. But when you return in a little while you are just in time to see the fly disappearing down the hole. How did they do it? Damned if you know."

I thought how right Whiteing's simile had been. Foreigners often laughed, or fumed, at the seemingly incredible stupidities and inefficiencies of the Japanese; at their endless bureaucratic rivalries and quarrels. The army jibed at the navy and the navy at the army and both at the government. Like scorpions, government bureaus stung themselves with their own tails. Definite answers on anything usually were impossible to obtain. Yet their trains ran on time, their merchant ships maintained clock-like schedules and now their armies had swept over eastern Asia like a storm. In time we would win it all back. We would give them an awful pasting; smash their cities, seize their conquered territories and every mandated island and write the peace in Tokyo.

We would squash them so thoroughly they could never rise again. But they would. Already they had won a victory we could never efface. They had demonstrated how the yellow man could fight the white man and win—if he had the will and the tools. Even when our armies returned, as they would, and beat them to a bloody pulp it would not prove—from a military standpoint and aside from the moral issue—that the Japanese had been wrong in trying. It would only demonstrate we won because we had more and bigger guns.

Perhaps a few hundred years from now, I thought, historians may record how the Japanese and Chinese and other Orientals swallowed what remained of the white race because of the incredible stupidities of Occidentals—who could not live with themselves because of the different colors of their politics, nor with Asiatics because of the different colors of their skins.

What was it I had learned as a kid in Sunday school? The words echoed in memory: "God made man in His own image and likeness."

How we are violating the image!

Why can't we look beyond the color of politics and skins to the souls He created, too, and see there our fellow men? But that is neither scientific nor economic and this is the white man's age of Science and Economics, of mathematical gods and controlled populations.

The Asiatics will continue multiplying, because they are not among those blessed with our birth control civilization, while we grow old and barren because children are not economic. Asia's peoples then will not have to have bigger and better guns because no matter how large or terrible our weapons they will do us little good. The "uneducated" millions of the Orient, who suffered little children to come unto them, will only have to pluck us as though we were a withered branch and drag us away, as the ants dragged the dead fly. They may not even have to pluck and drag us—only fill the vacuum created by our self-induced demise.

I stirred in the mosquito net as the Air Corps March sounded again, ending the concert. The saxophone was tooteling hot notes, cymbals were crashing, strings were zinging high, wild harmonies. The song was being played as though the players liked it.

I felt certain of one thing as I dozed off. The players did like it and they would not forget it, even after the Indies had been retaken and the Japanese had gone.

7

Just Another Day

HERCULEAN splashing at the bath tank and stentorian "good mornings" by the splashers awakened me and everybody else in the jail hospital one morning before dawn. The Twins were at it again.

The Twins were a pair of middle-aged Hollanders whose affinity was not blood relationship but something even more binding—a mutual determination to live their own lives in their own way regardless of their companions. One such way was pre-dawn bathing. It gave them first crack at the contents of the small water tank.

I lay boiling inside and wondering who would be the first to raise a protesting but futile voice; futile, for it would only start an argument and awaken still more sleepers. We had pleaded before with The Twins but they insisted on their "rights." Mutterings from Allen's corner told me he was fuming too. One small hope brought me a little comfort. Inevitably, some day The Twins would be clinic patients and I could burn their bottoms in a hot bath. But even that dream was spoiled by another thought as I speculated on medical ethics. Theoretically, a doctor was bound to treat his worst enemy to the best of his ability if the enemy should become a patient. I supposed the same code applied to all workers with the sick, even a non-professional volunteer like myself. Well, that killed any hopes for even indirect revenge on The Twins.

Daylight interrupted my speculations because daylight meant it was my turn to light the hospital fire and start boiling breakfast rice for dysentery patients. Morosely I arose and went out into the damp, chill air to struggle with the fire. The wood was both green and wet from night rain. It smoldered and smoked but would flame only sporadically when I created a draft by alternately fanning up a breeze and blowing myself dizzy as ashes swirled into my face and eyes.

The rice should have been cooked by roll call but when the bell rang I had just got the fire burning well. During the long wait for counting, the flames died and afterward I had to start fanning and blowing again. We supplied soft rice porridge not only to dysentery victims but to half a dozen non-hospitalized dyspeptics whose ulcers made them eligible. The dyspeptics were congenitally sour individuals whose dispositions matched their stomach linings. While I sweated over soft rice, flinching occasionally as little bubbles on its glutinous surface exploded and splashed blisteringly onto my bare belly, they stood around holding empty, accusing plates. One of them, he who had asked me for milk my first morning in jail, occasionally uttered a long, martyrous sigh.

At long last the porridge was cooked and served. Now to make myself a cup of cocoa and relax for a little while before the clinic rush began. Last night a fellow had traded me enough powder to make one cup of cocoa for enough tobacco to make two cigarets. He had brought a tin of cocoa powder into jail with him and now, after all these months, was using it to obtain tobacco. On the edge of the fire I had heated a small tin of water. I poured into it the precious cocoa powder, let it bubble momentarily, then retired to the clinic with my drink.

I had taken the first sip when in limped the martyrous dyspeptic. Among ourselves we called him Evangeline because he always had a long tale of woe.

"You must have swallowed your soft rice in one gulp," I said.

"I just couldn't eat it," he replied, "until the pain is relieved in this foot of mine."

"Clinic isn't open yet," I told him.

"I know," he said, "but my foot pains so excruciatingly I just couldn't wait."

"Can't you wait until I drink this cocoa?"

"I thought I smelled cocoa. Where did you get it?"

"From Tojo by special courier."

"Cocoa would be a great relief to my ulcer," he whined.

"Scram," I said.

"Look at that red line," he said, pointing to a spot just above his ankle. "Blood poisoning. I tell you I'm suffering."

A thin red line was there all right, extending about six inches up from his bandaged foot. Lymphangitis. But not an emergency. Five minutes while I drank my cocoa wouldn't make the slightest difference to it.

Had it been any one else but Evangeline I wouldn't have minded so much going to work immediately on his foot, but the combination of that whiner and my cocoa going cold, both climaxing the long battle with a stubborn fire and blistering soft rice, irritated me.

"Sit down," I said, "and wait until I drink this cocoa."

He sat down with a self-pitying moan. I took another drink. He whined again,

"I wish I could find cocoa somewhere."

"Oh, hell," I said, "you win. Shut up and take that bandage off your foot."

I walked out to the fire and looked at the five gallon kerosene tin of water being heated for baths. It was warm enough. I filled a tin and called Evangeline. By the time I had finished treating him the cocoa was cold. I set it back on the fire.

At that moment Evangeline hobbled over, pulled a

smoldering stick from the fire to light his cigaret and knocked over my cup of cocoa, spilling every drop.

There was a stunned silence while I mastered a blind urge to shove Evangeline into the fire and curse him as he burned; then I turned and stalked back into the clinic.

Chief Cook Beissel, who had just come from the kitchen, followed me in to ask if a certain camp member, notorious for his wheedling, had been in the clinic to complain of earache.

"Not yet," I said.

"Just as I suspected," said Beissel. "Next time he comes around I'll give him a real earache."

The scrounger had called at the kitchen on three successive nights and asked for hot water on the plea he needed it for a persistent earache. Beissel gave it to him but the third time he followed the man to his cell and caught him pouring the hot water on coffee grounds.

"Oh," explained the scrounger, "I don't put the water on my ear; I make coffee and it puts me to sleep so I don't feel the pain."

For men like the scrounger with their spurious aches, and hypochondriacs with their daily sob stories, Doc West and J. Drysdale, the hospital "chemist," had manufactured special sleeping powders and stomach pills. The powder was rice flour and the tablets were hardened rice paste— nothing else, but their psychological effect was wonderful.

Perhaps the inventive Drysdale could figure out something to silence The Twins at their early bathing.

"You bet I will," he told me when he came into the clinic a few minutes later. "Do they do it every morning?"

"Nearly every morning."

"Let me sleep in here tonight and if they wake me up tomorrow morning I'll go out and sock the blighters silly."

Doc West vetoed the offer.

"Direct Action" Drysdale we called the Scot, who had been a business executive in Malaya. In addition to mixing our genuine ointments and spurious powders he performed another invaluable camp service—manufacturing toothpaste which the hospital sold at cost. Drysdale's toothpaste formula was his secret, arrived at after long and tedious experiments with burned and ground bones, lime extracted from scrapings off whitewashed jail walls, a clay he dug up in the graveyard one day while helping bury a man, and various flavors ranging from a mosquito repellent known as white wood oil to the juice of small green limes. Whatever his exact formula, it was a triumph of ingenuity. And it worked. The cost came in buying the flavoring ingredients through a Chinese food contractor who brought our daily rations. As a profitable sideline to his toothpaste trade, Drysdale made toothbrushes from coconut and rope fibers.

Clinic hours were from 8 to 10 A.M. Doc had left and I was cleaning my instruments and tidying up about 10:15 when in walked a customer who, instead of waiting in line like every one else, had been sitting across the yard reading a book. Now he wanted service.

"Too late," I told him.

"I was busy and didn't notice the time."

"Nuts, I've been watching you over there reading a book."

Being tripped up annoyed him. He snapped,

"The clinic is here for service, isn't it?"

"During regular hours, yes," I said. "After regular hours, for emergency only."

Just then Jan Rombeek, a big Dutch sailor who worked in the kitchen, came in to have a foot dressing changed. We treated kitchen staffers whenever they could get away from their work. I swabbed and rebandaged the foot and Rombeek left. When I looked up the other man was still there. Only now he had removed his shorts and was waiting confidently for "Palembang Bottom" treatment.

The morning was nearly done. I had items to gather for the jail weekly newspaper, "Camp News," and this man

who would not inconvenience himself to take his turn in
line was insisting on special service.

"Okay," I said, "bend over."

He bent over with a smirk that said, "I knew you would
treat me."

I turned him around so his bare, spot-covered posterior
was to the door.

"Now take a deep breath," I said.

"Why?" he asked. "What's breathing got to do with it?"

"Do as you're told," I snarled, "or I'll ram these scissors
into you."

He inhaled.

"Now, hold it until I tell you to let it out."

He held it.

I tiptoed out of the clinic and began my weekly round
of news gathering.

As the result of a three-way tie which ended a voting
contest to select a name for the publication, Camp News
had two subtitles: Hot & Less Hot News, and Terompak
Echo. "Hot & Less Hot" derived from a peppery sauce,
called *sambal*, served daily with rice. The sambal came in
two strengths, "hot" for old Indies hands whose taste buds
had long since been corroded by fiery peppers, and "less
hot" for neophytes such as I. Hot sambal was so hot it
made a man's eyes water, his nose run, and caused fits of
sneezing; nevertheless, devotees relished it.

"Terompak Echo" derived from the clatter of our wooden
sandals on concrete floors. Terompak was the Malay name
for the sandals which we carved ourselves from firewood.
Terompak making was a major jail industry and the clatter
of terompaks day and night was a noise as familiar as our
own voices.

Our artist with the jaw-breaking name, Th. J. A. Ronkes-
Agerbeek, solved the three-way-tie dilemma with a cover
design incorporating all three ideas. The same cardboard

covers were used for each weekly issue, of which four copies were made, two in English and two in Dutch, and passed around from cell to cell.

Despite the contest and resultant cover, the newspaper continued to be known simply as "Camp News." We used the word "camp" because, although we lived in a jail, we called our community a camp. Camp members were called internees. The reasons were technical as well as psychological: technically, we were not in jail but in an internment camp for civilians; psychologically, "internee" sounded less harsh than "prisoner." And, finally, the Japanese explicitly told us more than once that we were in an internment camp and not a jail.

First call on my news gathering round was at the kitchen to get from Beissel the weekly figure on Japanese-issued, as distinct from Camp-purchased, rations.

In return for judicious bribes the Japanese permitted the Chinese contractor who brought our regular rations to bring extra rations also, which we paid for out of a common fund. Every man in jail was assessed for the fund whether or not he had money. This seeming magic was possible because a number of Hollanders had entered jail carrying extraordinarily large sums of money. The Resident of Palembang, an official corresponding to a Governor in the United States, in the name of the Dutch government borrowed from those men and loaned to penniless men who signed promissory notes payable, without interest, after the war.

British capital was small compared with Dutch and most of it was in Straits Dollars or Pounds Sterling, which gave both Dutch and British money lenders opportunity to exchange at exorbitant rates for their own profit. Eventually, due to the continued petitions from us, the Japanese stepped in and exchanged the money on a dollar-for-guilder basis, using Japanese invasion currency. Some money lenders were kind enough to make refunds to those for whom they had exchanged money at a high rate but others were not, using the emergency to fatten their pocketbooks.

Sporadically, but only half heartedly, we debated the pros and cons of the Resident confiscating all monies from every prisoner and thus creating a common pool that would accomplish two things: First, we could budget with certainty, knowing the exact limits of our financial resources. Second, it would conserve every penny by depriving wealthy men of spending money and thus eliminate the thriving black market. But the psychology of private enterprise was so deeply ingrained in us that such debates never progressed beyond the talking stage. Not even the absolutely penniless men were in unanimity on such a plan; for many already were able to make money in jail and they did not wish to surrender even tiny earnings over and above the common assessment.

Money was earned by various kinds of trading or manufacturing. I never failed to be astonished anew at the variety of tools disclosed on a walk through jail. Some were homemade, some were not. There were saws, hammers, hatchets, files, heavy chopping knives called *parangs*, pliers, screw drivers, and one man even had made a plane, carving it from a wooden block and fitting it with a metal cutter filed from a piece of iron. How they had acquired or made all those things was a mystery to me who had consistently flunked my manual training class as a boy in grammar school. After first confiscating everything with a cutting edge, the Japanese relaxed, evidently secure in the knowledge there was no place to go even if we did carve our way out.

Beds, chairs and stools were the most common manufactures. Empty rice sacks became "upholstery" while firewood properly tooled or cell door bars heated and bent to correct shape supplied the frames.

Trading of all kinds flourished, from simple barter to

complicated black market deals involving bribed guards. Black marketing really boomed when, under guard, working parties marched every day from the jail to a site on the outskirts of Palembang to build a camp of wooden barracks with palm-thatch roofs. Some day we would occupy the camp. Places on the working party were eagerly sought for three reasons: the guards allowed us to buy from peddlers at the site, and we could salvage precious small pieces of lumber; enroute, we passed within hailing distance of the Women's Camp and men could wave at figures they knew included their wives; we could breathe free air outside jail walls.

For a time in Palembang Jail it was possible for wealthy men, at a black market kitchen built behind the jail kitchen, to eat steak, chicken and duck while ordinary men lived on regular rations of rice and vegetables. Wiser men with money conserved their cash or converted it into barterable goods against the day when goods would count more than money. Or, through the Chinese contractor, they bought mosquito nets, mattresses, khaki clothing and tinned goods such as powdered milk and corned beef.

Less wealthy individuals obtained mosquito nets by clubbing together and buying one net which they cut into pieces. The pieces were fitted over small frames into which a man could put his head at night for sleeping. The rest of his body depended for protection on clothing, rice sack or blanket.

The Chinese contractor was an enterprising salesman who started in business with a pushcart and soon had a truck powered by Japanese-supplied gasoline. So successful was the arrangement to all concerned, including the Japanese, that we were able to set up a camp store, called a *toko*, selling at cost to internees. Because supply never equalled demand, a ration system was worked out whereby each block of cells got its quota of any incoming goods.

Another source of income to poor men was *corvee*, the

name we used for compulsory performance of necessary camp labor. Every able-bodied man had to take his turn on the various working parties—kitchen, sanitary, wood-chopping. A wealthy man could hire some one to take his place. Often such hiring was done, not because the hirer wanted to avoid working but to help a penniless man earn money.

All these activities required organization and we had one, headed by Dutch Controleur D. J. A. van der Vliet, who assumed command in the very beginning and did a splendid pioneering job. We worked out a system whereby elections were held every six months to determine leaders of the British and Dutch communities, members of the "Camp Committee," and the liaison man between the camp and Japanese.

Routine and humdrum as was our community life there was enough activity within it to furnish items for Camp News. Therefore, my weekly round always yielded something.

After obtaining the week's ration figures from Beissel I called on my next information source, Harold Lawson, the jail librarian, to learn how many books had been received during the week. Lawson, who had been a typewriter salesman in Singapore, had conceived and carried out the idea of buying books through the Chinese contractor. Japanese guards acquiesced. The contractor brought books which natives had looted from Dutch homes in Palembang when the residents were interned. Many an internee who donated to the library fund discovered he had paid for books stolen from his own house. Within a comparatively short time Lawson had built up a library of approximately one thousand volumes, half of them in English.

Against my better judgment I next called on Penryce, chairman of the British committee, and immediately became involved in a heated argument over censorship. He insisted on the right to approve or disapprove publication of anything concerning the British community, which at that particular time was quarreling over retaining him in office.

The fight was over whether or not we as a camp should pursue an "active" or "passive" policy in our relations with the Japanese. The "active" school, headed by Direct Action Drysdale and Bard Curran-Sharp, favored making formal, written demands on the Japanese that we be allowed to send our names to the International Red Cross and that we be given more medical facilities and better rations. The "passive" school, headed by Penryce and having the sympathy of Camp Leader Van der Vliet, opposed such action, saying it might provoke the Japanese and cause them to treat us still more harshly. I personally sided with the "active" school.

After a number of fiery sessions in the British committee, Curran-Sharp and Drysdale resigned their membership, to which they had been elected. Curran-Sharp posted a public notice of his reasons.

I wished to print in Camp News statements from leaders of both sides. However, Penryce refused to speak for publication, and further told me,

"I forbid you to publish anything about this matter."

"You're wasting your breath," I replied. "It's going to be published."

"I'll go to the Camp Committee and have the issue suppressed."

"Go ahead. You'll only hurt your own case by losing the support of many who now are behind you."

If things came to a showdown and the Committee supported Penryce, I knew Camp News certainly could be suppressed, but I doubted that the Committee would risk a showdown. Its members were firm adherents of the peace-at-any-price philosophy. They would compromise, I thought.

A compromise was worked out, before going to press, whereby several letters to the editor on both sides of the quarrel were published in the English edition but not in the Dutch. The basic issue was temporarily settled by the British community deposing Penryce from leadership and the next day promptly re-electing him but with a mandate to pursue a more vigorous policy toward the Japanese.

The whole episode sounds silly at this writing, but men do peculiar things in confinement. In fairness to Penryce and those who believed as he did I must say that the active vs. passive policy was a contentious subject throughout our imprisonment. The rightness or wrongness of either side was never decided satisfactorily.

After my futile argument with Penryce I dropped into the cell of New Zealand Burt to ask if he would give the next public lecture which Camp News sponsored weekly. Burt once had been a member of a British expedition to the Arctic.

"I think the boys would enjoy hearing some more about your experiences with Polar Bears," I said.

Burt agreed they would. His previous lecture had only scratched the surface of anecdotes about the adventure.

As we discussed it I looked around Burt's cell. Designed originally for one native prisoner, it was a little over five feet wide and nearly filled by the cement sleeping bench. Three men slept on the platform and Burt slept on the floor in the narrow space between the end of the bench and the door. Their bedding consisted of a rice sack apiece. Between their bodies and the concrete was one woven grass mat. There were no shelves or hooks on the bare walls, so their eating utensils and other belongings lay beside them on the bench or floor. The odor from an open drain a few feet outside the door filled the cell.

"You can almost cut it with a knife, can't you?" Burt remarked sniffing.

He waved a wad of papers.

"I found these in the trash can outside the guardroom," he said. "They're old prison records."

They looked as though they had been torn from a ledger. The pages were ruled in vertical columns and horizontal lines, with names of prisoners, their dates of admission and other data filled in.

"I'm going to use the unwritten spaces to keep a diary," Burt said. "I just wrote a note in it to the wife telling her it's the little things I miss most, things like shaving gear and handkerchiefs and a comb and needle and thread.

"I told her that confinement under these circumstances is making men irritable and we're all losing our tempers over trifles."

A cockroach appeared from under the bench, waved exploratory antennæ and started sidling along where floor joined wall. Burt whipped off his terompak, struck at the cockroach but missed. The insect buzzed its undeveloped wings and sailed across the room. Burt made another pass and it scuttled for the dark opening under the bench. Angered at his second miss Burt made a third vicious swing and lost his grip on the terompak which clattered out of sight under a bench. It must have hit a rat hiding in there for the startled rodent popped out of the black recess, leaped across the floor at our feet, shot out the door, cleared the walk in another jump and disappeared into the drain.

"What do you think of that?" Burt asked. "I'll bet the Japs had that rat wired. My wife would never believe it. Flying cockroaches and fifth column rats."

I left Burt and continued my rounds, exchanging gossip here and there and feeling around for the source of the latest fantastic rumor that Americans had landed on Bali.

Phoney rumors were my pet peeves. Few things nettled me more than hearing men solemnly proclaim as "facts" stories that could not possibly be true. Perhaps my special aversion to them sprang from having, as a reporter, chased down so many baseless rumors. Many tales bruited about Palembang Jail were so patently false they would have aroused only contempt in the most juvenile cub reporter. Yet men of supposedly mature minds accepted them. I thought they were bad for morale because they did violence not only to men's good sense but to their hopes.

The Bali story, I thought, was of the harmful variety. It sounded as though it had a source common to many previous yarns which stank. I decided to trace it. I had been backtracking and eliminating for several days when I left Burt's cell to resume the hunt. The finger pointed at a certain garrulous Hollander who was too coy about his source. He was sitting on a pile of firewood near the kitchen when I arrived to try again. We bantered the latest rumors for a while. Finally I tried a shot in the dark.

"A fellow told me last night where you got that Bali landing story."

"Nonsense," he laughed, "no one could possibly know."

"You mean no one outside your private circle, don't you?"

The laugh died and he looked at me suspiciously.

"What do you mean, private circle?"

"Oh, just the other members of the seance. He said you got it from a Ouija board!"

He started and swore. The shot in the dark had hit home.

"Who told you? We agreed . . . well, who told you?"

"He said he thought you moved the planchette yourself."

"I did not. We didn't use a planchette. And who was it?"

"He said you did. Where did you get it?"

"He lies. It was no planchette. We used a small pointer suspended by a string. None of us touched the string. Who told you?"

"No one told me. I just guessed."

He spluttered like an emptying fizz bottle but apparently decided to make the best of it.

"Don't tell any one else, will you? If you do, it will spoil a good joke."

He forced a laugh. "Ha, ha. A good joke, isn't it?"

He was trying to pass off as a joke his responsibility for starting not only the Bali landing story but others equally spurious that had falsely buoyed hopes of gullible fellow prisoners.

Months previously the spiritualist and a few others like him had labeled me a defeatist for insisting the war was going to last a long time and that we should conserve our resources for starvation days ahead. They resented Camp Committee efforts to curb individual spending and conserve our resources, as well as Camp News jibes at the black kitchen. This pseudo-spiritualist and two other men had once constituted themselves a deputation to investigate me. With long faces and grave voices they had asked if it were true I had said the war would last three or four years.

"That's correct," I answered.

"Impossible," they said. "We will be free within six months."

All this, the deputation's call and the conversation with the spiritualist, occurred in 1942, before the war was a year old. In April, 1942, those men had been confident we would be free by June. In June they were betting on August. In August they predicted, without qualification and with assurances of having "confidential information," that Japan would collapse by October 1st—1942! Ardently as we all longed for freedom and the war's end, I thought there was no excuse for such wishful prognostications.

I reminded them of the publicly announced Allied policy of finishing the job in Europe before turning full heat on Japan. That brought up another tender subject. They could think of the war in Europe only in terms of a second front on the Channel coast. North Africa and the Mediterranean were as secondary to them as the misty interior of China. I said that books and articles I had read on military strategy in the Eastern Hemisphere seemed pretty well agreed that North Africa would be a decisive field. We had to neutralize Dakar to safeguard our South Atlantic supply routes; and we had to control North Africa for the sake of Middle East oil and Mediterranean sea lanes; only then could we really crack down in Europe.

"And that seems to indicate, first of all, a second front in North Africa," I said, "if you see what I mean."

They did not and, fantastic as it may sound reading this in 1949, my words anent North Africa convinced the deputation that I was mentally off balance. In fact, one of the men, a little ferret we of the hospital staff nicknamed "Guy Fawkes," immediately began spreading a story I was losing my mind. When I left for Charitas without having been previously ill, Guy Fawkes cited that as proof of my insanity.

He told men who later told me, "Doctor West wanted to get McDougall out of here before the Japanese learned he was insane and did something to him."

The nickname "Guy Fawkes" was invented by Doc West, who said that, given a cloak and hood, the ginger-bearded little Dutchman would be a walking cartoon of the seventeenth century conspirator of that name notorious in English history. Guy was a furtive man whose childhood reading must have been loaded with spy stories. To him life was a vast, dark PLOT in which he was a counter-conspirator. He talked out of the side of his mouth and often looked quickly over his shoulder to catch any Japanese agent who might be spying on him.

In the beginning we had taken Guy Fawkes seriously because he was one of the senior government men. We could smile indulgently at his eccentricities because, we thought, he really had secret connections with the outside that enabled him to obtain authentic radio news. He would appear at the clinic regularly once a week and read news items from sheets of paper concealed in a book.

Perhaps he did have a genuine "pipe-line" during the first months of imprisonment for his reports certainly sounded conservative and authentic. But if he did have, he either lost it and reverted to other and less reliable sources or his outside informant did, because gradually the reports changed from what sounded like actual Allied radio announcements to stories that must have been dream world broadcasts.

The night before I had gone to Charitas Allen said, "I'll lay you five to one that within twenty-four hours Guy Fawkes will have the 'inside story' of why you went."

"That's no wager, that's money in the bank," I said, "but we could bet on what the 'inside story' will be."

Allen thought awhile, then decided,

"He'll say you've lost your mind and Doc had to get you out of here."

I didn't think Guy would go that far so I took the bet. My return from Charitas, of course, proved Guy's insanity story false, and when, in late November 1942, Singapore newspapers, relayed from the hospital, told of Allied landings in North Africa, my stock as a prophet soared considerably. Two of the deputation who had previously interrogated me called to apologize. Guy was not with them but later he began coming around again as if nothing had happened and resumed reading his "radio reports."

After uncovering the Ouija board story—which I could refer to only obliquely—I spent most of the afternoon typing Camp News and carefully working around two "holes" in the manuscript to be filled with cartoons by the staff artist, former police commissioner Ronkes-Agerbeek.

That night, as Allen and I sat discussing the latest genuine good news, an account in an old Singapore paper telling of fighting in the Solomons and admitting loss of the airfield at Guadalcanal, Guy Fawkes walked in.

"That is only a fraction of the truth," said Guy Fawkes, peering suspiciously under the clinic table. "The whole truth is that Americans have captured all of the East Indies except Java and Sumatra. Maybe they even have landed in Java but my source has not yet been able to confirm it and you know how careful I am about not accepting anything until it has been confirmed."

"Very interesting," said Allen. "Please go on."

Guy Fawkes tiptoed to the clinic door, looked out, tiptoed back again and motioned us to stand close to him.

"You must keep this absolutely confidential," he said *sotto voce.*

We crossed our hearts and bent down so our ears would be closer to the great secret about to emerge from behind Guy's ginger beard. He hissed:

"The Americans are about to land here. Soon we will be free."

This was in November, 1942.

Allen and I straightened up and looked at each other, then at Guy Fawkes.

I decided I was sick of the little man and his aberrations.

"There's an old saying in America," I said, "that goes, 'No matter how thick you slice it, it's still baloney.' Does that mean anything to you?"

I could almost see his brain cogs grinding as he frowned and thought and finally delivered the results of his cogitation.

"I suppose it is a code but I will have to think longer to learn its meaning."

Had anyone else replied thus I would have seen the humor but coming from Guy Fawkes it only intensified my aversion for the man. So for his benefit I spelled out the meaning of 'no matter how thick you slice it, it's still baloney' and concluded by saying, "That's what I think of your confidential information that all the islands have been captured except Java and Sumatra."

He stalked out of the clinic.

"You're on his black list now for sure," Allen said. "Now you'll never get any more news straight from the fighting front."

"We hope," I said, and began rigging my mosquito net with intentions of retiring early.

Just then Evangeline walked into the clinic.

"My stomach is simply awful tonight," he whined, "haven't you anything that will settle it?"

Evangeline's appearance, coupled with his act in the morning that ended in the loss of my cocoa, made a parenthesis around the whole irritating day starting with The Twins and their pre-dawn splashing.

"You humor him," I growled to Allen and walked outside, only to stumble over a stool someone had left in the middle of the walk. I limped back into the clinic, surveyed a long abrasion on my shin and reached for the bottle of potassium permanganate solution.

"Hold it a minute," said Evangeline, "there's a visitor on your neck."

He picked a familiar insect from my collar and held it up to the light.

"It's a big one," he said, and popped the fat, red bedbug.

8

New Year Inventory

THE Women's Camp crowned a low hill on the outskirts of Palembang. Every day our working party of fifty men passed within a few hundred yards of it on the hike from jail to the camp we were building for ourselves.

In pre-war Palembang what was now the Women's Camp had been a group of fourteen medium-sized houses comprising a compact little residential section of Dutch families. The Japanese had strung barbed wire around the hill and turned the area into an internment camp, packing in women and children forty to a house and ten to a garage. Between the lower houses and the barbed wire fence was a low retaining wall and an open space where women gathered daily to wave and call to the working party as it hiked past.

Once a week I laid off my hospital job and joined the working party in order to breathe free air outside the jail and see what I could pick up at the new camp site. Most of the building work was done by native laborers. We did little but go through the motions for the benefit of Japanese inspectors who came around infrequently. They appeared satisfied with our pretenses. It was a period of leniency. The working project lasted through the last half of 1942. It began when a Japanese civil administration superseded the military government of Palembang.

We marched to work in line, two abreast, with guards

95

flanking us and bringing up the rear. The guards during this period were not Japanese soldiers but native police, mostly Javanese, who had been members of the colonial police force before the war and who were as friendly to us as they dared be. They allowed us to wave and shout back to the women. The distance was too great to distinguish words but the women's concerted voices, high pitched and vibrant, made cheerful sounds. Husbands and wives had worked out methods of identifying each other by signals with hats or colored clothes. The signals were arranged by smuggled correspondence via the Javanese police, who also guarded the Women's Camp, or through the Charitas letter system.

The Javanese police sometimes carried other things than letters. One day I noticed an internee making what looked like splints. Since no prisoners had broken bones I displayed my curiosity. They were splints. But for whom?

"The Women's Camp."

"Women's Camp?"

"Yes. Mrs. Koenes broke her leg."

"How?"

"She was standing on a wall, waving to the working party, and fell off."

I laughed and told him, "You'd better make some more splints in case the Colijn girls fall off their roof."

The Colijn girls, Helen, Antoinette, and Alette, daughters of the oil man, did their waving from astride the ridge of a rooftop. Antoinette and Alette were 'teen-agers and Helen had just moved into her twenties. They were husky young women with strong lungs. Their piercing voices and wild gyrations as they signaled to their father in the working party caused our Javanese guards to remark they must be crazy.

I first met Helen when, after swimming all afternoon in the Indian Ocean, I was pulled into a lifeboat. She was the only woman in the boat and during the ensuing thirsty six-day voyage to Sumatra we became well acquainted. When we landed on the isolated southern tip of Sumatra the majority aboard elected to take the boat and sail to the nearest Japanese occupied port to surrender and obtain medical aid for a seriously wounded passenger. The rest of us, including Helen and her father, hiked north along the beach. On the third day we found another lifeboat and its passengers. Antoinette, Alette, and Oosten, the Shell executive, were among them.

A machine gun slug from one of the planes which sank our ship and strafed us in the water had ripped Antoinette's arm open to the bone from elbow to wrist. Salt was our only antiseptic and rags torn from clothing our only bandages. Wet dressings made from those materials kept Antoinette's arm from going septic. Although she must have suffered unmercifully during our three-week hike along the coast she never mentioned pain. She had her father's courage and tenacity and despite her wound was determined to escape with him if we could get away.

The girls were in Java when Colijn was captured in Tarakan and dispatched as a hostage under guard to warn authorities in another oil port, Balikpapan, not to destroy the installations before the Japanese arrived. If they were destroyed, said the Japanese commander, the women of Tarakan would be shot. Colijn escaped by a clever ruse. Balikpapan was razed by the Dutch to prevent its use after capture and Colijn went on to Java. His wife was among the women of Tarakan. After the war I learned the women were not executed as the Japanese had threatened, but Colijn had no way of knowing that when I met him fleeing Java.

The day before Christmas I marched out with the working party. As usual we began to wave and shout when in sight of the Women's Camp. But the women were silent, standing motionless in the open space. The Colijn girls on the roof were quiet too. Their stillness silenced us. We slowed to a halt and asked each other, in whispers, what was wrong.

The answer came in song. Across the no-man's land which separated us sounded the melody of "Come All Ye Faithful." Our guards were as astonished as we and let us stand there listening. The music softened on the second song, "Silent Night, Holy Night," and grew stronger on the third, a Dutch carol. Leading the singers was a woman in the habit of a nun. Her arm rose and fell, as though waving a baton.

The guards finally asked us to move on.

"Please walk," they said in Malay. "Japanese may come."

We walked, moving quietly and slowly in order to hear those voices as long as possible.

That was the second time the women had risked trouble in order to cheer their men. Months before, on the birthday of Queen Wilhelmina, a holiday the Dutch celebrate as do we the Fourth of July, the women astounded us by flying two Dutch flags. As the working party passed, the flags were raised from the Colijn girls' rooftop perch while other women on the ground waved colors of the House of Orange and cheered madly. Probably that was the only time between Palembang's capture and its liberation that Dutch colors flew in the city.

Wilhelmina's birthday is August 31st and on that date in 1942 we still had been able, by bribery and good luck, to purchase food enough to celebrate, even in a jail.

Still flush with guilders brought into internment, the Dutch had transformed the jail yard into a midway and staged an auction "horse race." Horses and riders were advanced by dice throws around a white-washed track. Financial proceeds were split between the kitchen and hospital funds. The day had begun with religious services and singing of a Te Deum. Father Bakker's choir gave its first official performance in the late afternoon. Dinner was colossal; it included meat and potatoes.

The birthdays of Princess Juliana * and her consort, Prince Bernhard, also were observed by extra food and coffee. Nor were Dutch holidays the only ones celebrated. The birthday of England's King George was marked by a special meal and, although there were only two Americans in jail, the Fourth of July was a big day too.

Festivities had begun early on that July 4, 1942, my first Independence Day in captivity. Everstijn, manager of the toko, had galloped into the clinic bearing two plates, one for Eric and one for me. Each plate contained two slices of *buttered* toast, a piece of canned salmon and two sardines, carrots sliced to resemble bacon, pickles and hot chili. On a piece of paper was written, "With compliments of the toko staff." Chief Cook Beissel came in a few minutes later with two more plates, each bearing one fried duck egg and a note, "With compliments of the kitchen staff."

Official congratulations by the Dutch and British communities were tendered by the Resident of Palembang, Oranje; the Burgomaster of Palembang, Hildebrand; the Camp Leader, Van der Vliet, and British Leader Penryce. They, and many others, called to shake hands, wish us a happy day and express hopes that "the Allies soon will be here."

The Pacific war was only eight months old on July 4, 1942.

The unexpected breakfast donated by the toko and kitchen staffs was only a starter. At noon we opened a long hoarded tin of bully beef and shared it with Father Elling, who had brought presents of tobacco.

That night Allen was host at a gala dinner in the clinic. The medicine stand was cleared of bottles, covered with my bed sheets and became a banquet table. Decorations

* Wilhelmina abdicated and Princess Juliana became Queen in 1948.

were three paper flags—Dutch, British and American—and green hedge leaves stuck into two measuring glasses. Around the table sat Camp Leader Van der Vliet, Oosten and Colijn, my companions of shipwreck and jungle trek; Chief Cook Beissel, Dr. Hollweg, Poet Curran-Sharp, Doc West, Allen, Eric and I.

Beissel himself cooked the dinner, a sumptuous *nasi goreng*—fried rice garnished with meat and condiments.

Dr. Hollweg astounded us by producing a fifth of English gin which he had brought into jail when first interned. We mixed the gin with water, flavored it with limes purchased through a guard, and had gin rickeys. Allen proposed the first toast. We all stood as he raised his tin cup and said:

"Gentlemen, I give you the President of the United States of America, Queen Wilhelmina and King George of England."

We drank.

That was the first time I ever felt genuinely patriotic on the Fourth of July.

Half a year had passed since that red letter day and here it was the day before Christmas and another surprising celebration. The women's Christmas serenade had been such an emotional surprise that working party members were silent during the rest of the hike to the new camp site.

When we arrived, we dispersed around the rectangular field where wooden barracks and a high barbed wire fence were rising. This area on the edge of the city long ago had been sectioned off into streets, but only a few houses had been built, and undergrowth covered the intervening fields. Malay peddlers hung around the camp site and haggled with us over prices. One peddler, by prearrangement, had a fried chicken for Colijn. During the morning Colijn slipped unobserved into some undergrowth on one side of the area. Then, on hands and knees or sometimes flat on his belly, he snaked through the area of fields and houses between us and the Women's Camp.

He reached the Women's Camp fence at a point which was screened from the sentry boxes by bushes. His three daughters were waiting, also by prearrangement. Gleefully they received the chicken and talked in excited whispers with their father. He kissed them, through the fence, then started the long wriggle back to our camp site. After the war Antoinette told me the sequel.

The farewell had been witnessed by another woman who betrayed them to the Japanese guard, hoping thereby to gain some advantage for herself. However, they were back in their quarters and the chicken was hidden before their betrayer returned with the guard, who took them to the commandant, who in turn summoned the leader of the Dutch women in camp. She was a nun, Mother Laurentia, a school teacher and musician. She it was who had led the women in their Christmas caroling to us.

Mother Laurentia listened to the betrayer's accusation. Coolly she told the woman, "You are dreaming. You never saw a man talking to these girls."

To the guard commander she said,

"This woman is not responsible for her actions. Please excuse her. Obviously a man could not come to our fence without your sentries seeing him. She is suffering hallucinations."

Convinced, the guard commander berated the woman tattle-tale and dismissed the case.

"That was the third time Daddy visited us at the fence," Antoinette told me. "They were happy moments. We admired him so much for coming. And how it bucked us up to have him right there."

They never saw him again. He was dead when liberation came.

As we hiked back to jail that Christmas eve of 1942, we discussed how best to reciprocate the women's carols. We were still debating when we reached the front gates and were counted through.

Shortly after dark, prisoners gathered in the yard while Reverend Wardle led Englishmen in singing Yuletide hymns and songs, creating an atmosphere for listening to Dickens' Christmas Carol. Reading key passages and synopsizing in story-telling fashion what lay between, Allen recited the tale of Scrooge and Marlowe, the Cratchets and Tiny Tim.

Christmas morning everyone went to church, some attending services of all three faiths, starting with the Catholics' High Mass at 6:30 A.M. The clergy had spent days disguising their Cell Block No. 3 as a church. They could not hide the barred windows or grey walls or cement sleeping benches but they softened them with greenery, flowers, fronds, and palm leaves. The working party had brought in the branches and shrubs; a Chinese woman brought the flowers to the jail gates—making a dozen trips—and two smiling Japanese guards had brought the palm leaves! Orchids and gardenias banked the altar. It looked as solid as one of marble, although beneath the flowers and the freshly laundered white altar cloths were only planks. Six candles flickered in tall, conical, painted candlesticks of cardboard which disguised beer bottles underneath. Behind and above the altar were murals painted by Father Bakker on cardboard screens of the folding type used by Chinese. The murals depicted Bethlehem's barren hills the night the shepherds and their flocks received angelic tidings of the Nativity. Where he had obtained the cardboard to make the murals and the paints to paint them was Father Bakker's secret.

Father Elling, the jail's most eloquent speaker in either Dutch or English—he had learned English that well since the previous April—preached the sermon. It was the second time he had given the same sermon and it was as appropriate to this occasion as when he first preached it, Christmas

Day, 1936, in Utrecht, Holland, when his parents, brothers and sisters and all their family friends gathered in the church to hear his first sermon as a priest.

Protestants as well as Catholics packed the cell and the area immediately outside it. After a special Christmas morning breakfast Colijn conducted Dutch Protestant services and Reverend Wardle preached a sermon and led prayers for men of the Church of England. Reverend Wardle for years had been in charge of a seamen's mission in Singapore and this morning he drew on that background to address his fellow castaways of the sea.

Christmas was a holiday from work. The Japanese had allowed husbands and wives to exchange gifts, via a special courier, on condition there was no writing except the recipient's name on or in the packages. So we had Christmas presents, although not of the sort usually associated with Christmas. They were whatever knicknacks the givers could fashion with needle and thread, or pocket knife, or cook from their scarce possessions. And somehow the ever-thoughtful women had managed to get the ingredients for toffee and paper to wrap the pieces in, and thus ensured every man a present of candy whether or not he had relatives in the Women's Camp.

An Australian jockey named Donnelly, the smallest man in jail, dressed up as Santa Claus and, accompanied by the five biggest prisoners as bearers, distributed the presents. I was flabbergasted when he marched into the clinic with a present from the Colijn girls, a notebook cover made of cloth and monogrammed.

Dinner that day marked the high point of food abundance in our captivity. We had a fat Christmas in 1942. Perhaps that is why I remember the first Yuletide so vividly. It was such a contrast to subsequent ones. Also, we still were balanced enough to appreciate life and each other and the spirit of the day. Starvation, disease, confinement, death and the bickerings of men had not yet distorted our perspectives. We could laugh and sing and perform such non-sense as serenading the small army of corveyers preparing dinner. The orchestra parked itself outside the kitchen. Clapping hands and stomping feet set a beat to which the workers chopped meat and vegetables and peeled potatoes, washed pots and pans and cut firewood. Chief Cook Beissel had been hoarding for this occasion. Also, he had used his diplomatic powers on the guards to get the necessary condi-ments for a true nasi goreng which literally means fried rice but actually connotes much more . . . just as the two words turkey dinner imply more than turkey to an Ameri-can. Beissel's only rival for food output that day was a Britisher named Knobby Clark who, from rice flour he ground himself and hard candies he made from palm sugar, steamed fifty "plum puddings" on a stove consisting of two kerosene tins set on a few loose bricks.

That night, beneath a black velvet, cloud-flecked sky, sprinkled here and there with stardust, Father Bakker's choir first sang the story of the Nativity. The kitchen porch had been transformed into a stage by judicious use of the church decorations: palm leaves, sarongs and the murals. Standing in a splash of light were the singers while beyond them in the yard's darkness men sat, squatted or stood, illuminated only by the glow of their cigarets. Tobacco and nipa leaves had been issued in the morning.

Beissel and Allen read the gospel story. When their voices ceased, Father Bakker raised his baton, swept it downward and the sacred cantata began.

One of the most difficult of all things to secure in Palem-bang Jail was silence for events such as lectures or shows. Always there were some disinterested individuals who spoiled things for others by talking, laughing or splashing. The greatest tribute to Father Bakker's genius was the silence he and his choir secured. After the singing started not even a cigaret was lighted as the music and the memo-ries it evoked held men completely hushed until the last notes throbbed and a full moon rose silvery and splendid to flood the jail yard and walls with light.

I have seldom seen an audience anywhere so moved by song as were my fellow internees that night in Palembang Jail. Most of them, I think, thanked God they were alive and asked Him to let their families also know.

In the Christmas issue of Camp News was a poem written by Allen, which I thought contained a message common to the hearts of most prisoners. Entitled, "To My Wife at Christmas," it said:

> "It needs no festal time to bring you to my mind,
> For every sunrise, every close of day, I find
> Your image by me, smiling, bidding me good cheer,
> Whispering our private nonsenses I love to hear.
> Yet to be parted at this season, for this cause,
> Seems doubly hard to bear; though if men break
>   the laws
> Of Him on high, they only have themselves to
>   blame
> For suffering; the Eternal Rules are still the same.
> Last year I hung a stocking, child-like, by your bed
> While you were sleeping; but this year my
>   thoughts instead
> And prayers and wishes to the stars and round
>   moon spoken,
> Are all the gifts that I can send to you for token
> Of all the joy there is between us, come what may.
> Have faith, my love, although the night is dark,
>   the day
> Will break, and peace and good will come to
>   men at last.
>   God bless and keep you always."

My own thoughts were summarized in one of the few editorials I ever put into Camp News. The editorial concluded by saying:

"Past Christmases were happier, we admit. But this Christmas need not be sad or gloomy. How lucky we are to be here, and not at the bottom of the Bangka Straits [where many were sunk] or in the Indian Ocean, or prisoners in certain other concentration camps. For there are worse. We have reasons to smile today. We are in good health; we are not starved; we are not cold. We are not being bombed or shelled or machine-gunned. Truly this is a wonderful Christmas because we are not among the maimed or dead. We are alive!"

Seldom have I appreciated Christmas more than that day as a war prisoner in a jail beside Sumatra's Moesi river, two degrees south of the equator. Different as was that Christmas to all of us, there was about it something which brought us closer to the real significance of the day than many of us had ever been. We had Christmas in our hearts, instead of on an electrically lighted tree or in gaudily wrapped packages from a department store.

On the day after Christmas we reciprocated the women's serenade. Father Bakker led his choir out as members of the working party. When within earshot of the Women's Camp the choir began to sing, first a verse in Dutch then a verse in English, "Come All Ye Faithful." The women were waiting, standing silently in the open space between their houses and the fence.

The choir walked as slowly as the men could move. The guards did not hurry them, but also did not let them halt.

"Come All Ye Faithful" was followed by "Silent Night, Holy Night." The Women's Camp was no longer within sight when the song ended but the choir swung into another melody, for singers knew the women could hear them still and would be listening even after the last note died.

We ushered in 1943 with a New Year's Eve show at which I was master of ceremonies. High spot of the show was intermission because a punch was served which was spiked by liquor two men had spent weeks distilling. Coils for their still were made from an electric wire conduit stolen from an abandoned house adjacent to the new camp site. The rest of the still was made of tins, bottles, and a metal firebox. Fermented rice supplied the mash. The final product was a foul tasting stuff but its viciousness was disguised by the punch it powered.

Clad only in a pair of shorts and squatting on the kitchen stoop sipping punch during intermission, I thought of the previous New Year's Eve, when Martin, Lee and I, wearing all the clothes we could find, shivered in a mud farm house and drank in 1942 with throat-searing Chinese wine while we waited to begin the most hazardous leg of our escape from Shanghai.

After the show, when everybody had shaken hands and wished each other Happy New Year, and gone to bed, I sat outside the clinic and, as men are wont when they have little else to do at such a time, reviewed the year and attempted a balancing of books. There were fewer items on the credit than on the debit side of the ledger but the black entries outweighed the red because my sense of values had changed considerably.

What I call my own private miracle had done that. After the ship on which I was escaping from Java was sunk in the Indian Ocean, I had swum up to the only lifeboat in sight. Its occupants turned me down.

"No more room," they said, and rowed away, leaving me to drown.

That was shortly before noon of March 7, 1942, approximately 250 miles southwest of Java. Death was a certainty. It was only a matter of time. Buoyed by my life belt, I spent the afternoon swimming and praying and thinking and weighing the values of life—balancing my own books.

Toward sundown a lifeboat mast appeared on the horizon. I swam toward it, but the sail was hoisted and the boat moved away. Another lifeboat came into view. It too was hoisting sail to go off without me.

"God," I prayed, "make that sail go down."

The sail collapsed.

The sail was hoisted a second time. Again I prayed. Again the sail collapsed. Twice!

I reached the boat and was pulled in. Crew members refused to go after another man who had been swimming behind me. Too many were in the boat now, they said. I was picked up only because I reached it under my own power. Had the sail's collapsing not delayed the lifeboat so I could reach it, I, too, would have been left behind. That is why I call the episode my own private miracle.

As I sat outside the clinic of Palembang Jail in the last minutes of 1942 and looked back, it was plain that the year just ending had been my greatest spiritual adventure. Its lessons had shaped a conviction that success is not measured by how high a man has climbed or whether the whole world knows his by-line; but by whether he has loved God and his neighbor, not with words only but with deeds. While swimming in the Indian Ocean and living in prison I had found what for me was the most important thing in life; and somewhere out of all the travail involved had come peace of mind.

My heart could sing and did as the guardroom clock struck two o'clock Tokyo time and it was midnight * and a New Year in Sumatra.

---

* The Japanese operated on Tokyo time throughout their areas of occupation no matter in what time zone. We internees kept our watches set on Palembang time, two hours behind Tokyo.

9

Barracks Camp–Harbinger of Evil Days

WE stripped the jail like a swarm of Mormon crickets moving through a grain field when we left it and moved to the new Barracks Camp January 16, 1943. The Japanese supplied trucks for our luggage, the first time they had given us anything but rations since our imprisonment, so we carried everything detachable. Even bricks from the bath tank floor were hidden in the debris we called our baggage—sacks, bottles, tin cans rusty and otherwise, pieces of metal and every stick of firewood stacked outside the kitchen. We left nothing but the walls.

The new camp covered a rectangular area 330 feet long and half as wide. Long windowless barracks of plank and bamboo with earthen floors and palm-thatched roofs lined the four sides. The short spaces between buildings were filled with solid wooden fence. A barbed wire fence surrounded the whole area and high sentry boxes in each of the four corners commanded views of the outer barricade and the inner yard. We had twice the space for walking and half again as much for sleeping as in Palembang Jail, and were anticipating the comfort of more living room, but we did not get it. More prisoners came. They arrived in a convoy of trucks: 126 men, two cats, four dogs, fifty-three ducks and one hundred chickens. And the men were well fleshed.

Not until we saw the newcomers did we realize how lean we had become.

They were the Dutch oil technicians of Standard and Shell who had been forcefully imported from Java to repair the damaged refineries near Palembang. They had successfully done so little that the Japanese sent them back to internment. However, they had been well treated, well fed and even paid for their time. With them they brought enough equipment to set up their own camp, complete with kitchen and first-aid facilities.

Not until they walked in on us did they know they were not to occupy a place by themselves. The surprise was mutual. When we had all unpacked, and individual living spaces been allocated, we found each man had a space six feet six inches long and twenty-seven inches wide for himself and belongings on the long bamboo sleeping benches that lined the barracks. Quarrels over who was infringing on whose space were frequent and bitter. Some men protected their rights by erecting tiny fences of sticks and wire on either side of their twenty-seven inch spaces. Others were more ingenious. They clubbed together into joint partnerships, known as *kongsies*, and enlarged their living space by various means. Those who had the necessary materials built bunks in tiers. This method allowed three men to sleep stacked one above the other, thus using only one bed space in the horizontal plane. The two free spaces served for storage and a place to sit. A few rugged individualists, using saws, cut their bed spaces from the bench and then elevated them like platforms, a few inches above the bench level. As bug life increased, those who could built lean-tos against the fence outside and slept there.

Food supplies diminished steadily from our first day in the new camp. As our diet deteriorated, skin sores and eye troubles increased. Men became night blind and by day saw double or were plagued by dancing spots. The queues of patients waiting for skin treatment grew so long that we called men up by blocks in the same way as for serving food. Hot baths were by appointment and only major cases got them because the water supply was so poor we often had no water at all.

Fortunately, we were able to increase our hospital space in the new camp. In fact, the Japanese allotted one entire barracks to the hospital and instead of bamboo sleeping benches, gave us individual wooden beds and laid a concrete floor to put them on.

As hunger preoccupied us we became calorie conscious, mentally translating every morsel of food into its components of vitamins, proteins, calories and other nutritive elements. The power packed by a few vitamins and fats was strikingly demonstrated when Doc West, after months of pleading, received a quantity of palm oil from the Japanese. Sumatra abounds in palm oil but for some reason our captors were reluctant to give it to us. Doc issued the oil, rich in Vitamin A, as medicine to men suffering night blindness. Their vision improved remarkably. More oil arrived and it was given to men with certain types of skin disease. Their sores healed.

Palm oil rations increased until, for a few months, it was possible to issue every man in camp five cubic centimeters —about one teaspoon—on his noonday rice. The effect was remarkable. Itching and burning skins were relieved. We slept better at night. Our dispositions improved and there was generally more harmony among us. And all because of a teaspoon of palm oil. That sounds small and is, but it was big to us who by late 1943 were counting things in grams and teaspoons instead of pounds or quarts. Peanuts, for example, were issued when available not by weight but by number. And salt, vital to our lives, was issued in ten gram (approximately 1/3 oz.) lots.

We moved to Barracks Camp during the wet monsoon. Rain fell steadily through January, February and March. Tons of rain, rivers of rain. The camp had excellent drainage—from one end to the other—where water piled up and earthen floors became ponds through which men waded to their sleeping benches. The yard was a quagmire of red, mucilaginous mud that gripped our wooden sandals, tore them from our feet and spilled us headlong into its gluey embrace. Falls were most frequent as we carefully picked our way back from the food lines, carrying a plate of rice— a heartbreaking mishap in prison camp.

Septic tanks, already inadequate for our numbers, over-flowed, their effluvia accentuating our discomforts and in-creasing disease hazards. Clothing, bedding and mosquito nets, wet from roof leaks, or clammy damp from moisture laden air, could not be dried because there was no sun.

Through April the rains diminished and the sun peeked out. Through May the sun shone all the time. It burned through June, July and August, drying up the land and the wells we dug when water from the city system failed. We dug the wells deeper, scraped muddy water off their bottoms and passed buckets hand to hand, chain fashion, to fill our tanks. There was no water for washing clothes and so little for our bodies that in time we stank nearly as badly as the septic tanks. Vermin thrived in the noisome barracks, swarming hungrily over us at night, biting with sharp, needle-like nips, adding their tortures to the burning skin itches which returned when the palm oil supply ended. The itch was especially fierce at night. A man's skin crawled so much that, to keep his sanity, he deserted his bed and walked up and down the yard.

Hunger and drouth raised special problems for chicken and duck owners. Should they keep the fowls and sell eggs, or kill them and sell meat? Eggs would be more profitable in the long run but the hazards against chickens living were numerous. A hen mistakenly wandered into the Australian section one evening and was quickly and silently strangled, plucked and popped into a cooking pot. Dogs, cats and rats also were their enemies. Fowls could not be kept in box coops all day and when released they might lay eggs off the family premises. Before liberating a hen to scratch in the yard the owner probed her with his fingers to determine whether an egg was in prospect.

One owner safeguarded his ducks by tying them to a small tree. Heat waves were raising dust in the yard and the panting ducks attracted the sympathy of a Japanese guard. He left his post, approached the ducks, studied their hobbles and went away. Presently he returned with a canteen of water, a cup, and a handful of rice. The ducks drank from the cup and ate from his hand.

Tempers shortened as conditions worsened. Internees became increasingly critical of their leaders. A movement started to unseat both Dutch and British members of the Camp Committee. The "oil block," which had been strengthened by the 126 newcomers, exerted its power. Although the oil men were themselves divided into Shell and Standard rivalries they had a mutual interest in being more strongly represented in camp government. The basic conflict over an "active" versus a "passive" policy toward the Japanese furnished fuel for controversy. But what finally brought matters to a boil had nothing to do with policy. Dogs caused the revolt which unseated Camp Leader Van der Vliet, British Leader Penryce and other committeemen.

The new oil men had brought four dogs with them. Three other dogs somehow found their way into camp and were adopted by non-oil men. Van der Vliet announced in July that he had been ordered by Palembang City officials to get rid of the dogs because Palembang was full of rabies. Dog owners accused Van der Vliet of lying. They said he himself wanted the dogs removed from camp and started the rabies story as an excuse. Van der Vliet hotly denied the accusations and said he was acting only under orders from the Japanese. Proof that Van der Vliet was telling the truth materialized July 14th in the form of the Palembang Indonesian dog catcher, complete with truck and assistants armed with clubs. Not a dog was in sight.

"Bring dogs in five minutes or we will go in and get them ourselves," the guard commander told unhappy Van der Vliet.

Five minutes passed, then ten, then fifteen, while Van der Vliet went through camp pleading with dog owners. Still they refused.

"Search barracks," the guard commander ordered.

Joyfully dog catcher and guards started through the barracks swinging clubs. Dog owners capitulated, produced their pets from under benches and saw them loaded into the truck and taken away. Then they turned on Van der Vliet with renewed fury, claiming that if he had resisted the initial demands the matter would have been dropped.

Van der Vliet resigned as Camp Leader. The Committee, which had supported him, called for a vote of confidence. The next day dog owners were summoned to the front gate and told by an Indonesian guard they could have their dogs back on payment of a dog license fee plus a "present." The owners paid; the dogs were returned. But the vote of confidence was held anyway and Van der Vliet and the Committee lost by five ballots.

An election was set for July 21st and campaigning began. I entered the political arena to root for Direct Action Drysdale, who decided to be a candidate when it was nearly too late to file because nearly all British signatures already had been secured for the petitions of other candidates. Sixteen signatures were required for each petition and I had obtained only fifteen shortly before filing time. Desperately I appealed to the sportsmanship of Wembley-Smythe.

"I don't like him," said Wembley-Smythe, taking a deep breath, "and I won't vote for him and I hope he's not elected because he is too headstrong and brashly unorthodox in his methods, but I'll concede he should be given a sporting chance to run for election. I'll sign his petition."

Many of his fellow countrymen were genuinely afraid that if Drysdale should become British leader he would so antagonize the Japanese that dire consequences would follow. Their fears dated from the time Drysdale dared a Japanese guard to shoot him and the guard backed down.

For a month after their capture in February, 1942, the Britishers had been forced to load ships in the Moesi river. The labor was strenuous and they were ot allowed to rest. Drysdale finally rebelled. He sat down on the dock and announced he was going to rest for ten minutes. A guard pointed his rifle at Drysdale, ordered him to get up and resume working. Drysdale refused.

"I'll shoot," said the guard, in Malay.

"Go ahead," Drysdale replied, and remained seated.

Other guards approached. Drysdale again was ordered to stand up and resume work or be shot. He again refused, and repeated his defiant,

"Shoot. I'll work when I'm rested."

Instead of shooting they reported to the officer in charge, who investigated and listened to Drysdale's demands that he and the other men were entitled to rest periods. He agreed. Thenceforth they were allowed rest periods. However, despite what Drysdale won for his companions, they were so frightened by his method—because the Japanese MIGHT have shot Drysdale and them, too—that they always mistrusted him.

My electioneering for Drysdale was in vain. He ran a poor third in the balloting. Colonial Officer Hammet was elected British Leader to replace Penryce. Standard Oil Engineer H. Van Asbeck, who was a baron of the Dutch nobility, was elected to replace Van der Vliet as liaison man between prisoners and the Japanese. That meant that in the eyes of the Japanese Van Asbeck was Camp Leader.

However, he actually was not because of a new system we inaugurated in our internal affairs whereby Resident Oranje reluctantly became Chairman of the Camp Committee and, as such, the real head of the camp.

The maneuvering necessary to get Oranje to take responsibilities many thought he should have taken from the very beginning, coupled with the entire episode of the dogs and the election, was a demonstration, in my opinion, of the scarcity and crying need of real leaders. Leaders were as necessary in prison camp as they are in the world at large. Our community of prisoners in Palembang was a cross section of society in general. Among us were all kinds of men, from ne'er-do-wells to tycoons of business, industry and government. And not one of them was a real leader. There were men of character and integrity, but in none burned that vital flame which inspires men to follow. None seemed able to really break down the barriers of nationality, blood or position that divided us. Instead of being brought closer together by our common troubles we seemed to grow increasingly suspicious of each other—suspicious that the other fellow somehow would get more than his share. And, as in ordinary life, the loudest complainers often did least to help either themselves or the community. However, I noticed one essential difference between Dutch and English malcontents. No matter how loudly the Hollander complained he usually worked hard at the job assigned him; while the British belly-acher was as lazy as he was obnoxious.

Oranje's aversion to being target for shafts from dissatisfied internees was one reason for his reluctance to accept leadership. He told me, when I asked why he did not step into the breach when Van der Vliet resigned,

"No matter who the camp leader is, he will be handicapped by his inability, in a showdown, to enforce his will because we have no laws and no agency to enforce them even if we did.

"It seems to be the nature of men in here to rebel against

authority unless that authority is their boss in civil life and controls their paychecks. I do not wish to make enemies in this camp who will remain so after the war."

There was also, I suspected, the matter of his dignity, both in relation to the Japanese and to us internees.

As Resident of Palembang, Oranje was our highest ranking official. That automatically made him the natural leader of the camp but he had declined from the beginning to assume office on grounds it would bring him into a relationship with Japanese authorities that would compel him to recognize them as the government of Sumatra. He refused to pay such recognition.

His objection was by-passed just before the election by a plan which provided for Oranje to be Chairman of the Camp Committee because of his position as Resident and without election. That would save him the "indignity" of standing election. The elected liaison man, whom Oranje would rank, would be Camp Leader in Japanese eyes but not in reality. Thus Oranje became a kind of power behind the throne while the ostensible leader was Van Asbeck.

"Politically, our lives in here are just as complicated as in ordinary life," I commented to Chief Cook Beissel after the election. "And just as in ordinary political life the most trifling thing sometimes will change history. Look what a few dogs started."

That reminded Beissel of a dog story.

"Did you ever hear of the American Pied Piper of Bali?" he asked.

I had not. Beissel told me.

Everybody knows about Bali but only those who have been there know about its pariah dogs. They are to Bali what the snakes were to Ireland and the rats to Hamelin town. An American woman tourist with a love for Bali, a large purse and a crusader's zeal, decided to do something about it. Beissel was one of the Dutch civil servants there at the time who cooperated fully, glad of a chance to reduce the island's canine population at no cost to the government.

The woman sent for an American dog exterminating specialist. He arrived equipped with catching devices and gas chambers. But he had not envisaged the size of his task. After long investigation, including a census that stopped after ten thousand dogs had been counted, the expert said the dogs would breed faster than he could round them up for gas chambering. Most of them would have to be exterminated by other means.

The government supplied him with rifles, ammunition and assistants. He organized what was probably a record pariah dog hunt. Beissel accompanied him on a half-day expedition wherein eleven hundred dogs were killed. He hunted and killed for eight months and finally quit in despair without any appreciable diminution of the canine population.

"What happened to the American lady?" I asked.

"I don't know," said Beissel.

Sea Lion Smallwood, who had waddled up to join the conversation, ventured an opinion,

"Maybe she joined one of your American birth control leagues to get a few pointers," he said, and laughed until he was purple-faced and breathless.

"Time to ring the tea bell," said Beissel, and started for the kitchen. I walked part way with him and asked;

"Are there any cooks among the new oil men?"

"I think there are several good ones," he said. "Why?"

"Oh, I was just wondering. Got nothing better to wonder about."

Actually, I was wondering how long it would be before someone would start a movement to get Beissel out of the kitchen. He was a prodigious worker and an excellent cook but that would mean little if rations got leaner and dissatisfied men started looking for someone to be the goat, since they couldn't vent their anger on the real culprits, the

Japanese. Psychologically, that factor of being helpless to combat the real cause of our hunger probably played a large but unrealized part in our internal bickerings. We couldn't get at the Japanese so we substituted whipping boys who were the current powers in camp life. Petty hates, as well as malnutrition, floods and drouth, were our companions in Barracks Camp and harbingers of evil days ahead.

10

Verities: Mundane and Eternal

DENTIST HARLEY-CLARK, who with Dr. Hollweg had been taken away from Palembang Jail to work in a hospital for natives, was returned to us in Barracks Camp. He said the Kempeitai appeared at the hospital, brought him back to internment but arrested Dr. Hollweg and took him to their own private jail. Harley-Clark moved into the eight-foot-square hospital staff room occupied by Allen, myself, a New Zealander named Wilson and numerous rats who lay low by day and frolicked around at night. The dentist brought with him two small sacks of green beans which had to be protected against the rats. We decided the safest place would be hanging in midair, suspended on a wire from the ceiling.

Careful calculations showed that if the beans were hung in the exact center of the room they would be four feet from any wall, too far for a rat to jump. We retired that night feeling sure the beans were safe. But next morning holes had been gnawed in the sacks. Rats had proved they not only could reach the wire but shinny up and down it. Harley-Clark fashioned a conical tin guard around the wire and we retired the second night, certain they could not get around that rat guard. They did.

We greased the wire before going to bed the third night. Strange noises awakened us. I switched on the electric light we were allowed to burn in the clinic. There was a rat crouched on the tin guard. Frightened by the light he had paused for a moment in his frantic efforts to go back up the wire. Then he resumed them, but the grease was too thick and slippery. He would start up and slide back, start up and slide back. He tried again and again until finally, either baffled or exhausted, he stopped, clung to the rat guard and watched us. Perhaps it was my imagination, but I fancied his sharp features were wrinkled with bewilderment. Now was the time for us to act.

"He's yours," said Harley-Clark, "I can't reach him."

I grasped a club we had made for this specific moment and stood up to swat the rat. He must have read my mind. In one enormous leap he sprang from the tin, cleared the four feet of space to the wall and scuttled out the window. Harley-Clark took his beans to bed with him after that.

We had long hoped that Mehitabel, the cat who moved into the clinic bedroom with us, would prove the answer to rats but our hopes were killed and my faith in cats forever dashed by Mehitabel's base treachery. Mehitabel was lured into our room by blandishments of food and luxurious shelter. She had just given birth to two kittens in another part of camp and wandered into our room obviously house hunting. Under his bed, Allen had an empty, fiberboard suitcase with a hole in it. We put Mehitabel in the suitcase and turned it so she could come out the hole. Delighted she emerged from the hole, mewed her thanks and scampered out the door. Ten minutes later she returned carrying a kitten. A second trip brought the second kitten. Our next problem was to keep Mehitabel from moving elsewhere when the kittens were older.

We reasoned that if she were treated royally she would not want to leave and so we squandered precious food on her. Our most treasured possession was a bottle of rendered pork fat which had cost us much negotiating and twenty guilders. Fat was the closest thing to meat we had tasted since early days in Palembang Jail. Every other day members of our kongsie got one teaspoonful each of melted fat on their rice. Mehitabel was included. She loved it. Occasionally our rations included dried fish and we divided those with her. I had acquired some powdered milk I was saving for lean times. Mehitabel got that too.

We cherished her by day and at night watched her kittens so she could feel free to roam as she wished without fear of harm to her offspring. At first she would not leave them for more than a few minutes at a time. To ease her mind Wilson and I became kitten sitters. When Mehitabel mewed desire to roam one or the other of us would take the kittens into our mosquito nets. Satisfied, she would leave and be gone for hours. The arrangement pleased Mehitabel so much she took to waking us up three or four times a night: first to give us the kittens, then to get them back; then to give them to us and so on. Exasperating, but we endured it cheerfully. We wanted Mehitabel to be happy.

She consumed our pork fat and my powdered milk. The kittens grew large enough to roam around themselves at night. They expressed dissatisfaction with the suitcase so we made them a new bed. They became very temperamental but we put up with all their whims because we knew the kittens soon would be large enough to catch rats. In fact rats had completely avoided our bedroom since Mehitabel's arrival.

But when the pork fat bottle and the milk powder tin were empty Mehitabel deserted us. She took the kittens to another part of camp where she got nothing but indifference and had to forage for herself. Why? I'll never know. But I'll never trust a cat again, especially a lady cat.

Among necessaries of life difficult to obtain in prison camp were false teeth. If a man lost his real teeth he was in a bad way.

Dentist Harley-Clark one day told a nearly toothless

customer, "If somebody will donate a spare plate, I can help you."

But no one had teeth to spare until Whitey died. He went suddenly and unexpectedly during the night. We carried him from the ward into the clinic and laid him on a bench to wait until the guards produced a coffin. They had a rule bodies had to be in coffins when they were taken out for burial. I was looping a rag around Whitey's head to hold his jaw shut when I remembered Harley-Clark's promise.

"How about it, Doc?" I asked West.

"Good idea," he said, "maybe Harley can use them."

So I removed Whitey's plates. Harley-Clark went to work on them and in a few days another man was eating with Whitey's false teeth. But he never knew whence they came.

The camp orchestra tripled in size with arrival of the new oil men. They brought enough wire with them to supply strings for a half dozen guitars and two bull fiddles. Finding only two guitars in camp and no bull fiddles they made the instruments themselves. Such an orchestra could not be wasted on small scale productions so we staged larger ones every month on the night the moon was full. Master of ceremonies for several productions was an English planter named D. F. Pratt, the nephew of an English actor, William Henry Pratt, whose Hollywood name is Boris Karloff. Pratt's jokes were translated into Dutch by Controleur De Jong, who also possessed the best baritone in jail and sang Malay love songs and lullabies. If I were a girl in love and my boy friend could sing, there are few melodies that would please me more than those the Malays sing when the moon is full. My favorite was *Terang Boelan*, which means Clear Moon.

When Pratt ran out of jokes his place as master of ceremonies was taken by a young radio announcer from Singapore named Andrew Carruthers, who organized a production team comprising Poker Shark Attenborough, an Australian consular service man named John Quinn and a rotund jokester named Magnay. They staged most of our shows until illness halted them. A revue written entirely by Librarian Lawson climaxed our monthly concerts. Lawson composed a tuneful theme song named "Singapore Way" and built around it a show for which we rehearsed nightly for a month. Eric Germann and I played the parts of husband and wife. By wearing backwards, with appropriate stitching, a man's black satin dressing gown, inserting the halves of two coconut shells into a home-made brassiere, donning a tight fitting turban bonnet and lavishing Chinese cosmetics in the right places, I made a passable looking wife. Except for Eric's beard, which he declined to remove, we might have been the gum chewing American tourists we were supposed to represent. Lawson's show was our last concert of magnitude, because hunger was beginning to take its toll. More and more men were cracking and becoming physically unable or psychologically unwilling to participate in theatricals.

When our diminishing food supplies were augmented with soya beans we whooped for joy, only to discover in a few days that they went through us like beebee shot. Many internees could not digest the beans no matter how long they were cooked. Individual men solved the bean problem by grinding them into coarse flour which was roasted, then sprinkled on rice. An Australian named Marning made a mortar and pestle from a tree stump. He drilled a hole perpendicularly through the stump, burned out a hollow depression, carved it smooth and had a mortar. The pestle he made from a stone fitted onto a long, heavy wooden handle. He rented the mortar and pestle for a percentage of flour ground.

Germann and Canadian Christie also went into the milling business, using a coffee grinder. They charged thirty-five cents a kilogram (seventeen cents a pound) for their labor and figured two hours of grinding per kilogram.

In Barracks Camp our horizon, instead of being a jagged profile of stone wall and tiled roofs as in Palembang Jail, was a far-flung line where green trees met blue sky. Evenings, therefore, we could marvel at the fantastic grandeur of tropic sunsets and, as dusk deepened, watch lines of flying foxes winging from their jungle lairs in search of food. The flying fox is a species of large frugivorous bat with a fox-like head. As the weird creatures beat slowly along not far above the tree tops, with their four and five foot wingspreads, they looked enormous. They reminded me of vampire bats of fiction, so sinister did they appear as their dark wings flapped silently overhead.

Immediately after sunset a solitary flying fox, as if reconnoitering, would wing slowly over camp from east to west and disappear. Soon came the advance guard of from three to ten, directly on the trail of the leader and flying wide apart. Behind them came groups in close formation and then the main body. Hundreds of fox-bats, flying so low it seemed we should have heard the beat of their wings, but there was no sound. They might have been shadows, they were so quiet. Stragglers brought up the rear and when even the last stragglers should have passed, along would come a single bat, like the solitary leader. We never saw them flying eastward for they returned during the night. Occasionally I thought I saw single flying foxes silhouetted against the moon. But I was never sure. They might have been ordinary, smaller bats which frequented our camp and ultimately furnished an article of diet for starving men.

While trying to determine one night whether the silhouettes were flying foxes winging high or ordinary bats flying low I saw my first moonlight thunderstorm.

The moon had risen full, peering over the edge of the world like an enormous bloodshot eye dwarfing everything of earth. As it floated free of the horizon, it bled white and shrank until it was just the moon, inanimate in space and reflecting its cold, second-hand light that glimmered dully on nipa palm leaves which thatched our roofs. The shadows of men walking in the yard gradually shortened as the moon rose higher.

In the north thunder muttered, like distant guns, and in that direction the stars were blotted out. Slowly the curtain which obscured them grew and blackened and moved like a flood across the sky. Thunder sounded with a crunching and grinding akin to rocks moving unseen but terribly alive within the waters of a flash flood down a western arroyo. And, as in such a flood, the earth trembled from their force.

But an invisible, supernal dyke halted the flood before it could invade the southern sky and drown the moon. Instead, it piled up higher and higher in the heavens until it seemed higher than the moon. Convulsively, with blinding lightning bolts and ear-shattering thunder claps, the giant sought to burst its bonds but the dyke held—a celestial equator splitting the sky into northern and southern hemispheres of storm and calm so that the moon could ride down the middle serene and unafraid.

"Awesome spectacle, isn't it?" crackled a husky, penetrating voice, and Wembley-Smythe ambled across the moon-bathed yard. "Too beautiful a night to waste sleeping. Let's take a few turns around the quadrangle."

We fell in step.

"Nights like this almost make me believe in a personal God and a hereafter," said Wembley-Smythe.

I asked him in what kind of God he did believe.

"Oh, a vast, impersonal Intelligence that started things spinning and hasn't bothered much with them since."

That started us debating again about the origin of things and he reminded me of our unfinished discussion in Palembang Jail.

"Do you really doubt the existence of God?" I asked.

"Or are you only throwing it out as a bait for argument?"

He laughed and said, "I suppose I do believe in God. It is illogical to say things simply started by themselves. There had to be a first cause and we call it God. However, I'm very doubtful there is a hereafter of any kind, a heaven or hell or anything else, beyond the grave. When the end comes, well, I think it simply will be the end. That is why I am neutral on the so-called eternal verities, but obviously you are not. Why take your beliefs so seriously?"

"Because we can't be neutral about religious truth any more than we can be neutral about mathematical truth," I said. "One is as true as the other. But we quibble about religious truth because it entails obligations on the believer. If believing seven times eight equals fifty-six also meant that we had to keep the Ten Commandments and go to church on Sunday, there would be a hell of a lot of debate over whether or not seven times eight really did equal fifty-six or some other sum; and men would split up into mathematical sects, each one giving a different answer to seven times eight, yet each one declaring that it had the only correct answer."

"It's not quite that simple," said Wembley-Smythe. "You can demonstrate with chalk or beans or your fingers that seven times eight equals fifty-six but you can't demonstrate so easily which of the claimants to religious truth is right, or whether all of them are wrong."

I agreed that demonstrating religious truth was not as simple as reciting the multiplication table but insisted that with good will on the seeker's part, truth could be found and had been found by countless millions since Christ walked among men.

"You've got to want to find the truth and accept it without reservations when you find it," I said. "Recognizing truth and accepting it as your standard of life are two different things. You can recognize it and not accept it."

"What if I neither accept nor reject what you call truth, but maintain a neutral attitude?" he asked.

"You cannot be neutral," I said. "Being 'neutral' to God is tantamount to denying Him. Christ Himself said, 'He who is not with Me is against Me.' Those words are either true or not true. There is no middle way. You are either for God or against Him. You make the choice. If you're against Him during your life on earth you'll be against Him in the next."

"Go on," laughed Wembley-Smythe, "say it. If I'm against Him here, in the next I'll fry."

"And without benefit of palm oil," I quipped. "Seriously, however," I said, "this internment can be a blessing in disguise for all of us because we've got so much time to think and figure out what counts most in life."

"You're right there," said Wembley-Smythe, "although I really don't need *all* the time we're having to think it out. But go on, what else do you think?"

I said I believed the really fundamental battle lines of the world were not between the currently contending armies but between forces fighting to control the souls of men and such forces were on both sides. Whatever the military results of the war the struggle for men's souls would go on.

"We can't be neutral any more than a soldier in battle can be indifferent as to which side wins, his or the enemy's. Neutrals will perish wondering what struck them."

"If you're going to perish," said Wembley-Smythe, "what does it matter whether you die knowing or not knowing what hit you? You will be dead anyway."

"Your body will be dead, yes, but not your soul," I said. "How do you think a neutral soul will fare when it stands in judgment before God? There's a passage in the New Testament that gives a good hint. It goes something like 'because you are neither hot nor cold but lukewarm I am about to vomit you out of my mouth.'"

"You're too vehement," said Wembley-Smythe, "and

we're right back where we started. In the last analysis you have to accept on faith that you have a soul that is immortal and that it will be judged after death. None of those beliefs is demonstrable."

"Not by test tube methods, no," I agreed. "But faith in the eternal verities is not a matter of test tube proof. It is belief because of the veracity and authority of a witness whose veracity and authority are unimpeachable. It is believing a thing because someone who knows and who would not deceive you tells you it is true. Faith is neither a pious feeling of sweetness and light nor a haunting premonition of doom. It is as solid and real as the air in your lungs or as the certainty that there is another side to the moon or as the knowledge that seven times eight does equal fifty-six."

"You mentioned believing a thing because someone who would not deceive you tells you it is true," said Wembley-Smythe. "There's the weak link in your reasoning. You are accepting someone else's word."

"Certainly, we go through life accepting other people's words for most of the things we think and do. If your mother tells you about an episode in her childhood do you dispute it because you weren't there? Or do you call Einstein a liar because your mind can not grasp the theory of relativity? All of recorded history is taking other people's words for things that happened. You take almost anybody's word for anything except the most important thing—that you have an immortal soul. I take Christ's word there is a hereafter because my reason tells me He proved beyond all doubt that He was a qualified authority to speak about the hereafter."

Wembley-Smythe remained unimpressed.

"We'll simply never agree," he said. "I'd like to know whether there is anything after death, but I don't. And I doubt very much that there is. As I said before, when the end comes, well, I think it simply will be the end.

"If I'm wrong I'll find out when I awaken someday standing outside the Pearly Gates; and if I'm right, there won't be any awakening at all, will there? Just an eternal blackout. How dreadfully boring if one were compelled to be aware of it!"

We walked in silence for a while. The moon was drifting westward to retire. We decided to follow suit.

"Good night," we told each other, "good night."

11
The Reckoning

THE Japanese cracked down in the third quarter of 1943. The crack-down came in the form of a well planned pogrom throughout southern Sumatra both inside and outside of war prisoner camps. In Palembang itself Ambonese died by the hundreds and Chinese by the score. The mortality rate among interned Hollanders was considerably lower. I know of eight who were beheaded and perhaps a score who were sentenced to seven-year terms at hard labor in special Kempeitai prisons. Indirectly, however, hundreds of prisoners died during the next two years because rations were drastically reduced.

Looking back it is apparent that the Kempeitai began preparing for the purge nearly a year before it happened. A preliminary was building of Barracks Camp which began coincident with stories in the local Malay language newspaper condemning rumor mongering. Shortly thereafter, and while we were still in the jail, newspaper announcements said all radios in possession of natives had to be reported for inspecting and licensing. Unlicensed radios were forbidden. Javanese guards told us that "licensing" meant that all radios capable of receiving short wave broadcasts were confiscated.

A front page Malay language editorial signed by Lieutenant General H. Kasai, Governor of South Sumatra, said, "Natives are filled with propaganda that the Allies will land here and destroy the Japanese. Such reports are false and ridiculous. The Allies could long ago have been destroyed completely.

"However, although the Allies will never be able to resurrect their strength sufficiently to land troops in force here, they probably will attempt air raids or try to land small groups of men by submarine. Therefore, the people of Palembang must expect anything but also must have confidence in Nippon's strength and once again hit at the false propaganda from the enemy which is being spread by radio or other means."

We had just finished translating the editorial and were discussing it when a trumpet sounded somewhere outside. The notes came closer and closer. Whoever played them was moving along the street toward the jail. The music sounded high and clear and grew louder. We ran to the front gate to peer out and see who the player was. We were just in time to glimpse a bicycle ricksha bearing a passenger who was blowing the trumpet. The ricksha peddled slowly past. The music died away down the street, playing the same tune over again, "Whispering."

It started us whispering among ourselves. Were unknown native friends outside trying to tell us something? Fanciful as it sounds now, at the time it was incredibly heartening to prisoners grasping at straws of encouragement. From that day onward we began to hear persistent rumors of arrests among Palembang's Ambonese and Chinese population.

After we left the jail and moved to Barracks Camp, Javanese guards confirmed the rumors as facts and told us that we had been transferred so the jail could be used as a Kempeitai prison.

In July, 1943, news of Allied landings in Sicily, of Mussolini's "resignation" and the succession of Badoglio appeared in the Malay newspaper. Joy swept Barracks Camp. But on the heels of our elation came ominous developments in Palembang. Nearly all Ambonese men in the city and many women were rounded up and crammed into Palembang

Jail. Javanese guards said the Ambonese were bound hand and foot, tied in twos, back to back, and given water only once a day. Most of them died.

Illicit radios and arms were said to have been found in homes of Ambonese who were accused of operating a Dutch sponsored underground.

Dr. Ziesel of Charitas hospital was arrested.

A friendly Japanese doctor told Dr. West that a radio transmitter had been discovered operating somewhere on the coast; therefore, we could expect more prisoners to be crowded in with us.

"When we are going forward and winning," said the doctor, "we must take prisoners and intern them; if we lose and retreat, we must take more."

He unsheathed his sword and pointed to stains on the blade near the hilt.

"Two heads," he laughed. "Cut off in Malaya."

He sheathed the sword and said he would like to help us but he could not. He had been ordered to be more strict on admitting prisoners to Charitas. As for food, we would get less because "rice is so expensive."

Kempeitai agents called at Barracks Camp and took away Resident Oranje and his secretary, an Indo-European named Lubblik-Weddik. Lubblik had been the chief guitarist of our concerts. Soon the Kempeitai men returned and removed more government servants plus four bankers and two coal mine operators. Most of them, including Oranje, were returned in a few weeks, badly frightened men. They had seen companions—who did not return—emerge broken from torture grilling by the Kempeitai who accused the Dutch of having instituted and financed the alleged Ambonese underground.

Kempeitai headquarters was in the former residence of a Dutch banker named Geroms, who was among those arrested. Ironically, Geroms died in his own house after weeks of torture. Prisoners in the room next to his said

Geroms defied his inquisitors to the end. They could hear blows rained on his body and Geroms, between moans, jeer at his torturers:

"Hit me again. Hit me again. When the Americans come they will hit you."

"When the Americans come," was a popular phrase among the Dutch and, judging from newspaper editorial fulminations, was also frequently whispered among the natives. Our Indonesian guards said it when Japanese were out of earshot, but they used it with different shades of meaning, contingent upon whether they were Javanese secretly friendly or Malays many of whom were hostile.

Oranje returned to Barracks Camp convinced there were informers among us who told the Japanese everything we said or did. He ordered Camp News discontinued and all back numbers destroyed. Because of increased clinic work I had ceased editing the newspaper shortly after coming to the new camp. My successor as editor was the Australian consular man, John Quinn. Whether Quinn destroyed the back numbers issued during his editorship I didn't ask but I considered mine too precious as souvenirs to be burned. Instead I buried them. Nick Koot, the young Shell Oil engineer who told me the glass eye story, made the necessary container for me. Using empty cans and solder, he fashioned a cylinder of two thicknesses of tin with insulation between the layers. Acting on a hunch that the Japanese soon might search the camp I decided also to bury my diaries.

The bicycle inner tube I had bought before my capture, also on a hunch, now proved its worth. We cut it into strips and used them to seal three wide-mouthed bottles which once had contained quinine tablets. Inside the bottles were my diaries. Where to bury them worried me next.

The best place, I thought, was under the cement foundation of the hospital. Even if the camp were destroyed the foundation would still be there as a landmark after the war. But digging under the foundation unobserved was impossible in a crowded camp filled with curious eyes. It had to be done so openly that no one would be curious. I enlisted the aid of the hospital general handyman, J. F. Jones, who could hammer, saw, or excavate with impunity. Jones dug a shallow trench alongside the foundation ostensibly to change the course of the water pipe running to the hospital kitchen. At distances of 27, 30 and 33 feet from the southeast corner of the foundation he burrowed under the edge of the cement and inserted the tin and the bottles. Then he filled in the trench, loudly berating people who kept changing their minds about where a pipeline should be laid.

One week later Kempeitai agents thoroughly ransacked the camp. That was the first and last time the Japanese ever did a complete job of searching us. And even that job was poorly executed. The searchers tired quickly, too many bugs. For an hour or so they were painstakingly thorough, and since they began with the hospital they went through it inch by inch, but after a few hours they grew careless and the last stages of the search consisted in little more than a helter-skelter tearing apart of men's belongings and scattering them on the ground.

Next day trucks disgorged a score of sick men at the gate. Charitas had been closed and its patients returned to their respective camps.

The Japanese had been gradually tightening up at Charitas ever since the previous January, when Mrs. Curran-Sharp, wife of our camp poet, was caught smuggling sixty-two letters into the hospital. She was not punished, individually, the Japanese said, because the letters only proved the men had been smuggling letters too. From that time on it became more difficult to get patients into Charitas. Surgeon Peter Tekelenburg and Mother Alacoque, the hospital superior, sent word to us they feared Charitas would be closed eventually. Their fears materialized in September, 1943.

Dr. Tekelenburg accompanied the patients to Barracks Camp. He moved into our hospital staff quarters and gave Dr. West what small surgical instruments he had been able to salvage and hide in his pockets.

"You had better keep these," he said, "because I fear the Kempeitai are going to arrest me."

They did, and also Mother Alacoque who had been sent to the Women's Camp. Later, the Japanese informed us they had sentenced Dr. Tekelenburg and Mother Alacoque to seven years in military prison for "aiding the enemy." The enemy was us. The doctor and the nun were paying for the letters and money smuggled through Charitas to the men's and women's camps.

The Kempeitai charged that the money was connected in some way with the alleged Ambonese underground. They said the Ambonese and Menadonese in Palembang had collected funds to give the Allies should the Allies invade Sumatra. However, the Kempeitai never did discover Dr. Tekelenburg's radio or that news from it was relayed through Charitas. If they had, he and Mother Alacoque probably would have been executed, as happened to another man, in another camp, whose hidden radio was discovered.

Not until after the war did we learn the ultimate fates of those arrested. Dr. Tekelenburg and 171 Ambonese and Menadonese were manacled to long chains and transported to a prison camp named Soengei Liat on the island of Bangka. Only seven survived the war. Dr. Tekelenburg was among the dead. In another group fifty-one Ambonese were shot, beaten, or stabbed to death October 30, 1943, on the edge of a large pit on Palembang's outskirts.

Dr. Ziesel and nine Ambonese were executed, by beheading, November 9, 1943. Oranje's secretary, Lubblik-

Weddik, with three Chinese and some Indonesians, was executed November 14, 1944.

Mother Alacoque and four Ambonese women sentenced to prison with her survived. The nun was forced to kneel, hour after hour, with her hands behind her and her head bare and bowed, while she was grilled by Kempeitai inquisitors. They learned nothing from her.

Among other Dutch executed in 1943 and 1944 were Resident Myndersma, of the Lampong district, in whose possession the Japanese found a quantity of letters written by internees to their wives in Java to be smuggled by a native courier; Police Commissioner Kamphuis, of Tandjong Karang, who confessed to hiding a radio; Resident Maier, of the Benkoelen district, and three other men, Veer of Tandjong Karang; Walter of Tandjong Enim, and Stammershaus of Lahat, all accused of either destroying money so the Japanese could not confiscate it when they first arrived or of helping finance the alleged underground. I was never able to confirm to my own satisfaction that a systematized underground, directed by the Dutch, really had existed in south Sumatra, although one did operate in some other parts of the Indies.

Bishop Mekkelholt was among those who returned from Charitas. He brought copies of the Singapore newspaper, telling of a second exchange of nationals between the United States and Japan. With sinking heart I saw I had missed another chance. The second exchange ship, like the first a year before, would pass through Sunda Straits where my lifeboat had made landfall in 1942.

I did not know, of course, that on the ship was prisoner of war mail and in the mail a card I had written the previous March. It arrived home two days before Christmas, 1943. That was the first news they had of me after Java fell. United Press followed that lead, through the International

Red Cross, and in 1944 received word that my name was no longer among prisoners of war in Sumatra. They decided then, as did almost everyone except my family, that I had died after writing the card.

On September 14, 1943, within a few days of Charitas' closing, we were ordered to pack for a move to an undisclosed destination. We hoped it would be to Java, where we understood war prisoners were better fed. Our spirits were especially buoyed by a paragraph in the Palembang newspaper which said a repatriation ship was leaving Batavia, Java, September 23rd. We had wild hopes that some of us, at least, might sail on it.

We were cheerful men as we marched through Palembang before dawn and boarded a boat in the Moesi river. When daylight came we were moving downstream, toward the sea, and our hopes of going to Java soared.

But our ebullience changed to apprehension when the boat left the river mouth and, instead of turning southward to pass through the straits which lie between Sumatra and the little island of Bangka, continued right across them and by midafternoon approached the island itself.

Ever since arriving in Palembang Jail I had heard tales of the horrors of Bangka Straits and Bangka Island and its port of Muntok. Forty-odd ships—ranging from less than 100 to several thousand tons—jammed with refugees fleeing Singapore, had been sunk in the Straits in February, 1942. A majority of the estimated three thousand passengers on them perished. Most survivors swam or floated ashore on Bangka beach and, after being rounded up, spent a harrowing month in the prison at Muntok. Everything they had since experienced was as nothing, they said, compared with the Bangka Straits and Muntok Prison. They talked as though they had been delivered from the jaws of hell instead of from a man-made jail.

As we approached Muntok that September afternoon,

Eric pointed out a distant promontory, scarcely distinguishable in the haze. On the other side of the promontory, he said, was a lighthouse which had been a saving beacon to some of his companions but to most had been only a light which blinked tantalizingly in their eyes as they drowned.

On the beach, not far from the lighthouse, Eric had been executed and left for dead by a Japanese patrol.

12

The Saga of Eric Germann

ERIC GERMANN, my American fellow prisoner, was the only man I ever met who was executed and lived to tell about it. His adventure began when, wearing a pair of high leather boots and a fireman's helmet donned while helping fight Singapore's bomb-set conflagrations, he boarded the S.S. *Vyner-Brooke*, a 700-odd ton passenger-freighter built for and named after the Englishman known as the White Rajah of Sarawak, in Borneo.

When Eric first saw the vessel in burning, bomb-shattered Singapore harbor he thought he was looking at a marvelously reduced copy of a large Cunard liner. For war purposes her white surface had been painted battle-ship gray, her bridge bundled up with mattresses, her windows and portholes covered and she was armed with a rack of depth charges, two Y guns and a three-inch anti-submarine gun.

"She looked tough, chunky and reliable," said Eric, "and I sure was glad to get aboard her."

Most of the 250 passengers were women, children and old men, plus a few able-bodied fellows like Eric who had been given special permits to leave beleaguered Singapore. Sixty-three Australian army nurses were assigned cots on the promenade deck. White European civilians packed the dining saloon and Eurasians were jammed in the after-hatch. Remaining passengers were sprawled about the decks, corridors and companionways. The forward hatch held the Chinese crew which had been replaced in operating the ship by some Malays with British naval ratings and a few British army lads picked up because of their previous marine experience.

The *Vyner-Brooke* threaded her way through the harbor's mine field, closely followed by another refugee-laden vessel, the *Mata Hari*. Aboard the *Mata Hari* were Doc West and Direct Action Drysdale. The two vessels moved slowly past the inferno of burning oil tanks that was Singapore's oil storage depot on Bukum island, past the hulk of a blazing ship, away from the flaming glow of the water-front and its lurid reflection in the harbor; moved out of ear-shot of rumbling guns and exploding bombs, straight south into the quiet night.

Eric went to sleep lying between a grossly fat English civil engineer whose most recent job had been camouflaging Malayan airports, and a middle-aged couple from South Africa, Mr. and Mrs. Buridge.

Six Japanese bombers found the *Vyner-Brooke* about 2 P.M. February 14. She zigzagged so successfully that twenty-six bombs missed her but the twenty-seventh smashed through the forward hatch, exploded inside the ship and blew a hole in the keel. A Malay crew member rushed onto the deck from a passageway. His hair and clothing had been burned off, leaving only his shoes, belt and shreds of his shorts which were still smoldering. The Malay's body was covered with immense, flat blisters and yellow froth exuded from his mouth and eyes. He tried to speak but could only gurgle incoherently. Eric extinguished his smoldering shorts and asked two nurses to take him to a lifeboat.

The *Vyner-Brooke* was filling rapidly and listing. Life belts had been issued the night before and passengers instructed that, in case of sinking, they were to descend into the water via ropes or Jacob's ladders and wait to be picked up by lifeboats and liferafts. The boats when lowered would still be secured to the ship by long drag lines. The rafts would float free as the ship sank. There was little talking and no panic as the order was given to abandon ship, only a general uncertainty what to do.

Looking over the side Eric saw that the last boat he had helped lower had lodged directly beneath a water condenser outlet and was rapidly filling. He hopped over the rail, slithered down a Jacob's ladder and into the boat. He loosened the drag line, allowing the boat to drift farther back and out of the outlet's path. Then he discovered the real reason it was filled with water. Bomb fragments had holed it, as well as three other starboard lifeboats. Only their sealed, empty air tanks kept them afloat.

Women were coming over the tilting sides of the *Vyner-Brooke* in a steady file, lowering themselves into the sea and bobbing helplessly away with the current. Eric realized that they would be swept away from any possible assistance before the liferafts would float free. He determined to get back on deck and, despite contrary instructions, to shove off the liferafts.

He had to swim from the lifeboat to the ladder and, even with his life belt, his heavy boots dragged him under, but he made it. Eric was an expert swimmer and once had been a lifeguard at a New York boys' camp. Hooking one leg over the ladder's lowest rung and with his face underwater he shucked off his life belt as being too cumbersome for movement, then unlaced and removed his boots. Descending women, still wearing their high heels, used his head as a stepping stone into the sea. Each time he removed his face from the water to gulp air he berated the women for their inconsiderateness.

"I should have saved my breath though," he told me, "for as I began creeping up the ladder they cursed me, and just as fluently as any man. But they had a peculiar reason for swearing at me. They shrieked that I was crawling up the ladder as they came down just so I could look up their legs!

"Such modesty stunned me. I wheezed myself to the rail without being able to think of a reply."

Eric reached the deck only to have four-year-old Mischa Warmen thrust into his arms. Mischa was the son of a White Russian couple from Shanghai. When the first bombs fell Mischa's panic-stricken father leaped overboard. His wife screamed,

"He can't swim. Somebody save him. He can't swim!"

"I'll get him," yelled a British soldier and jumped into the sea.

He reached Mr. Warmen but the frightened White Russian seized him around the neck and both men disappeared. Mrs. Warmen collapsed. She was unable to help either herself or her son as the *Vyner-Brooke* sank. A soldier assisted her over the ship's side and someone else handed Mischa to Eric.

"Don't be afraid," Eric told the child. "We're just going to jump into the water for a nice, cool swim."

Calmly Mischa put his arms around Eric's neck. Eric held his hand over the child's mouth and nose and jumped. Mischa was quiet and smiling when they bobbed to the surface and they both laughed.

Eric swam to the nearly submerged lifeboat and placed the child inside. The fat civil engineer was floating nearby screaming for help. Eric thrashed after him, silenced his cries, towed him to the boat, boosted him in and told him to look after the child. A wounded soldier was Eric's next customer. Six or seven people in all got inside the boat and cut the fall line. Eric clambered in himself, picked up an oar and pulled. The boat was barely afloat, crowded and ringed with people clinging to the looped handlines on the sides.

Screams from a nearby liferaft attracted attention of rowers. They were amazed to see a woman being pushed off the raft by other women. She swam to the boat screaming for help. Eric recognized her as a Eurasian hairdresser named Marie, who had busied herself on shipboard helping old people and the sick. The all-white occupants of the raft would spare no room for a Eurasian.

"Take her back or we'll capsize you," Eric yelled.

His rowing companions supported him, cursed the women for their hard-heartedness and maneuvered the boat alongside the raft as though to carry out their threat of capsizing it. The women pulled Marie back aboard.

The *Vyner-Brooke* turned turtle and disappeared in a smear of fuel oil. One Japanese bomber returned to the scene, skimmed low over the sea, machine-gunned a lifeboat and flew away.

Ginger Sedgeman, chief mate of the *Vyner-Brooke*, swam up and joined the ring of people clinging to the hand lines. Three empty liferafts floated into sight. Men swam after them, attached them to the boat with a long line. Everyone except rowers then was transferred to the rafts and the long pull began to Bangka Island, just visible in the distance.

After sundown they saw flashings from two lighthouses about five miles apart on the coast. Midway between them burned a large bonfire. They pulled for the fire.

Water covered the boat seats on which they sat to row. A breeze sprang up, chilling them through their sodden shirts. Eric removed his, handing it for safekeeping to the fat civil engineer who had proved so useless at an oar he no longer rowed. The engineer let the garment float away.

They landed near the bonfire about half past eight and found around it approximately thirty survivors who had reached shore earlier. The *Vyner-Brooke* First Officer was there, some soldiers, sailors, nurses and civilian women and children. Eric sat hunched on the sand, his knees drawn up and his head between them. Despite the fire he shivered. He resolved to walk higher up the beach, find dryer sand and dig into it to escape the wind.

As he gathered his strength to move three nurses walked out of the darkness. They said a companion was lying wounded on the beach about a mile away. Would some men go and carry her in? No one responded.

"She can't walk," said one nurse. "Somebody must get her."

Pretending not to hear, the watchers only stared into the fire. They were tired themselves. Eric's head was clearing of its dizziness. He stood up.

"Come on," he said harshly, "who'll go with me?"

Only one man replied, an English boy who had rowed on the same seat with Eric in the lifeboat.

"I'll go," he said, and left the fire.

Using two borrowed shirts and two oars, they improvised a stretcher. The English lad made a final plea.

"Won't somebody else come and take turns carrying her?"

No answer.

"To hell with you then," he said and with Eric set off down the beach.

They found the nurse, her left breast nearly ripped off by a bomb fragment, and carried her back. Eric was so tired he nearly vomited from fatigue. He staggered higher up the beach, near the jungle edge, where lay the bones of an old fishing hut. Finding a section of woven palm leaf roofing he stuck it into the sand for a windbreak, scooped out a hollow for his body and lay down. Sleep came instantly.

The next day, Sunday, more shipwreck survivors joined the group. They spent the day foraging on the jungle edge for coconuts and pineapples and for material to make stretchers to transport the severely wounded. Malay fishermen appeared late that afternoon with bad news. Bangka was entirely in Japanese hands. The nearest food or habitation was the occupied port of Muntok. The fishermen led them along the beach to where a path emerged from the jungle. They said it was a short cut to Muntok.

Sedgeman volunteered to hike into Muntok and request a Japanese military escort to give the refugees safe conduct past any hostile patrols into internment. It was agreed he should leave early next day. By nightfall there were gathered on the beach approximately 70 men, women and children, many in need of medical attention. Mrs. Warmen was among them, reunited with her son Mischa. Marie, the hairdresser, also was there, an unpopular reminder to the women who had shoved her off the raft and been compelled to take her back again.

The Malay who had been so severely burned by the bomb-flash on the *Vyner-Brooke* had been brought ashore in a lifeboat but died shortly afterward. He was buried in the sand, after much tugging and pushing, because rigor mortis had stiffened his outflung arms and legs and he wouldn't fit into the narrow trench scooped out for him.

Sedgeman left for Muntok Monday at daybreak. Shortly after he had gone a metal lifeboat drifted ashore bearing six soldiers. One was mortally wounded, died within an hour and was buried beside the Malay. Another, named Kingsley, became the sixth stretcher case. The other five stretcher cases were Mr. Buridge, the South African, who had a bomb fragment in his kidneys; an elderly retired magistrate from Malaya named Watson, the nurse with the ripped breast and two civilian women with shrapnel wounds.

About nine o'clock it was decided that the civilian women and children, led by an elderly Australian miner and two soldiers whose arm wounds prevented them from being stretcher bearers, should start along the trail. Able-bodied men and twenty-one Australian nurses would follow with the stretchers. The nurses had fashioned a Red Cross flag to carry at the head of their own procession and each of them had an indentifying arm band. Mrs. Buridge elected to stay with her husband and so joined the nurses.

Hardly had the first group disappeared when out of the same trail came Sedgeman leading ten Japanese soldiers and a tiny officer wearing a long sword. The officer ordered the men and women to form two lines, then barked at his men. Four soldiers took up sentry posts on the flanks of the lines. The officer surveyed the group in silence for so long that, one by one, all but eight men broke rank and resumed work on the stretchers. The officer conferred with one of his soldiers and finally, by gesturing, ordered the eight men who were still standing in line to walk down the beach. He followed with six soldiers, two of whom carried a machine gun. The four sentries remained, bayoneted rifles at ready.

The soldiers and their eight prisoners climbed over a small promontory of rocks and driftwood about two hundred feet away and disappeared. Three shots, exploding in quick succession, sounded from beyond the promontory. After a long silence another shot was heard, but muffled, as though the gun muzzle had been pressed against something soft. Then another silence.

The stretcher workers looked apprehensively at each other but, except for a murmured "afraid they're gone," no one spoke.

Soon the officer and two soldiers reappeared, climbing over the rocks. They returned to the stretchers and ordered the remaining ten men to march. Chief Mate Sedgeman, the First Officer and another man, pointing to their epaulettes, protested they were officers and expected treatment appropriate to their rank. The Japanese officer shouted them down.

Eric and Sedgeman were ordered to lift the old magistrate, who had been sitting up in his stretcher, and carry him between them. Slowly the doomed prisoners walked toward the promontory. Eric suddenly grasped at a desperate straw. He stopped and called to the officer. The procession halted.

From his shorts pocket Eric pulled a swollen, water soaked wallet containing his passport and $900 in twenty-dollar bills.

"I hoped the passport with its gold seal would impress him and he might change his mind," Eric told me.

The officer studied it intently but ended by throwing it on the sand. In drawing out the passport some of the twenty-dollar bills also had come with it. Sight of them in Eric's hand caused the officer to burst into a furious tirade. Obviously he thought Eric had tried to bribe him.

Picking up a piece of driftwood he swung it at Eric's face. Eric warded off the blow with an upraised hand and threw the wallet and its contents after the passport.

"I won't need the money any more," he thought.

He and Sedgeman then picked up Magistrate Watson and labored down the beach. They had difficulty getting him over the pile of rocks and driftwood and the officer motioned them to leave the magistrate. They placed him so he was sitting leaning against a log and shook hands with the old man.

"Goodbye," they told Watson, and climbed down the rocks onto the beach.

They were in a small cove. At the water's edge, lying face down, sprawled the bodies of those who had gone before them. Eric saw only seven bodies. He wondered about the eighth. Remembering the first quick shots he presumed the eighth man had made a dash for the sea and been cut down by rifle fire. The last muffled shot must have been the *coup de grace* for some one who did not die quickly enough. The others had not been killed by bullets. That was obvious from the wound in the back of the body nearest him, the young Englishman who had helped him carry the nurse to the fire. There was a short red wound under his left shoulder blade. The instrument that had made it, and similar wounds on the other bodies, was a bayonet.

Three soldiers stood near the bodies, wiping their bayonets with rags; polishing them carefully as though anxious to have naught but the cleanest steel for the next job.

A machine gun was ready to sweep the little strip of beach should anyone attempt to run.

Eric and his companions were ordered to stand in line facing the sea. He noticed two men blindfold themselves with their handkerchiefs. He was impressed by the quietness of the entire tableau. No one spoke. He looked out over the water. The hazy sky and sea seemed especially beautiful this morning.

"What a stupid way to die," he thought. "And what a strange ending—here in the morning sun on a strange island, far from anything familiar or any friend."

He recalled the assortment of unusual places he had visited during a wandering life, but none more strange than this. He thought of his family—his brother and his brother's wife and his mother. They would never know how or where he died.

In his mind's eye he saw his mother as she taught him his prayers when he was a child. Across the years he heard her telling him,

"Eric boy, if you are ever in danger, put yourself in God's hands and say His prayer."

He began, "Our Father, Who art in heaven, hallowed be Thy Name . . ."

At that moment the First Officer, standing on the other end of the line, dashed for the sea. The machine gun chattered. He fell to one knee, rose, stumbled again as the firing continued and slumped to a halt on his right shoulder directly in front of Eric. He was dead, bleeding from a multitude of holes.

Eric continued praying, slowly and with more fervor than he had known existed in him. He was saying "deliver us from evil" when he was aware that he was no longer standing but instead lying face down on the beach. His hands were clasped under him, pressing palm upward at the right side of his chest. His face was turned slightly to the left. His mouth was open and full of sand and water. That is, it would be full of water one moment and empty the next. He realized the reason—tiny wavelets on the outermost edge of the sea were surging and receding, surging and receding. His mind was clear. It told him to lie relaxed and still as death and to let the waves bob his head. It told him that with each incoming wave his head could bob naturally and turn sideways just a fraction of a hair. On the incoming rise he could inhale slightly and quickly, like a swimmer; and, as the wave receded, exhale slightly and slowly . . . but so minutely the Japanese could detect no movement. They were shooting men who moved.

He heard noises of a man vomiting and thrashing as though his body were flopping up and down on the sand. A shot cracked. Silence.

He heard a moan almost in his own ear and felt a body writhe against him. BANG! The body lay still.

His own guts crawled and the back of his neck felt as though a rifle muzzle were breathing down it. What wind he had inside him he held, waiting for the bullet to crash into his skull. But it did not come. And did not come. AND DID NOT COME!

By playing dead successfully he might avert it altogether. He knew he might be dying from a bayonet thrust but he was unaware of pain.

Metal struck against metal. Feet scuffed. Probably they were dismounting the machine gun. After that the only sounds were lapping water. However, he did not move, except for an almost imperceptible twist of his head with each wave so he could look, eventually, along the beach. He got his head around so that he could peek between his eyelids and see a southward section of the beach. No Japanese. But he could not risk their being just out of range, sitting at the jungle edge watching. Slowly, he let the waves turn his head until, after an interminable time, he could look north toward the promontory. No Japanese. But he waited. And it was well he did. Two soldiers appeared on the rocks and surveyed the cove. One of them waved a small flag, as though signaling by semaphore to where the other soldiers must be with the nurses. The Japanese disappeared.

Still Eric lay there, straining his senses to detect the slightest sound behind him. How long he waited was impossible to know. He wished he could estimate the time so as to guess whether all the soldiers reasonably could be presumed to have gone.

Finally he decided to act. He tested his legs, his hips, his arms for life and found them responsive. The moment of preparing to spring up was the tensest of his life. He suffered agonies of doubt in the time it took to gather his muscles. What if they were still there, waiting to cut him down? He took his hands away from his ribs, turned them over to press against the sand and push him upward. He counted.

"One . . . two . . . three!"

And, flexing his knees beneath him, he sprang, hurling his body sideways and whirling to scan the beach. It was empty but for the dead. In the instant that his eyes flicked over their still forms one body especially stamped itself on Eric's consciousness. The corpse of the fat civil engineer was sitting upright, its sightless eyes looking out over the Straits. Eric ran up the slope into the jungle.

Thorny undergrowth cut his bare feet. He ducked back to the beach and ran south, skipping in and out of the trees and looking back to see if he had been spotted. For about a mile he ran like that until he came to a stream flowing into the sea. Turning up the stream he scrambled along until he was invisible from the beach. Then he lay on his back and rested.

After a while the pain came and he examined his wounds. The pain filled his back and chest with a dull throb. Blood oozed from a wound on his lower right chest where his hands had been clutched when he found himself lying on the beach. Reaching around he felt another wound on his back, opposite the one in front. The bayonet had gone into his back and out his chest.

He wondered why he was still alive and how long it would take to die if he were bleeding to death inside. He figured the bleeding must be mostly inside because there was surprisingly little outside. Still, if he was bleeding to death internally he would be weaker and have difficulty breathing. And he felt all right, except for the pain and fatigue. He could only wait and see what developed. He waited, lying there all day and all night, fighting mosquitoes and ants. Next morning he ventured to the jungle edge and peered out. Nothing. Crossing the stream he headed south, hoping to find a *kampong*—as a Malay village is called—where he could get food. He met three disconsolate survivors of another ship walking north. They said the lighthouse further south had been bombed and gutted. Eric led them north, back across the stream, to the fatal cove. There were the bodies of his executed companions. Sedgeman it was who had moaned and writhed against him and been silenced by a bullet. The fat engineer still sat there, one leg doubled beneath him, his wide open eyes staring at the water. On the pile of rocks and driftwood, still leaning against the log where he had been placed, was the old magistrate. His skull had been bashed in. Flies buzzed around the mess that had been his head.

Eric found the nurses too. However, they had been shot, not bayoneted. The bodies he examined had single bullet holes at the base of the skulls. Rifle shots. He wondered at no evidence of machine-gunning. He presumed, from the way they were widely scattered along the water's edge, that some bodies had floated away when the tide went out. Four bodies lay huddled in one group and three in another. A red-haired nurse was lying higher on the beach than the others. Her skull had been crushed but the sea had washed it clean. Flies were everywhere.

The stretchers also were where they had been left and in

them the patients lay staring sightlessly at the sky. Two stretchers were empty. One had been the old magistrate's and the other the wounded soldier Kingsley's. What had become of Kingsley? Buridge, the South African, and the three women had been bayoneted in the chest. Thinking perhaps Kingsley had survived bayoneting and crawled into the jungle they searched the immediate area and called his name. No answer.

Still scattered on the beach were some of Eric's twenty-dollar bills. He did not bother to pick them up. Of what use was money? What he needed was food.

Abandoning the search they continued north, ultimately met some Malay fishermen who gave them water but had no food to spare. Muntok was the nearest food. It was that or starve.

In Muntok Japanese soldiers received him casually and directed him to a cinema where he found the women, children and old men who had walked away from the beach Monday morning. They had met the same patrol, guided by Sedgeman, which had executed Eric's companions.

Why had the first group been ignored and the second slaughtered? Inexplicable Japanese.

Not only did the fate of a prisoner vary according to the individual Japanese who found him but also according to the particular moment the Japanese found him. The Japanese soldier seemed to possess the personality of a Dr. Jekyl and Mr. Hyde. He could be gentleman or beast with equal naturalness and facility. However, except for war time conditions on battlefield or in prison camp, the gentleman prevailed in all the Japanese I have ever personally known. In their own country, where I worked before the war, I never experienced an unkindness or a discourtesy.

Soon after Eric's arrival refugees in the cinema were moved into Muntok Prison. There Mischa Warmen's mother died of pneumonia, leaving her little son an orphan. There, also, Eric learned why he had seen only seven bodies in the cove when his group arrived for execution. The eighth man, a *Vyner-Brooke* crew member named Lloyd, had run into the sea before the Japanese set up their machine gun. Three rifle bullets clipped him superficially but he dove, swam under water and made good his escape.

The most fantastic climax occurred when one of the Australian nurses, Miss Vivian Bullwinkle, staggered into Muntok Prison with Kingsley, the missing stretcher case. Miss Bullwinkle was a tall, slender girl in her twenties with light brown hair and grey eyes.

Testifying at a War Crimes trial in Tokyo in 1946 she said that after slaying Eric's group the Japanese soldiers returned from the cove polishing their bayonets. Standing in front of the nurses they unhurriedly continued the job until rifles and bayonets were scrupulously clean. Then they ordered the nurses and a civilian woman (Mrs. Buridge) to line up at the water's edge and walk into the sea. Shots sounded.

"I saw the girls fall one after the other," said Nurse Bullwinkle, "then I was hit."

She fell into the water but did not lose consciousness. Like Eric she played possum, pretending death but managing to breathe as the waves washed her back onto the beach. When she was sure the Japanese had gone, she testified, "I sat up and looked around. Then I took myself up into the jungle and became unconscious."

When she awakened and returned to the beach she found she was the only survivor of the women. Kingsley was alive and she managed to get him into the jungle; then she foraged for food. Wives of native fishermen supplied her food for about ten days, until Kingsley became strong enough to walk with assistance and they hiked to Muntok. The effort was too much for the soldier, however, and he died in jail within a few days.

Miss Bullwinkle said the bullet which felled her entered her back at about waist level and passed straight through.

Like Eric's bayonet thrust it missed vital organs and the wound healed rapidly.

Doctors could hardly believe the facts to which Eric's wounds were testimony. They concluded the bayonet must have slid between lung and liver without seriously damaging either. They attributed the absence of infection to the thoroughness with which the Japanese cleaned their bayonets. Eric's explanation was simpler. He said, "The Lord was with me."

13

Out of the Bangka Straits

THE most envied people in Singapore just before that shattered colony surrendered to Japan were the lucky persons permitted to get away. Their less fortunate fellow colonials could only wait for the Japanese to enter and intern them. But all the lucky ones were not so lucky after all. Approximately 3,000 are estimated to have perished under the guns of a Japanese task force in or near the Bangka Straits. The *Vyner-Brooke*, with Eric Germann and the Australian nurses aboard, was only one of approximately forty vessels sunk and another twenty captured.

*　　*　　*　　*

The *Giang Bee* found herself being circled by Japanese destroyers near the mouth of the Straits. She hove to and signalled that aboard her were women and children and that, if spared, she would proceed under orders. The Japanese appeared willing. A small boat put out from a destroyer. It had covered a quarter of the distance when two Dutch bombing planes appeared, attacked but missed the destroyer. The small boat turned back.

Soon came signals from the destroyer giving *Giang Bee* passengers thirty minutes to abandon ship. If they did, for nearly half of them it would be as swimmers because there were not enough lifeboats. Robert H. Scott, Chief of the Far Eastern section of the British Ministry of Information, whose last job in Singapore had been to get war correspondents safely out of the city, and Lieutenant E. P. C. Langdon volunteered as emissaries to plead with the Japanese. A dinghy just large enough for two men was lowered over the side and Scott and Langdon rowed as hard and as fast as they could row for the destroyer. The sun had set. Soon it would be dark.

Aboard the *Giang Bee*, lifeboats were being prepared for lowering. Jimmy Martin, a tough little Australian jockey, was working on one of them. Nearby was an injured man and his wife and their two blond children, aged four and six. The man had been carried aboard with two broken legs. Now he was doomed. Lifeboats were only for women and children and a skeleton crew to row. Jimmy heard the wife ask two men who were standing by idle to help her move her husband into a more comfortable position.

"If you'll give us a kiss, sister, we'll move him," one of the men replied.

"I'll do anything for my husband," she said, and kissed them as her husband watched, helpless.

Just then a warning shot was fired by the destroyer.

"Abandon ship!"

Women were ordered into lifeboats.

"Hand me the children," Martin said.

"No," said the woman. "If my husband can't go, none of us will."

She removed her own life belt, then the life belts of the children. When Jimmy last saw her she was sitting on the deck, one arm around her husband's shoulders, the other around her children.

Jimmy and his helpers loaded one lifeboat and started to lower it. A davit rope broke and the stern end dropped, spilling its cargo into the sea.

"I thought the most terrible sounds possible were from horses being burned to death," Jimmy told me in Palembang Jail, "but the cries of those women and kids when the davit rope broke were worse."

Scott and Langdon were halfway to the destroyer when it opened fire. Twenty minutes later the *Giang Bee* sank. They changed course to avoid the destroyer and rowed slowly, debating whether to pull toward Sumatra or Bangka Island. A voice hailed them from the darkness and a hand grasped the gunwale. They pulled in W. Probyn Allen's 240 pounds. A few minutes later they hauled another man from the dark water. When they got him into the dinghy Scott said to Langdon,

"One of us had better get out and walk. Another half inch and the gunwales will be under water."

They all laughed. The latest passenger was a rubber planter from Malaya named H. P. Kendall. He was bigger than Allen; not as broad but taller, around six feet two with a barrel chest and huge stomach. Scott and Langdon were good sized men themselves.

Together they debated the wisest landfall. They suspected Bangka was already captured but Sumatra might still be free. Scott knew the approximate direction of the mouth of the Moesi river, up which lay Palembang.

"Let's try for the Moesi," he said.

Two days later they grounded the dinghy at a Malay fishing village on the Moesi shore. Villagers gave them water and food and shelter for several days but declined to keep them longer, fearing reprisals from the Japanese who meanwhile had captured Palembang and were masters of southern Sumatra. Surrender was their only course. Barefooted they hiked to Palembang. Scott, Kendall and Allen were put in Palembang Jail and Langdon in one of the Military camps.

In another part of the Straits a heavily loaded lifeboat pulled laboriously for Bangka Island. Clinging to its sides and stern were eight men for whom there was no room in-

side. Their ship had been sunk in the afternoon. The clinging men grew weaker as the hours dragged. They discussed
with the lifeboat's skipper their chances of being allowed
inside the boat.

"Not a chance," said the skipper. "Under no circumstances can any more enter."

"Then there's no use hanging on longer," said one of the
men, "Cheerio."

He relinquished his hold and vanished. Three others followed suit, with a "cheerio" bidding those in the boat
goodbye. By morning only one of the eight still hung on.
He was H. E. M. Mason, a 63-year-old rubber planter.

"I'm too stubborn to die," he quipped. "You can't get
rid of me."

When the boat reached shore he waded up the beach
under his own power, stretched out on the sand and slept.

The 600-ton *Li Wo*, coastal steamer of the China traders
Jardine & Matheson, found itself in the middle of the
Sumatra-bound Japanese invasion convoy. Aboard the *Li
Wo* were 120 men, mostly sailors from the British battle-
ship *Prince of Wales*, which with the *Repulse* had been
sunk off the Malayan coast. R. L. McCann, an Australian tin
miner, was one of the few civilian passengers. He told me
that the *Li Wo's* skipper, Captain Tom Wilkinson, didn't
waste a second debating his predicament.

"We'll go down fighting," Wilkinson declared, "and
we'll take one of those Japs with us."

The *Li Wo* had a submarine gun forward and thirteen
shells. Captain Wilkinson picked out a small transport for
his target and, ordering full steam ahead, charged the transport. Whether Wilkinson's audacity took the Japanese
completely by surprise or whether they simply failed to spot
the *Li Wo* in time, McCann did not know. But the little
vessel managed to shoot all thirteen of its shells—setting the
warship afire—and then ram the transport.

The impact stove in the transport but did not hole the *Li Wo* below the water line. Not yet mortally damaged and her engines running, she could still fight. Wilkinson ordered full speed astern.

The *Li Wo* backed off. She surged forward for another ramming attack but by that time a Japanese cruiser had its guns on her and blew the *Li Wo* out of the water.

McCann was one of thirteen survivors.

Lieutenant Colonel Lang of the Australian Signal Corps had just lain down to sleep for the first time in forty-eight hours---because he thought his military launch had safely run the Bangka gantlet—when shells blew the launch apart. In the few hectic moments before the launch sank, Lang noticed a patriotic young corporal seize the boat's ensign, wrap it around himself and jump.

Lang jumped also. He noticed the launch's bathroom door floating beside him and clung to it. He was still tired so he decided to sleep in the water. He tied his feet to the bathroom door, lay back in his life belt, and slept. When he awakened, the door was supporting three other men, a brigadier general, a cook and the young corporal still wrapped in the ensign.

The hazy outline of a mountain peak indicated where lay Bangka Island. They debated whether to stay with the door in hopes of drifting ashore or to leave the door and swim. The cook, a poor swimmer, chose the door. The general, the corporal and Lang elected to swim. They bade the cook adieu and struck out.

During the long afternoon Lang went blind from sun glare on glass-smooth water. He followed his companions by sound. The corporal began talking nonsense.

"I'm going upstairs for a drink," he said.

"Better wait awhile," said the general.

"No, it's just upstairs."

Lang heard a gulp and the corporal ceased talking. After a while he asked the general what happened.

"He went under," said the general.

Night soothed Lang's eyes. Sight returned and he could see the Bangka lighthouse flashing ahead. When the sun rose next morning, he and the general still were paddling in their life belts. The sun rose higher, scorching their heads unmercifully. Lang's eyesight again blanked out. The general began talking nonsense.

"They should have served lunch before we left the ship," Lang heard him say. "We'll see they do it next time."

He jabbered for a long time, then said,

"I'm going upstairs for a drink."

Lang heard him gulp and guessed he was drinking sea water. He heard him choke, gurgle, and thrash his arms spasmodically. Then silence. Lang could feel the general was slumped forward in his life belt, his face in the water. He remembered the general had a clasp knife in his trousers' pocket, because he had used it to cut the water-swollen knots of the rope which bound his feet to the raft. The knife would be valuable ashore. With one hand Lang held the general's collar while with the other he searched for and found the knife. Then he let go of the collar. Now he was alone and blind.

He became aware that his own mind was beginning to wander, that his thoughts were fuzzy. He knew something was wrong because every once in a while his brain would wake up and tell him it had been dreaming. He had a strong feeling that he need not swim any more because he might be swimming in the wrong direction; that if he only rested and took a drink everything would be all right. But some inner compulsion kept him from drinking and some inner strength kept him paddling. Night came again and with it vision and the Bangka lighthouse. It flashed and flashed and flashed until he became irritated and wished it would stop. Then he was aware that he could see the lighthouse itself, and the reason he could see it was because the sky was lightening on another dawn.

Something bumped one knee, then his other knee. He put his hands down into mud. He crawled forward into a mangrove swamp and kept crawling and splashing through the swamp until he was on dry land. His next knowledge was that he was in a hut being given water by a Chinese man.

Lang told me his experience when we met in Charitas Hospital.

Vivien Gordon Bowdon, 57-year-old Australian Trade Commissioner to Singapore, had served his government in Japan and knew the language, and also the diplomatic immunities to which he was entitled. When Japanese soldiers in Muntok began stripping him and his companions of their valuables he remonstrated, censuring the soldiers in Japanese.

His companions, who told the story to me, did not understand what he said but his words enraged the soldiers. They marched him off, around a building and out of sight. After a long interval shots were heard and the soldiers returned without Bowdon. A Chinese resident of Muntok later managed to talk to Bowdon's friends and tell them what had happened.

He said he was looking from a window of the building behind which Bowdon was shot. He said Bowdon had been forced to dig his own grave. As the soldiers held rifles on him he used his hands and a board to scoop a shallow trench in the sandy soil. Nearby grew some flowers. Bowdon was ordered to pick a handful, then stand in the grave. While he stood holding the flowers, he was shot.

The S. S. *Mata Hari*, which had followed the *Vyner-Brooke* out of Singapore, docked at Muntok without a scratch. The Japanese had allowed her to surrender and destroyers escorted her into the harbor. That was fortunate, not only for her 400-odd passengers but for other hundreds who were interned in South Sumatra for the war's duration, because aboard the *Mata Hari* were two doctors and a small trunk full of medical supplies. The doctors were West and J. G. Reed, who also had been on active duty in Malaya.

The *Mata Hari's* passengers, plus another estimated 400-odd bedraggled men, women, and children who came out of the Bangka Straits, were jammed into old Muntok Prison and an adjoining building which, prior to the war, had been used as a quarantine depot for coolie labor in the island's tin dredging operations. The depot was a U-shaped, concrete building divided into long, narrow rooms containing cement sleeping benches.

The prison next door had been built originally for life term prisoners but when a newer penitentiary was constructed on another island, the Muntok structure had been turned into a pepper warehouse.

Bangka Straits survivors slept on top of pepper sacks in one half of the prison, while the other half was occupied by 600 Chinese coolies in the last stages of starvation and disease. The coolies were labor conscripts, swept off the streets of Hongkong after that city's capture, herded aboard ship and into the holds. They were kept under hatches for six weeks during the trip south, then dumped off at Muntok to work on the airfield. But most of them were too far gone to work. They could only die. And die they did, every day, lying in their own filth, filling the jail with a stench that was a blow in the face to newcomers. Since not enough coolies were fit for work, the shipwrecked white prisoners took their places, marching each dawn to the airdrome, where they labored under the muzzles of machine guns, and marching back each night.

Doctors Reed and West set up a makeshift hospital in

the quarantine depot which went by the name of the dredging company that owned it—Bangka Tin Winning. One patient was a Royal Air Force lieutenant with two shattered feet needing amputation. West and Reed pleaded in vain that he be sent to a Japanese field hospital for the amputation that would save his life. Finally, they decided to operate themselves. The trunk of medical supplies contained no anesthetic except morphine and little in the way of surgical instruments. They had no saw. A 60-year-old refugee named W. R. Roberts made a saw from a barrel hoop. He cut a section from the hoop, heated and straightened it, then filed in the necessary teeth.

The lieutenant was tied onto the top of a wooden table and kept under morphine while his feet were severed with the barrel hoop saw. He recovered from the operation only to die of dysentery.

Three Australians removed a wooden door from the Tin Winning offices, cut it up and made a coffin for the lieutenant. He was buried next to Kingsley, who had been brought in by Nurse Bullwinkle, in the Dutch Cemetery about a mile from the prison.

Conditions in Muntok Prison and the depot worsened as time passed. The places were foul, swarming madhouses of sick and hungry men, women, and children, and disease ridden coolies who daily furnished fresh corpses for burial.

In the last week of March, 1942, the prisoners were divided into groups. Women, children, the sick, and men unfit for work were shipped to Palembang and interned separately. Military prisoners, and Dr. Reed, were sent to concentration camp. Civilian men, and Dr. West, were put in Palembang Jail. Able-bodied civilians were sent to the Shell refinery at Pladjoe, across the river from Palembang, and put to work loading ships. Later, in April, they joined us in the jail. That was when I met Eric.

Throughout my incarceration in Palembang, men shud

dered when they spoke of Bangka Island and cursed at mention of Muntok.

*   *   *   *

Now, in September, 1943, our prison ship was docking in Muntok harbor. Trucks waited at the jetty. Except for drivers and soldiers, not another person was in sight. We clambered into the vehicles with our luggage and they lumbered through the deserted town. Windows and doors were closed. The only inhabitants seemed to be soldiers posted at each intersection along our route. Had the buildings been in ruins the town would have been almost as empty as a ghost city through which I walked while crossing the no-man's land between Occupied and Free China during my escape from Shanghai.

The trucks stopped in front of a high stone wall surmounted by barbed wire. In the middle of the wall was a double gate of solid, iron-studded wood. In one side of the gate was a grilled peephole. We looked at the wall and the gate and our hearts stood still.

"Muntok Prison," whispered Doc West. "It's Muntok Prison."

The guard commander inserted a key into a ponderous lock, turned it with both hands and pulled mightily. The non-peephole side creaked open. He squeezed into the opening so he could get his shoulder behind the gate from the inside and push. Other guards then pulled and pushed open the peephole side. Evidently no one lived now in Muntok Prison.

Inside the gates of thick, heavy wood was a short corridor, then two sets of barred iron gates. Guards clanged them open and we walked through into an empty, barren yard surrounded on three sides by vacant cell blocks. The fourth side, toward the gate, was enclosed by two high fences. The first fence was iron grill; the second barbed wire, curved inward at the top. It was Palembang Jail on a larger, grimmer scale. The walls were higher, the cells larger and the general surroundings worse. The sepulchral stillness of the place, like a waiting grave, chilled us. Of all the memories of my life that awful silence, utter and absolute, is the strongest.

I had heard of Muntok Prison as a bedlam of moans and screams and tears and milling humanity; of filth and dirt and disease and corpses of Chinese coolies whose gangrenous limbs were rotting before they died. But there was none of that now. Instead, Muntok Prison was uninhabited and clean. A bomb-wrecked cell house had been repaired. The barbed wire atop the wall was new and taut. Even the gravelly yard had been neatly raked. It was as though an old charnel house had been purged of corpses and cleaned and swept especially for us. But the odor of decay remained in the air, oppressive, frightening.

Wordlessly, because we were beyond words, we lined up for counting. We had walked into a tomb and we knew it. A feeling of death squeezed my vitals like a closing hand.

Bangka Island grew pepper and produced tin but no food. A sentence read to me by Controleur De Raat from a Dutch encyclopedia ran through my mind with the intonations of a dirge:

"The Island of Bangka is known for its production of tin and pepper and the high incidence of beri-beri and cerebral malaria. . . ."

14

McDougall's Bedroom & Morgue

DAYLIGHT faded during the counting—our first roll call in Muntok Prison. Puzzled, I looked up. The sky indicated that although the sun was low it had not yet set. Dusk was coming early to the jail yard because walls were high, cell blocks dark and we did not have the vistas of Barracks Camp. Spectacular sunsets no longer would parade their grandeur. We could not see them. Nor would flying foxes wing overhead because on Bangka there was nothing for them to eat.

Counting finished, we bowed, guards saluted. They pointed to a wing of cells bounding the yard's east side. Into the cells we went. They were large rooms of stone and concrete; each, as we learned by later measurement, 45 feet long, 22 feet wide and 15 feet high. Even the Japanese realized, however, the cells could not hold us all. They decided the problem temporarily by decreeing each man would have the space of one straw mat, about 6½ feet long and slightly over two feet wide. Mats were placed side by side and end to end without even walking aisles between. I was so tired I slept almost immediately.

Guards turned a deaf ear next day to pleas that we be allowed to spread out and occupy other empty cells—more prisoners were coming. They arrived in groups as the Japanese closed other small civilian internment camps in south Sumatra and consolidated all internees in Muntok Prison. We thought we had been crowded in Palembang but we had not known what real crowding was. There, men at least had shelves to sleep on. Except for one cell block there were no shelves in Muntok Prison. Men lay on the floors with their belongings. By October 10th there were 685 men inside a place built for a quarter of that number. When everyone was settled we were able to re-arrange our spaces so that there was at least a narrow aisle beside each row of mats.

Despite crowding we were cheered for a few weeks by an increase of rations, principally dried fish. But, when boats ceased bringing more prisoners from Sumatra, they also stopped bringing food.

Every inch of the prison was combed for nails, bits of wood or metal. Direct Action Drysdale noticed a chicken scratching persistently at a spot which had been a bomb crater when he was there in 1942 and had been filled. He dug where the chicken scratched and found a soldier's aluminum mess tin and some bits of metal which he made into wrist watch bands and sold to the guards.

Commandant of Muntok Prison was a sad-faced little Japanese civilian whom Doc nicknamed "Peanut." He talked and acted as though he was genuinely sorry for our predicament and in many ways he did his best to help us. Peanut blamed food shortages on the military who, he said, hogged available supplies and would not cooperate with the Japanese civilian administrators. He said we would be better off if the military would take back control of internees.

Peanut was concerned at our mounting sick rate and contrived to find extra food for hospital patients. The Chinese contractor, who had been brought from Palembang, said the little commandant himself scoured the island for supplies. Peanut found papayas, eggs and small amounts of unpolished red rice, more nourishing than ordinary white polished rice. Seldom did he bring in more than a few papayas or a dozen eggs at a time but what he did bring helped sick men immeasurably.

Peanut's greatest contribution to prisoner morale was news. We were starved for news, having been cut off from the undercover newspaper and radio sources we had in Palembang. Peanut filled the gap. He could speak and write crude English and he issued written "communiques" that were gems of backward sentences and twisted grammar but the content was dear.

His usual procedure was to summon Doc West. While Doc sat answering polite but vague medical questions, Peanut would be writing a translation of a Japanese newspaper or mimeographed army bulletin. Occasionally Doc even procured one of the papers, to be deciphered by a priest, Father P. H. van Gisbergen, who, from his knowledge of Chinese and with the aid of a Japanese dictionary, made rough translations. Thus we learned American forces were suffering colossal defeats on various Pacific islands; but each defeat apparently resulted in their gaining possession of the island.

We wondered what would be Peanut's fate if his superiors discovered he was relaying us war news.

Flowers for funerals were another of Peanut's innovations. And he kept the coffin supply abreast of demand. Since a body had to be carried outside in a box and we were without cold storage facilities in a tropic climate, it was important that a coffin be available not too long after death. Therefore, when a man was dying the guards were notified so a box could be ordered from the Chinese coffin maker who nailed together wooden planks supplied by the Japanese. The working party, whose job it was to carry in the boxes, also sometimes arranged with the coffin maker—for a substantial bribe and large profit for himself—to put food inside an incoming coffin. That was one black market source. Peanut not only saw that the coffin supply was adequate but with each furnished a huge wreath of brilliant flowers—yellow frangipani and alamanda, purple bougainvillea, red hibiscus, blue and white passion blossoms, crimson four o'clocks. He attended all funerals, standing with bared head during services.

Doc West told him that if he rustled more food instead of flowers we would need fewer coffins. Peanut replied that he was very, very sorry, but his superiors would not allow more food; therefore he bought the flowers with his own money. He was such a nice little guy we believed him.

Peanut's communiques relating Allied successes touched off a flurry of betting as to when the war would end. An Englishman named M. L. Phillips, known in Malaya for his stable of race horses and gambling luck, offered to wager 25,000 guilders or its equivalent in Straits dollars—payable after the war—that we would be free by January 1, 1944. He had no takers because no individual would bet that kind of money and Phillips refused to wager against a pool. However, his offer engendered such gambling optimism that bettors in the five and ten guilder class raised their antes to fifty and one hundred guilders. Controleur De Raat believed the war would end by November 1, 1944, and bet me fifty guilders to that effect. I picked June 1, 1945 as my date and bet twenty-five guilders we would not be free until then. A half dozen listeners jumped at the wager and such a heated argument developed over who got first crack at the bet that it ended by no one's taking it.

We had to depend entirely on our own hospital facilities. There was no Charitas in Muntok to take our critically sick or send us medicines. Our hospital was assembled in a group of storerooms and solitary confinement cells along the south wall and was separated from the rest of the prison by a barred iron fence. I spent all my time in the hospital dressing major skin cases. Out-patients were treated in the clinic on the other side of the fence inside the prison yard proper, because it was easier of access.

Three more doctors came with the new prisoners: Hollweg, who had been released by the Kempeitai after months of solitary confinement; and two other Hollanders, A. P. A. Boerma and Willem von Woerkom. Hollweg took charge of the clinic, assisted by Allen and two other dressers; Boerma and Woerkom divided the cell blocks between them and treated in their cells men who were too sick to walk to the clinic but not sick enough to be considered major cases eligible for the precious space in our hospital.

When Dr. Hollweg returned to us in Muntok Prison he found that our hospital had grown from a two cell affair with a staff of four, as it had been in Palembang Jail, to a major institution with a staff of forty. He may have resented, despite the fact it was the Camp Committee's request, that Dr. West continued as head of the hospital. Dr. Hollweg's attitude toward Dr. West and his staff became distinctly cool. No longer was he the raconteur who entertained us with tall stories, as of old. Instead, he seldom spoke to us except on medical matters.

At one end of the hospital, next door to a crude one-holer which served us, was a cubicle containing a miniature, unused bath tank. We were so cramped for space that when Doc suggested I convert the cubicle into a private bedroom by covering the tank and sleeping on top of it, I gladly acquiesced. Next to food and news, privacy was the most precious commodity in jail. The tank top, covered, was just wide enough and long enough to sleep on. Between the tank and the door was room for my jail-made chair of wood and rice sacking. I could study—shorthand and Malay—and read in solitude.

Weeks passed. Doc had another idea. A dying man was entitled to privacy if he could get it. There should be some place he could lie besides shoulder to shoulder with other patients. Sometimes men groaned in coma for days before death came, and that was hard on other patients.

We agreed that when a man was on his final lap of life he could die in my bedroom. I would sleep elsewhere until it was possible to move back.

I changed places with dying patients so frequently that in time my sleeping quarters became known as "McDougall's Bedroom & Morgue." Its reputation was so notorious that we put patients in there only if unconscious or too far gone to care. Only one other man besides myself slept in the room and left under his own power. He was a patient who fooled us by recovering.

Near my "Bedroom & Morgue" was a windowless solitary confinement cell we used as a storeroom. There it was we performed a secret autopsy. A man died after an illness that for a time baffled doctors who differed among themselves as to whether or not it was an intestinal obstruction. West and Boerma believed it was an obstruction and that only an operation would save the patient. Hollweg believed the cause was something else.

On the other side of Bangka Island, at Pangkal Pinang, was a Japanese hospital. Military authorities refused to allow the patient to be taken there. When he died the doctors decided to perform a post mortem examination, both to settle their own dispute and for the sake of other men who might become similarly ill. The autopsy had to be secret, not only from guards who might interfere but also from fellow prisoners. The fewer who knew the better. Resident Oranje gave permission.

We did not notify the Japanese of the death until too late for burial that day. We carried the body into the storeroom for encoffining but, instead of nailing down the lid after the guards had viewed the corpse and were satisfied the man was dead, we merely pounded to make a noise.

Handy men of the hospital staff were G. P. Harrison, assistant chief engineer of the Malayan Railways and R. E. Earle, Chief Electrical Engineer of the Singapore Harbor board. From barbed wire they fashioned retractors to hold open the abdominal incision. From the key opener to a sardine tin they made a surgical needle. And by unraveling a piece of canvas they made "surgical thread," to sew up the incision.

After the inside guard made his half hourly round at 3:30 A.M. Harrison, Earle, West, Boerma and I met in the storeroom, sealed the door behind us with a tarpaulin and blankets and went to work. Earle sat outside to watch for light leaks. The light was from an oil lamp and flashlight the Japanese allowed us for hospital use.

We removed the coffin lid and laid it down gently. The dead man had been a big fellow. He had gone in without difficulty when his corpse was still warm and pliable but now rigor mortis had wedged his wide shoulders against the sides of the narrow box.

"Tip the coffin on its side and pry him out," West suggested in a whisper.

Harrison vetoed that as "too apt to make a noise."

"We can do it with team work," Harrison said. "Each of us get a hand hold somewhere on the same side, underneath him, and pull up when I count three."

We each squeezed one hand under him and put the other on the coffin edge for leverage.

"One, Two, Three!"

Up came the left shoulder. We laid the body on the cement floor and the autopsy began. Boerma's scalpel sliced into cold flesh and moved downward, Harrison and I crouched on opposite sides of the body, holding open the incision with our crude retractors. West held the flashlight.

The flickering oil lamp, on the floor at the foot of the corpse, threw our shadows on walls and ceiling in monstrous caricature. Since ventilation was cut off by the blocked doorway, air in the concrete chamber became oppressive. The doctors consulted in occasional whispers. For long intervals the only sounds were those heard solely in these certain and peculiar circumstances: the faint tearing of parting flesh; tiny protesting suctions of viscera pulled from lifelong habitations.

At last they found it. The fatal adhesion two doctors believed must be there and the third had doubted. While probing in the cavity they explained to Harrison and me in whispers what had happened. They held up the affected organs and showed us how death had come about and how it might have been prevented had operational facilities been available. They decided that no matter how desperate a gamble an emergency operation might be in our circumstances it would be the only possibility should such a case occur again.

They replaced the entrails, pulled the incision together with large stitches and we lifted the body back into the coffin and pushed the shoulders down. The doctors left. Harrison and I washed the floor and waited for morning roll call. When it rang, filling the yard with clangor, we nailed shut the coffin.

After roll call I moved back into "McDougall's Bedroom & Morgue" and lay down for a short rest before beginning daily hospital rounds.

15

Malaria

A PREMONITORY chill, like a cold wind, passed through me and was gone during church services Sunday morning December 12, 1943. My eyes were acting strangely, my teeth were on edge and I felt light headed. A second chill prickled my flesh into goose pimples. Five minutes later a third came, then a fourth. By the time Mass ended I was shaking uncontrollably. I walked back to the hospital and asked Dishwasher Banks if he could find me an extra blanket. He brought his own and threw it over me where I lay in my Bedroom & Morgue, shivering as though I had stepped from a Turkish bath into a refrigerator.

Cold was welling inside my guts like an icy fountain, and soon diluted the warmth of a hot drink Banks also brought. The chills ran in cycles of intensity. First would come a warning flutter, a trembling that would rise swiftly to a crescendo of bone-rattling paroxysms. Then would follow a period of uneasy quiescence while I waited for the next one. The intervals between spasms grew shorter and their violence greater. They began in the very center of me, in my stomach where something tensed and writhed, sending tremors outward and setting up muscular vibrations which spread in ever widening circles until even my fingers and toes twitched and my teeth became chattering castanets. Shudders ran along nerve and sinew and bone in continuous waves, cold and hot by turns and accompanied by thirst and nausea.

There was a grand climax of convulsion, then gradually the trembling decreased as if its own violence had generated heat to melt the chills. Before the last fluttering died I glowed from an inner fire, a steadily burning dry fever that mounted during morning and afternoon, turning my head into one throbbing pain which crowded vision from my eyes. The room swam in a hot mist.

An indescribable depression obsessed me, filled me with forebodings. Dreams which were not really dreams, nor yet hallucinations, but formless terrors of the mind, stalked my room, settled shapelessly beside me on the bed. I was conscious, aware that the indefinable things which troubled me were imaginary, but that knowledge was no comfort. Rather, it whispered of insanity.

I thought of a husky young Dutch engineer who had died several weeks before from a sudden and undiagnosed fever. He had walked into the hospital complaining,

"Something is wrong with my head."

He had a temperature of 39 Centigrade (102 Fahrenheit). During the fourteen hours before he died his temperature rose to 41.8 C. (107.2 F.) Doc listed the cause of his death as "pyrexia of unknown origin." The phrase ran through my mind as I lay awake, fuzzy-brained and burning. Did I have the same thing? What was it? The sentence from De Raat's encyclopedia flashed like a neon sign:

"The island of Bangka is known for its production of tin and pepper and the high incidence of beri-beri and cerebral malaria."

Cerebral malaria was the deadliest kind.

"If it doesn't kill you," Hollweg once said, "it often leaves you silly in the head. Better die than have your brain burned out."

His words danced through my mind in a silly song to the tune of "Here We Go Round the Mulberry Bush!"

"Better to have your brain burned out, brain burned out, brain burned out. Better to have your brain burned out so early in the morning."

Sleep must have interrupted the song because suddenly I was awake, clear minded and clammy with sweat. The fever was gone, replaced by rivers of sweat and tons of soggy blankets. The headache was gone too. It was night. Clarity of thought brought increasing sensitivity to the cold stickiness of my surroundings. I began to shiver.

"No more of that stuff," I said to myself, "I'm getting up and get dry and warm."

My bed on top of the tank was four feet off the floor. I slid from the tank. My feet touched concrete but there was nothing between feet and hips. My knees folded like jackknives and I sat down. Nor could I rise. I remained sitting leaning against the tank, until old Kendall who had replaced Prior as ward matron, came clumping by on one of his hourly trips. He lifted me back into bed.

Sleep refused to conquer my restlessness and cold. When daylight came I tried again to get up and walk. Success. Shakily I made my way outside into the sun and sat down. Doc West came along.

"Get back in bed," he said. "Sun's not good for you."

I attempted to rise and could not. My knees were unhinged. He helped me back to my feet and boosted me into bed. Immediately shivering began. Harrison appeared with a hot drink. Fever replaced the chills. Dreams came that were not dreams because I was awake, and not hallucinations because I saw nothing; nevertheless, they were real and unnerving.

Talking was relief so I talked aloud, to myself. Frequently the words I heard had no connection with what I thought I was saying. Talking was an escape valve for the pressure inside me. The pressure made me want to get up and run, anywhere just to be running, away from the walls of the room which were closing in, away from the hard mat which galled my hips and shoulders, away from dully aching bones. If I could run I could leave the pressure behind. But my legs wouldn't run. If the pressure got any higher it would blow a little hole in the top of my skull and escape with a whistle. I didn't want to be a whistle. I managed to sit up and immediately began to fly.

Arms seized me, pushed me back to the mat.

"Hey," said a voice, "you nearly fell out of bed."

My eyes focussed on a face.

"Boswell," I said. "Norman Boswell."

"Yes," said the face. "Doctor West said you wanted to talk to someone."

So I began talking about Shanghai restaurants, describing in detail every place I had eaten there and many which were purely imaginary.

"You don't mind if they're imaginary, do you?" I asked Boswell.

He did not reply. I looked carefully where he had been sitting. He was not there. Instead, West and Engineer Harrison were looking down at me. I tried in vain to tell them what strange thoughts were ballooning in my mind but my tongue wouldn't cooperate. It spoke not what my brain ordered but only words without meaning. Frantically I tried to tell Doc I wasn't delirious, that it was just my tongue not working. But the words that came only made him laugh and tell me to go to sleep.

Not only would my tongue refuse to obey, my brain also played tricks.

A thought would flash into consciousness, then as suddenly vanish, leaving the impression it had been a good thought but no recollection of its substance.

It was like fighting drowsiness when driving an automobile. The mind goes blank for split second intervals until fear rings an alarm and you see the road again. You're scared stiff you'll doze off and smash up; but you can't stop driving. Rationality came like that, in sudden spurts, with knowledge there were blank or delirious spaces between.

I was helplessly and miserably aware of the addled state of my mind and tongue. I have distinct and vivid recollections of the episodes described here. They occurred during the first forty-eight hours of the fever. After that, Doc later told me, my conversation was limited to two endlessly repeated words: "Skip it."

There are a few more shadowy memories of peering through a mosquito net and saying "hello" to silent figures sitting beside the bed. Eric was there, and Father Elling and Father van Gisbergen, the translator, and Father Bakker. Next is a dim memory of being carried in someone's arms. After that was the awakening.

I was lying in a bed not my own and in a room not my own. Father Elling's face was just above mine but his voice came from a distance. He was saying,

"Merry Christmas!"

Again I awakened. It was night. A light was burning nearby. A ward attendant named Koopal was shaking me. He put his lips close to my ear and asked,

"Do you want to hear the choir?"

"Why?" I wondered aloud.

"Christmas Eve concert," he said.

Yes, I wanted to hear it, but I could hear nothing. Wondering what Koopal was up to I fell asleep.

When I awakened again it was day. Visitors were in the ward, shaking hands with patients. But no sounds came from their moving lips. All I could hear were bells. They rang so long and steadily I realized, finally, they were not bells. The ringing was in my own ears.

I tried to sit up. Someone noticed my efforts and propped

me up with a board behind my back. Doc West strode up, grinning.

"I'm deaf," I told him.

He leaned down and shouted.

"Quinine!"

That also explained the shuddering bitterness of my mouth. Harrison appeared with a cup of something to drink. He spoke into my ear.

"Have a Harrison eggnog."

I drank. It did taste like eggnog. I started to ask "how come eggnog?" but the effort to speak was tiring. I dozed off. Next day Koopal brought a bowl of rice gruel in which had been broken a soft boiled egg. Talking was easier. I asked about the egg.

"From Peanut," said Koopal. "Christmas present."

Doc was there again, grinning as usual.

"You can have an egg every day as long as there are any. And here's something else."

He put a spoonful of Australian tinned butter in the gruel. Where he got it I didn't know. He made light of thanks.

"Skip it," he said. "We're trying to get you back on your feet. You can have a spoonful every day, while it lasts."

Other friends brought me extra bits of food. Eric and Canadian Christie procured a coconut and made a pudding of shredded coconut meat and rice. Mike Treurniet, one of the clinic dressers, owned a duck. He killed it and made broth. Harrison and Kendall gave me slices of papaya, secured through the Chinese contractor. Gradually my ears stopped ringing, my strength returned.

On New Year's Day Mike Treurniet gave me a genuine American cigaret. He had brought a tin of cigarets into internment and saved it to open for some celebration. Often we had solemnly but indecisively discussed what the occasion would be.

"Where's your will power, Mike?" I asked when he

handed me the cigaret. "Couldn't you wait for the big day?"

"We're celebrating you," he said. "Last week we thought you might not be around for New Year's."

"Nuts," I said, and breathed the first ceremonial puff. "Anyway, here's to 1944!"

I blew out a lungful of smoke.

"Happy New Year," said Mike.

Deeply I inhaled again, right down to the innermost crevices. What blissful pleasure to blow out American smoke and watch it float away, mingling with the thin spiral from the cigaret end.

Then came payment time—the reaction of giddiness and a pounding heart.

"Hey," said Mike. "You better not smoke any more."

An itch followed the fever, making sleep impossible. The night of January 3rd the itching felt as if a host of little worms with red hot bellies was wriggling on my chest. I rolled and tossed and scratched. The tormentors only spread out, creeping over my stomach and down my legs. I pulled the hair of my head as a counter irritant.

From the Bedroom & Morgue, from which I had been moved to make room for a dying man, sounded long drawn moans and occasional cries. Each outgoing breath was an exhalation of woe. Whether he was conscious or unconscious I knew not; or if conscious, whether his moans were from pain, loneliness or despair. Hour after hour the groans continued. Somewhere outside the jail a dog began to howl. The dog's howling and the man's cries blended in a harrowing harmony. Together with the itch they made my bed unbearable. I got up and managed to totter out of the ward. The night attendant grabbed me.

"What in hell are you doing out of bed?"

"The itch," I said. "Got to have fresh air."

The attendant eased me into a wicker lounge chair that was used daytimes by a paralytic.

"Want a smoke?" asked the night man.

"Sure, got one?"

"A real one, too."

"From Mike?"

"No. Guess after you taste it."

He walked to the oil lamp in the ward, lit the cigaret and, returning, handed it to me. Already I had caught the odor and knew whence it came.

"Smells like Tokyo."

"Right. The guard gave me a couple. New Year's present. He said New Year's was the Japanese *hari rayah*. Did you know that?"

Hari Rayah is the Malay term for a Big Holiday.

"Yes," I said. "I knew it."

Because New Year's Day is sacred to the Japanese—the biggest day of their year—my escape from Shanghai had been facilitated.

On New Year's morning, 1942, I was lying in the bottom of a sampan in a canal west of Shanghai. Further progress along the canal was barred by an iron gate which let down into the water from a railroad bridge above. On either side of the canal lay a heavily garrisoned village. Japanese and Chinese puppet guards were on the bridge. A Chinese official in the puppet Nanking regime was scheduled to appear at the bridge at 9 A.M. and pay New Year's Day compliments to the Japanese garrison commander and his troops. The Chinese was scheduled to do it because he was secretly a Chungking man and the guerrillas who were smuggling us out of Occupied China had so arranged with him.

In the sampan with me were my fellow correspondents, Robert "Pepper" Martin and Francis Lee, and several guerrillas.

Promptly at 9 A.M. the Chinese official appeared with his retinue at the bridge. The Japanese guards retired to a nearby tea house to drink a toast, in saki, to their Emperor. When their ringing Banzais sounded, bribed puppet guards

on the bridge raised the iron gate, our sampan shot through
and the gate dropped down behind us. Sixty-six hours later,
about 3 A.M. January 4, 1942, we crossed the last barrier—
the Nanking-Hangchow highway—and stepped into Free
China.

Now it was about 3 A.M. January 4, 1944. I took the
last drag from the cigaret and asked the attendant where he
had been New Year's Day, 1942.

"Right here in Sumatra, working in the oil fields."

My ears were clear enough by now to hear little sounds—
the scuffle of boots in the nearby guardroom, the rattle of
wire as rats scampered, like tight rope walkers, along the
top of the fourteen foot fence which separated the hospital
from the jail yard. Once Doc West and I shook the fence,
unbalancing a rat. It fell with a plop to the cement and
lay there stunned. We were too surprised by our success
to kill it before the rat recovered itself and scampered away.
In Palembang Jail one morning Allen and I awakened to
see a rat crouched, perfectly still, with its nose just touching
the edge of the hole where it lived. At first we thought the
rat was mad, then we realized it was dead.

"Heart failure," said Allen, "right on his own doorstep."

Toward morning the dying man's groans faded to a death
rattle. When the rattle ceased the attendant investigated.
Returning, he said,

"He's gone."

I wondered aloud how long it would take to get a
coffin.

"We have one already," said the attendant. "The one we
ordered for you."

He wasn't kidding either. A little chill settled in my
stomach.

Weeks later I asked Father Elling if it were true I had
been that close to death. I had been. Two days before
Christmas he had kept vigil at my bedside, hoping I would
recover consciousness long enough to receive the Last Sacra-

ments. Having nothing else to do while waiting, he had composed part of a sermon for delivery at my funeral which he thought would be Christmas Day.

Unlike the young engineer who had died too suddenly to establish a malarial pattern, my illness ran a sufficient course, from December 12th to 26th, with the climax on the 23rd, when, instead of killing me, the fever unexpectedly broke. Luckily for me Doc West had a small supply of quinine. Palembang had been a malaria free area and I was the first of the Bangka cases. Consequently his slender stocks of quinine had not all been used. Luckier still, he had found, by accident on the 22nd, some pills of an unusual variety of quinine which my system absorbed more readily than the ordinary kind. The new pills tipped the balance in my favor.

In all the long, terrible months ahead of us in Muntok Prison, no other man survived cerebral malaria.

By January 15th I was able to walk as far as the kitchen where were some scales. I weighed 46½ kilograms (102.3 pounds). Just what I had weighed as a schoolboy in the ninth grade. I remembered the figure well because the day I weighed it had been a big one in my school life. The scales then proved I was over 100 pounds and could practice for the football team.

Doc laughed when I told him.

"You'll soon be casting a shadow," he said. "Two weeks ago I'll bet you didn't weigh ninety."

That night I lay awake thinking of my good luck in surviving and contrasting my two trips in two years down into the valley of the shadow of death. The first trip had been in the Indian Ocean after my ship sank. Then I had been keenly aware of my predicament and for nearly an entire afternoon had swum and thought and prayed. But on this second trip I had not even been aware of the danger until it was over. How blindly and in ignorance of his peril can a man slip out of life!

16

How Men Starve

MALNUTRITION is like age. It creeps up on a man but not without warning because an empty belly is its own perpetual alarm. For just as a man awakens in the morning and his joints tell him he is getting old, so the hungry man awakens and swollen limbs tell him he is starving to death.

Like cold, hunger numbs the body and the mind. No matter how vividly hunger is described it can not be understood until it has been felt. I thought I knew something about hunger after seeing so much of it in China. I thought I knew it intimately in prison where men were dying around me and I nursed them as my own stomach crawled with the ache for food. But I didn't really know about hunger until I awakened one morning to find my own feet swollen. Then I knew.

Unless you who read this get that way you won't know either. So there is little use trying to describe how hunger feels. All I can do is tell what we who were starving did.

Whether hunger changes a man's essential character is debatable. I think it does not. Others differ. They say, for example, that hunger makes thieves of men who otherwise would never dream of theft. I say that they were already thieves at heart and hunger only brought it out. The man who would steal from a starving neighbor was dishonest about lesser things in normal life. Men of stronger conscience would die before stealing from a hungry fellow prisoner.

Hunger throws into bold relief a man's true self. It strips away the false front behind which hypocrites masquerade. From others it removes the mediocrity which disguised them as only ordinary men and reveals the hidden rock of noble character.

Hunger, in my opinion, does not change the intrinsic things that make one man good and another bad. It only accentuates the stuff of which a man is made. His reaction to the realization that he is dying of starvation depends on the kind of man he is. He may quit trying and lie back on his mat in a state of apathy, or he may work still harder to live. If he is a quitter and does not try he also usually is a chronic bellyacher. Loudly he denounces as incompetent or dishonest his leaders and all workers. But he himself will not lift a finger to help anyone. If he is a worker he redoubles his efforts to earn money or acquire food by handicrafts, trading or black marketing. The entrepreneur falls into two classes: he who works solely for the purpose of keeping himself alive and he who works for profits he can bank after the war.

The man who works for post-war profits operates openly as a loan shark or racketeer trading on the cupidity or hunger of his fellows. Such men are not peculiar only to internment camps.

The honest worker will stay honest, but he will use every honorable means, no matter how desperate or fantastic, to obtain food.

When all the chips are down it is the man with the will to live, and the ingenuity to use the will, who survives. And, in addition to will and ingenuity, he must have something else: some call it luck.

A man I'll call The Droop was an example of survival through blind luck, or the inscrutable designs of Providence, call it what you will. He was an Englishman in his fifties who had been invalided by heart disease before the war. His chances of surviving even the excitement of the Bangka Straits had not been considered good and the odds against his surviving the privations of prison camp were astronomical. But he did. Throughout internment he did not lift a finger to help himself unless no one else would lift it for him. He walked out when freedom came, a living example of sheer luck.

But whatever their natures, their characters or their luck, hungry men have one thing in common: the continuous thought of food. Awake, the hungry man talks about food and schemes how to get it. Asleep, he dreams about it. When a man is starving, life reduces itself to a never ending quest for something to eat. All other material things are secondary.

Between a man who is hungry but not yet starving and a man who is actually starving there is a distinct difference. The hungry man begrudges the scraps the cat must eat to live. The starving man eats the cat. The hungry man curses the rats which plague him. The starving man eats the rats. The hungry man wishes he could eat leaves. The starving man does eat them.

Not every one in Muntok Prison, of course, was starving. Just as in any famine-ridden land there are those who have plenty, and if not plenty at least enough, in prison there were those who somehow managed to supplement their diets. Kitchen staff men were the best nourished. They were well padded and in no danger of beri-beri. Next in order of nourishment came successful black market operators and their more prosperous customers. Some black marketeers and kitchen workers actually grew fat. Members of the working parties whose jobs took them outside the jail to cut wood or tend gardens frequently were able to trade with natives who hid in nearby shrubbery, or with Indonesian guards who were not averse to supplementing their meager salaries with a quick profit.

The friendly Javanese police who guarded us in Palembang were replaced in Bangka by Indonesians of various races, mostly Sumatra Malays. They were volunteer soldiers, members of a Nippon-recruited "People's Army," known by the Japanese designation of *Haiho*. Many of them were thugs openly hostile to whites but nearly all of them were susceptible to bribery. Every shift of guards had a few Japanese soldiers in it but the Japanese could not be everywhere at once.

A standard and strictly legal source of extra nourishment was given as payment for the heavy jobs that had to be done to keep things going. The time came when it was impossible to maintain our self-run jail facilities—cooking, cleaning, nursing, wood cutting, coffin carrying, grave digging—without giving extra food to workers so that they would have the strength to carry on. Therefore, men doing certain jobs were allotted "calories"—100 grams of food more per day than the rank and file of non-workers. The necessary amount was deducted from camp rations. However, "calories" did not guarantee a man sufficient strength to carry on. If he burned up more energy than he could replenish, he dropped out of the working party.

In my diary is the comment:

"Truly, as a man told the Camp Committee today, only those fortunate enough to get extra food in one way or another will walk out of here when freedom comes. So it is understandable why men, after they have eaten, lick their plates like dogs."

Luckily for me, the period of acute food shortage did not begin until I had recovered from the bout with cerebral malaria and had returned to work. Doc West's gifts, the extras from other friends and the small reserve I had saved from better days against such an emergency, put me back on my feet. Another important factor was that by nature I am thin and therefore did not have so much to lose when I lost, or so much to put back when I recovered.

Rice was the backbone of our diet—our bread and meat. The other staple was a potato-like vegetable known as *ubi kayu*: that's Malay for wood root, and a singularly descriptive name. It is the Malaya and East Indies variety of the tropical South American plant known variously as manioc or cassava. Tapioca is one of its many by-products. Ubi kayu is an edible tuber below ground and a long stemmed, half-shrubby plant above. We ate not only the root but the leaves. Dutch doctors said the topmost cluster of leaves contained Vitamin B. Why only the topmost and not the others is one of Mother Nature's mysteries. The leaves must be well boiled in order to be chewed successfully. The root is a pure starch and has two layers of skin, the outer layer being poisonous—secreting hydrocyanic acid.

By March, 1944, our daily diet per man had fallen to 130 grams (4½ ounces) of rice plus varying amounts (100 to 300 grams) of ubi root and leaves and a large tablespoon of evil smelling fish sauce. Occasionally and irregularly this diet was supplemented by bits of dried fish, one per man, about the size of a domino, and infinitesimal amounts of maize, green beans or palm oil. Fish sauce was made for two reasons: there was too little to serve any other way and the fish had been dead so long that boiling and spicing with pepper was necessary to make them palatable. Hungry as we were, many men, including myself, could not stomach the sauce. These rations were divided into two or three meals a day, depending on the amount of ubi kayu available.

Breakfast was an ubi kayu porridge known as *ongel-ongel*, a name which tickled my fancy because it so well described its substance and the sensation of eating it. Ongel-ongel was a tasteless, grey-white, transparent liquid when hot; cold, it hardened to a rubbery gelatin. Cold ongel-ongel looked so much like a poultice I decided to try it as such on the festered hands of a Frenchman named Albert. It worked. After two days I removed the poultice by dissolving in warm water. Albert's hands were white as a fish's belly but the blisters had been drawn.

Unfortunately, ongel-ongel was too scarce a food commodity to be used on other blister patients, and even had it been plentiful I doubt that it would have proved practical on our most annoying blister areas—Palembang Bottoms. Hot water remained the universal remedy. So large did the hot bath trade become that Shell craftsmen built a special boiler for the hospital. Two oil drillers ran it, Nick Koot who made the containers in which I buried Camp News, and Peter de Groot, a barrel-chested husky who spoke seven languages and coaxed the boiler fire in all of them. They constructed a sitz bath by cutting a gasoline tank in half and beveling the edges. Customers were handled with assembly-line precision; twenty minutes per patient and thirty or forty patients per shift. Reserved seats only.

Toward the end of March Peanut announced that he had wonderful news for us. The military would take back control of prison camps April 1st.

"You will receive more and better food," he said. "I am happy for you."

As a sign of his happiness he issued his most memorable communique. It said American forces had turned the Marshall Islands into a vast "floating airdrome" and that the Pacific war would end in April, 1945, just one year more.

The promised ration improvement did not materialize under military administration; but we were given monthly stipends of one and one half and later four guilders per man per month. The entire amount was put into the kitchen fund but there was little the Chinese contractor could buy.

Every ounce of incoming food, both Japanese issued and contractor purchased, had been weighed on our kitchen scales to check both on Japanese promises and the contractor's honesty. The new commandant confiscated the scales, saying, "The Japanese army is honest. We give full weight as promised. And if we do not give full weight the reason is because there is not enough to be given."

The commandant amazed us April 27, 1944, by including us in a Japanese celebration of Emperor Hirohito's birthday. Every prisoner received two cookies, one banana and two ounces of *arak*, a raw alcoholic drink. He further cheered us by announcing that rations would be increased in May and that our hospital would be enlarged by being moved next door into the building that had been a coolie quarantine depot for the Bangka Tin Winning Company. The hospital would occupy one wing of the building and the other wing would be used to house 250 prisoners and reduce crowding in the jail.

The hospital was moved, rations did increase but only for two weeks; and instead of two hundred prisoners being transferred to the Tin Winning building's other wing, two hundred new prisoners arrived. The newcomers were pale as death, unbelievably emaciated and, by the alacrity with which they obeyed, even anticipating orders, we could tell they had been well broken. For two years they had been jammed into locked cells of the jail at Pangkal Pinang, capital of Bangka Island. They had not been allowed outside their cells even for exercise. Our freedom to move around inside the jail and run our own internal affairs surprised them. What delighted them most, however, was our food. Our food—on which we were starving!

E. M. C. Aubrey-Scott, 25, a skeleton-thin Englishman who was brought directly into hospital, began to cry when he received his first meal in Muntok prison.

"This is heaven," he said over and over in a choking voice.

"What's the matter?" I asked him.

"This food," he said, as the tears came. "It's so wonderful. You cook it yourselves."

In Pangkal Pinang jail the food, already cooked and little more than slop, had been supplied by a piratical Indonesian contractor. Pangkal Pinang Jail had been run entirely by Indonesians who, judging from tales told of them, were much worse than Japanese.

Despite the privations they suffered, however, Pangkal Pinangers were free from disease, except for a few pellagra cases like Aubrey-Scott. Malaria, severe beri-beri and dysentery had not yet visited them. But Doc West said it would not be long.

"They are in such poor condition," he said, "that they'll go quickly when they get our dysentery and malaria."

Prophetic words. Within six months half of them were dead.

But how desperately they fought to keep alive! Their efforts were reflected immediately by that barometer of desperation, rodent prices.

The price of cooking-rats, which had been retailing at one to two guilders, soared to five. They were hard to catch. Mice went to two and one half guilders each. A member of the British committee, and not a Pangkal Pinanger, who had a standing offer of one guilder for a rat and fifty cents for a mouse, was indignant when the price zoomed to five and 2.50 respectively.

One of the Pangkal Pinang men uncovered a nest of newborn mice.

"How much will you give me for them?" he asked the Britisher.

"Two guilders and they aren't worth that, they're so small."

"Three," demanded the salesman.

They compromised at two and one half. The buyer ate them raw because, he explained, "they are too small to cook. They'd disintegrate."

Bats were numerous when the Pangkal Pinangers arrived,

but their numbers rapidly dwindled as hunters stalked them day and night with homemade butterfly nets.

Ants, red or black but red and fat preferred, became a source of grease to flavor rice. I never tasted them myself but gourmands who caught and fried them said they were not bad. The chief selling point of fried ants was that grease of any kind was nourishment.

The Tin Winning building was a structure shaped like a block U. Between the wings of the U was a rectangular concrete platform called a *pendopo*, about 150 feet long and one third as wide. It was roofed but open on the sides. In prewar days it had served, probably, as an open air dining hall. On either side of the pendopo was a strip of grass; on the open end of the U was an area of weeds, tall grass and a few trees, the whole enclosed by a barbed wire fence and a thick hedge.

Pangkal Pinangers quickly combed the weed grown plot for grubs. When the grubs were gone they plucked the grass and weeds and tree leaves and boiled them. Nor were Pangkal Pinangers the only ones. British planters from Malaya and Dutch burghers from Palembang followed suit.

The dogs that had precipitated an election crisis in Palembang would have been among the first things into cooking pots had they been around after the ongel-ongel days began. But they had been killed and buried shortly after arriving in Muntok Prison because they no longer could be fed and death was more merciful than starvation.

Mehitabel the cat and her offspring, on whom we had lavished our pork fat, had been allowed to live only because they could exist on rats. But they did not live long after the Pangkal Pinangers arrived. A cleaning gang found their heads and hides in a septic tank. Two dogs and a monkey which somehow got into the yard were next.

A hospital ward attendant told me that on his shift one

day he caught two patients in the lavatory eating maggots.

"Holy Mackerel," I said, "we'd better guard the mortuary at night or they'll be gnawing on the corpses."

Such a strange glint suddenly appeared in his eyes that I thought about it for days afterwards. That man, I thought, was up to something.

Long afterward, when I no longer worked in the hospital, I learned what it was. He told me himself. Whenever a man died during his shift he inspected the dead man's mouth for gold teeth or gold fillings. If there were any he removed the teeth.

"I got a kilo of rice from a Haiho for each gold tooth," he said, "and smaller amounts, depending on the size, for a filling.

"The teeth weren't hard to pull out. You know, I noticed that the gums of most men became very soft and their teeth got loose when they died of beri-beri. And if they weren't loose I used a pair of pliers. The difficult part was doing it unobserved."

He laughed ruefully.

"Sounds terrible to say I pulled dead men's teeth, doesn't it? But that wasn't as bad as eating maggots."

I agreed that it was not.

Bats, rats, grubs, ants and maggots were protein and men were dying for lack of protein. A man's muscles are protein. If the body can't get protein any other way it feeds on the muscles until none are left and a man looks like the living skeleton in a circus side show.

The mind deteriorates too. Lack of protein affects the brain. Memory suffers, the power of concentration goes. Study becomes more and more difficult and finally is abandoned. A deadly lassitude lays hold of men. They cease to care about anything, even about eating. If friends do not snap them out of their inertia they simply disintegrate and die. When an internee's mind went his body soon followed. Fortunately, very few serious mental cases developed. We all became a little warped, I think, before the end, but only a small number completely lost their minds. And those few soon died. The body seems to reach a certain stage beyond which only the will power to survive will keep it alive.

Max Breuer, 34-year-old dark-skinned Indo-European policeman, whom we had written off as a chronic malaria case doomed for the beri-beri ward, was an example of the will to live conquering a body seemingly scheduled to die. For months he lay in the fever ward, apathetic between his spells of shivering and sweating. His malaria was not severe, like cerebral, but was chronic and slowly wearing him down. Something, I don't know what, snapped him out of his apathy. He began to fight. He asked Doc West to move him out of the hospital proper to what we called the Old Men's Ward, in the opposite wing of the Tin Winning building. There, convalescing patients and old men were more or less on their own but still got hospital food.

Every morning Max dragged himself out to the weed lot and picked and boiled a mess of "greens." Soon he was cooking not only for himself but for others and charging for the services. With the money, he bought black market condiments to flavor his "greens," and made more money to buy more condiments plus food for himself. His body grew stronger. By nature he was a heavy-set, muscular fellow. His wasted frame began to fill out. He left the Old Men's Ward and moved into one of the Pangkal Pinang cells where death had thinned the population so there was plenty of room. In time Max became a fat black-market operator because he had the guts and the will, plus the ingenuity.

Wembley-Smythe had the guts and the will but not the ingenuity. When Beissel lost his job as chief cook—because the oil men got control and ousted him—Wembley-Smythe lost his job too. He was too clumsy for any but kind hearted Beissel to keep on the staff.

Cut off from calories he had received as a kitchen worker and congenitally unable to do anything to help himself, he had to depend entirely on camp rations. They were not enough to give his body the strength to resist chronic malaria and septic sores. He began to fade. The future looked grim for Wembley-Smythe, with whom I had debated immortality after the moonlight thunderstorm.

Another fatal weakness in prison camp was an inordinate appetite for sweets or fancy things—for dessert instead of the main course. Numbers of men with such appetites succumbed by their own folly.

They sold their rice, the bulk of our diet, in order to buy tastier morsels on the black market: bits of fish, minuscule prawns, palm sugar, bean curd cakes or even fried ubi. Such tidbits, they said, satisfied their hunger more than rice. Others sold their rice in order to buy tobacco. Tobacco was solace for empty stomachs. It soothed nerves rasped by confined living. It helped bridge the aching gap between 6:30 A.M. porridge and mid-afternoon rice. But it was not food. And those who sold their rice to buy tobacco or other luxuries inevitably ended in the beri-beri ward.

Disposal of dead men's effects became a major problem. The hospital benefited by getting their rags for bandages but disposition of more useful articles and money caused endless bickering and quarrels among neighbors of the deceased. Ghoulish "friends" frequently could not wait for a man to die before they began looting his possessions. A partial solution to the problem was obtained by having all internees fill in brief, prepared forms, appointing executors of their jail estates. Since most men died in hospital we became watchdogs of their effects, fending off the efforts of executors or would-be executors to get possession of their belongings before they were turned over to the Camp Committee which "probated" the estates according to the wills.

As theft and chiseling became more frequent the Camp Committee drafted a system of laws and penalties and established our own private jail within our prison to punish offenders. The jail was the room in which we had performed the secret autopsy. Men caught stealing food, clothing or other things were locked in it for various periods. Chiselers were those men who by various stratagems, such as appearing twice in a food queue, got more than they were entitled to; or who shirked compulsory corvee when they were not sick. They were penalized by being deprived of rations in varying amounts for varying times, depending on the severity of their offense.

Weaklings and dolts, ghouls and thieves, fools and mere good hearted bunglers were more conspicuous than men who lived or died quietly but gallantly; nevertheless, we had our share of brave and self sacrificing men, such as the father who every day gave part of his food to his sons. On the principle they needed it just as much, probably more, boys under sixteen were given extra calories, the same as workers. So the particular Dutch father I refer to was not morally or otherwise obliged to give away a single fraction of his food to his sons. But he did regularly and is numbered among the dead.

There was a *kongsie* of four men, three of whom fell ill. Two lay side by side in hospital in the beri-beri ward and the third lay in his block with chronic malaria. The fourth man, a slender, middle-aged Englishman who looked as though a strong wind would blow him away, worked desperately to save them. By buying and selling, working and scheming he managed every day to get something extra for his friends. It looked for a while as if he would save all three but the beri-beri victims finally died. When they died the friend was able to concentrate all his efforts on the chronic

teen brothers of the Bangka mission headed by Monsignor Bouma. The priests were of the same order to which Father Bakker belonged, the Congregation of the Sacred Hearts of Jesus and Mary, famous for an illustrious member known to the world as Father Damien of Molokai, the Hawaiian leper colony.

I think that something of the fire that burned in the heart of Father Damien burned also in the heart of Father Bakker. Although he never said a word it was obvious from his actions that Father Bakker dedicated himself to the task of saving his fellow missionaries, especially Monsignor Bouma, from the beri-beri ward.

Bishop Mekkelholt did for the Bangka missionaries what he could but he had his hands full trying to keep his own priests and brothers from Sumatra alive. The Bangka clergy had to depend mostly on themselves.

So Father Bakker cooked and scrubbed, bought and sold. One of his business enterprises was selling cigarets rolled in paper instead of nipa leaves. The papers were torn from breviaries. Every bit of extra food he earned went to feed the sick. He was burning himself out. But instead of reducing his self-imposed tasks of helping his friends, in order to help himself, he merely cut down on his personal pleasures, such as studying and composing, and devoted the time saved to assisting his helpless companions.

They were helpless in two ways. The Pangkal Pinang Jail had sapped their vitality. And they did not have the necessary ingenuity. Unlike the Sumatra missionaries, Monsignor Bouma and most of his men seemed unable to cope with the exigencies of black market barter or the sheer struggle for survival. Consequently, the task fell on the shoulders of a few practical priests like Father Bakker. As the lean months passed the burden proved too much. Father Bakker's limbs swelled; his feet and hands began to bear the familiar lesions of malnutritional disease. Malaria bouts increased in frequency. By the end of 1944 he could not even direct the remnants of his beloved choir.

As deaths mounted so did our protests, written and verbal, to the Japanese. On June 19th Captain Seki, commander of all south Sumatra internee affairs, moved his headquarters to Muntok and replied in person to our pleas. Every man who could walk—there were 910 in prison then and about 200 too sick to attend—stood at attention in the long open air pendopo to hear Seki speak. His words were translated into Malay by a Japanese interpreter who was the most hated man in Muntok.

Seki said our prospects were for more work and less food. We must grow our own food or starve. No more rice would be imported from the Sumatra mainland. Rations would be reduced fifteen per cent immediately. We must furnish 200 more men for cultivating outside gardens—and the gardeners would get no extra nourishment for their efforts.

Seki said he was sorry for the old men and the sick but that Japan had not started the war. Bangka was a war theater with the imminent possibility of action. Japanese soldiers must come first in food consideration. He concluded his talk by saying,

"Please do not get sick, so that when the war ends you can all go home."

Derisively we laughed and hooted. Seki looked at the interpreter and the interpreter exploded into a tirade of abuse for our insult to the captain.

The fifteen per cent reduction made it impossible for our kitchen crew to stretch rations into three meals a day. Thereafter we had only two and no more ongel-ongel.

July 31st the Camp Committee handed another letter to Seki:

"It is now no longer a case of the older and weaker men dying through under-nourishment. Young men in their twenties who but recently went out to work in the vegetable gardens at your request are dying, after a brief illness, owing to lack of resistance as a result of under-nourishment. We state plainly that, if our food supply is not quickly improved, the health of the camp will be completely undermined and the internees will succumb to fatal illnesses in increasing numbers. And this with the full knowledge of Nippon authorities, whose attention we have repeatedly drawn to the seriousness of our situation.

"We fully understand that the war effort is of primary importance in your eyes. We realize that the food situation may be difficult. But we can not understand that a responsible Japanese government and the Japanese Military Authorities will stand by idly while the death rate amongst internees increases at such an alarming rate as has been the case here.

"Our letter addressed to you and dated July 8th has remained unanswered. The situation is serious. Only quick and radical improvement of our food supply will prevent disastrous consequences. We rely upon you, as the officer in charge of this internment camp, to realize the gravity of the situation and to take all steps in your power to forestall a catastrophe."

Seki did nothing to forestall it. Rather did he worsen matters by moving the Women's Camp from Palembang to Muntok, thereby placing an added strain on Bangka Island's dwindling food supplies.

17

The Beri-Beri Song

ON A bright June morning in 1944 I first heard the weird wailing that came to be known as the beri-beri song. None who sang it lived to disclose the reason but we had an uncanny feeling the singers were conscious of their act. Why they did it remains a mystery, the answer to which lies buried in rows of graves beneath the pepper trees of Bangka Island.

Beri-beri patients lay in a ward identical with others in the prison hospital. Concrete platforms forty feet long and eight feet wide lined either side of the room, with a narrow walk between. The same number of men lay shoulder to shoulder on the benches which sloped slightly from the wall downward to the aisle. A small ledge ran along the foot of the shelves and kept things from sliding off onto the floor. Liquid suppurating from pores of swollen victims ran in little rivulets down the slope and collected along the ledge.

Not all patients were filled with liquid. Many were little more than skeletons. Two types of the disease were most common in Muntok: hydropic, or "wet," wherein victims filled with water, and atropic, or "dry," wherein they dried out and shriveled up like angleworms in the sun. Why some shriveled and others swelled I don't know. Both types started the same way. First symptoms appeared four months after our ongel-ongel diet began. And the first deaths were in May, one month after initial symptoms.

Beri-beri is a malnutritional scourge caused primarily by lack of Vitamin B in the diet. Protein deficiency is a secondary cause. First symptoms usually are swelling—caused by oedema—of the feet, numbness of certain areas of the legs and a peculiar walk: the victim "slapping" the ground with his feet and staggering as though intoxicated. The swollen flesh is flaccid and, if squeezed, fingerprints remain as though pressed into wet clay. As the disease progresses, serous fluid fills and expands tissues of the entire body and, in a cold, steady stream, sweats through distended pores. The peritoneal and pleural cavities fill and the victim literally drowns in his own juice.

The wet type is deadlier than the dry. I can remember no hydropic case recovering after having reached an advanced stage, whereas there were several recoveries from the advanced atropic state.

Response to proper and early treatment is remarkably fast. In Muntok, proper treatment meant food containing Vitamin B and protein. The green bean known as *kachang ijau* is fabulously rich in Vitamin B and when obtainable in sufficient quantity worked unbelievably rapid cures. If the patient could digest them the beans were eaten raw after being soaked overnight; then the water was drained off and the beans were allowed to stand another twelve to twenty-four hours, until they began to sprout. At that point, due to some internal chemical change, the bean was richest in Vitamin B content. As the bean sprouted the Vitamin B content decreased and Vitamin C was built up. Patients suffering skin lesions caused by Vitamin C shortage were fed well-sprouted beans.

Kachang ijau's magic was demonstrated on our first two cases of pronounced oedema: an Englishman named Grixoni and a Dutch Catholic brother. They expanded like balloons. Within one week Grixoni's weight shot up 19.8 pounds and the Brother's 26.4, due entirely to water in the tissues. Doc West obtained enough kachang ijau, through a Japanese guard and the black market, to feed them large amounts. In a few days the swelling began to subside. In two weeks they were completely "deflated." The Brother survived internment and Grixoni died, but months later and of malaria and dysentery, not beri-beri.

Men who lay in the Muntok beri-beri ward were those for whom there was not enough kachang ijau and who consequently could not be "deflated" like Grixoni and the Brother.

If they lay there long enough they developed one, or two or sometimes all three painful complications: creeping bed sores, septic legs or beri-beri blisters. The septic legs began as deep ulcers, usually below the knee, and kept expanding, sometimes completely encircling the leg. Our only treatment was soaking in hot water, cutting away dead tissue and applying wet dressings. Maggots invariably invaded those particular wounds and assisted in the scissoring process. Doctors said the maggots actually were beneficial but patients complained of pain and itching.

The blisters usually occurred on thighs grotesquely swollen by oedema. The blisters were enormous things, tense with serum and sometimes extending from knee to groin. They erupted with astonishing suddenness. Puncturing and draining alleviated pain but the victim was doomed because flesh beneath the blisters was dead. Medically the condition is known as "hydropic necrosis of subcutaneous tissues." Both septic and blistered legs invariably were fatal, death resulting from general toxemia.

The first high-pitched, long drawn notes of the beri-beri song awakened me one morning before roll call. They were a song-like wail such as I imagined keening might be. Curiosity impelled me to rise, slip my toes into a pair of sandals and explore along the hospital veranda, tracing the noise to its source. One after another I passed the two fever wards, the beri-beri ward, the septic ward and came to the dysentery ward. The noise then sounded behind me. I had overshot the source. Turning back to the septic ward I went in, walked down the aisle and joined the attendant who was leaning over a 40-year-old rubber planter I will call Maurice.

Maurice was not in the beri-beri ward because in addition to that disease he was covered with septic sores. He had been the "pretty boy" of our community, spending hours in finicky cleaning and washing of his person and clothing, gazing into a tiny hand mirror and combing and recombing, combing and recombing his thinning hair. Now his dandified body, from scalp line to toes, was a solid incrustation of scabs and pus. He lay flat on his back, his knees drawn up so that the soles of his feet rested on the bench. His hands were folded over his chest and the fingers picked at each other. His eyes were open and peered intently at the ceiling, as if trying to discern some dimly seen object above him. And he was singing. Not with words, but with a long drawn a-a-a-ah which rose and fell in a tune strangely similar to "Waltzing Matilda." I stepped up on the bench beside him and, squatting down, asked if he wanted anything. Changing a dressing frequently eased the pain of serum filled sores. He rolled his head to look at me but continued the wail. Again I asked him,

"Do you want something?"

He stopped singing, closed his mouth, opened it as though he were about to speak, but did not. While I felt his pulse he rolled his head back to his former position, peered at the ceiling and resumed the song.

The sack he used for a blanket had been pushed aside. I pulled it back over him and stepped off the bench. The attendant wondered aloud if we should call Doc West because Maurice was keeping everyone awake. We decided not. Roll call soon would sound anyway. I looked around the gloomy ward. It was always dim inside because the only windows were at the end next to the door. Here and there men were propped up on their elbows, watching. A patient requested a light for his nipa straw cigaret. The attendant brought him the small night kerosene lamp and lit it. Another man called for a bedpan. The attendant hurried to him. I walked out into the open to breathe the clean air of dawn and listen to the birds bustling in the durian trees beyond the fence.

The singing grew louder after roll call. Doc West tried to quiet him but Maurice would only pause momentarily, look at Doc as a blind man looks in the direction of a sound, working his lips as if trying to speak, then resume the wail. Around seven o'clock the song changed to loud groans and cries. We collected our breakfasts of boiled ubi and tried not to hear Maurice while we ate.

After breakfast I worked as usual in the septic ward where Maurice lay next to a rabbit-like little man I'll call Bunny. While I was dressing Bunny's sores Maurice suddenly galvanized into action. With a raucous groan which set my teeth on edge he slowly rose from the bench to a sitting posture. It was as though a corpse on a morgue slab had sat up to look around.

He was in the grip of a violent muscular contraction which affected all parts of his body. The cords of his neck and throat were taut and distended. His fingers became talons reaching for some invisible thing. His lips drew back from his teeth in a sardonic, skull-like grin. So widely staring were his white-socketed eyes that the lids appeared torn from them. Wildly he stared at whatever it was for which he reached and tried to grasp and convey to his half open mouth. I decided he was trying to bring air to his bubbly lungs.

He rolled from side to side, throwing his arms and hands over Bunny, then twisting to the other side and trying to climb the wall, then rolling back again to half embrace

Bunny. It was almost as though he hated Bunny and was trying to take the little man with him into some realm of nightmare.

Bunny was too weak to move. He had a hole in his lower abdomen where yesterday Doc Boerma had cut into his bladder and inserted a drain tube as a desperate expedient to lessen his last agonies. Bunny could only plead:

"Keep him off me. Please."

A morphine injection gradually quieted Maurice. His writhing decreased to restless twitching, his breathing became stertorous. An hour later he suddenly became quiet. I felt for his pulse. It was not. As I held his wrist Maurice relaxed, tension drained from his muscles, his jaw sagged as a last exhalation emptied his body of life.

The following morning I noticed that Bunny paid no attention to flies which settled on his face.

"How are you?" I asked.

"It's no use, Mac," he replied. "I'm finished."

Trying to convince him otherwise would have been mockery. I thanked him for the language lessons he had given me before his illness and asked if there was anything he wanted done.

"Will you pray for me?"

I promised I would. He thought of something else.

"If I act like Maurice," he said, "hold my hand. I don't want to go that way."

Bunny sang the beri-beri song two mornings later. He was spared the convulsions Maurice had experienced. He drifted from song into coma while I held his hand. When he was past knowing whether or not he was alone I returned to work. He died that afternoon.

Next singer was a man of 29 we called The Gow. He burst into a wild, frenetic wail about seven A.M. But, unlike the two before him and the scores who followed, we were sure The Gow knew what he was doing.

"Why are you singing?" I asked him.

"I have to," he said between snatches of the dreadful melody. "I have to."

That was the nearest we ever came to an answer. Like Maurice, The Gow went into a long series of convulsions, but unlike Maurice he remained, apparently, aware of his actions although powerless to stop them. His lips formed the same death's head grin, his eyelids disappeared behind his eyeballs, his body tensed and writhed and twisted. He clawed for air.

Acting on a theory that the wailing and convulsions might be caused by an acute shortage of salt in the body, Doc put a tube into The Gow and poured a salt solution into his stomach. He finally quieted, drifted into the inevitable coma and died in the afternoon. As we carried him from the ward other men on the bench, who looked as if they were going to go in the same way, watched uneasily.

The fourth song filled hospital rooms the following morning. I was talking to a 37-year-old English seaman nicknamed Flash when he broke into loud wailing. It was like watching a man go insane.

Flash had been shipwrecked and survived wearing nothing but a pair of shorts. He acquired little else during internment. All his possessions were on the bench beside him. They totaled four empty tins, two of them rusty; a battered enamel plate, a wooden spoon and a metal fork, half of a coconut shell, a bottle from which the neck had been broken and a half finished dart board. He had worked on the dart board intermittently for two years. Flash was a fighter but the odds were against him because, like Wembley-Smythe, he had not the necessary ingenuity or the luck for survival. He was a scrawny fellow when I first met him. Now his grotesquely swollen body was wracked by malaria and incrusted with ringworm, itch and septic sores. But he remained cheerful, frequently smiling and deprecating his ills, often apologizing for the "trouble" he caused hospital attendants.

Flash expressed concern for the first time over his condition when pains wracked his chest and arms the night after The Gow's death. He asked the night man how sick he was. The night man did not have the heart to tell him. When the day man came he would not tell him either. Eric and I visited Flash before breakfast. We knew he wouldn't be around much longer and we liked him. Eric had just lit a cigaret and placed it between Flash's lips when an abrupt, hoarse, involuntary cry wrenched its way from the sick man's throat.

Flash looked at Eric, then at me. Fear was in his eyes, but he said not a word. The cigaret had fallen to the bench. Eric picked it up and replaced it between Flash's lips. Flash took a few drags then shuddered violently, dropped the cigaret again and cried a second time. The paroxysm passed as quickly as it had come.

"I'm sorry," said Flash, "I can't help it."

About half past eight I was working nearby when Flash again groaned loudly. I asked him if he wanted another cigaret.

"I'd like it if you have one," he said.

I walked down to the staff room, selected a nipa leaf, placed a few grains of tobacco on it, rolled it and returned to Flash. He smiled his thanks and said,

"Don't go away, will you, if . . . if . . ."

"Okay, Flash. I'll stick around."

I lit the cigaret and was about to put it between his lips when, as though a switch had been thrown in his brain, Flash passed from reason to delirium. He talked nonsense, then began to sing. The tune, as with Maurice before, was not unlike "Waltzing Matilda." Convulsions followed. So did the shot of morphine, the coma, the stertorous breathing.

Because he had asked me not to go away I put a stool on the bench beside him, in the space left vacant by Bunny's death, and waited. Other patients glanced apprehensively in our direction. Hospital visitors wandered in and out, staring as they passed. Attendants hurried up and down the aisle, wielding bedpans. Tommy Thomson, the hospital quartermaster, made his rounds taking orders for soya bean cake available only to sick men without stomach or intestinal troubles.

Preacher Gillbrook, who had been a lay "interdenominational" missionary in North China, came in, said he guessed Flash was a Church of England man and intoned a prayer. The morning dragged. Tiffin time approached. Flash's breathing was more labored, his pulse weaker. I wondered,

"Will he die in time for me to eat?"

Food was served to patients. The man who lay next to Flash was an English engineer whose swollen limbs had more and deeper sores than any man in the ward. He used chopsticks to eat his rice because they stretched out his meal. Many of us used them because we could eat one grain at a time that way and make 130 grams last an hour. Each time he raised the sticks his elbow grazed Flash's left shoulder. Flash died at 1:25 P.M. I pulled the sack over his face and rose stiffly from the stool. The chopsticks had not missed a beat.

I walked into the staff room just as Eric returned from the food serving line carrying his plate and mine. Flash had died in time for me to eat.

After dinner we lifted Flash's body onto a stretcher and carried it into the bamboo and palm shed built beside the hospital for a mortuary. An empty box was waiting. We put Flash in and nailed down the lid. The coffin gang slung ropes around each end of the box, then, like Chinese coolies, looped them over carrying poles which rested on their shoulders, toted the coffin to the front gate and lowered it to the ground.

Father Bakker, with the remnants of his choir, was waiting at the gate. He raised his baton. The choir began "Abide with Me." When the song ended, the pallbearers, three to each side, lifted the coffin onto their shoulders and were counted through the gate. Behind came six alternate pall-bearers, including Eric and myself. We traded off every quarter of a mile. Two guards carrying bayoneted rifles led the procession, two more brought up the rear. The road wound through a green, park-like section of Muntok. Men usually liked to go on funerals because of the walk.

The cemetery, an old one laid out by the Dutch, who had colonized Bangka and developed the pepper plantations and tin deposits, had been expanded for internees and was growing rapidly. Mounds of red laterite marked the resting places of prisoners who had preceded Flash. Six open graves waited for succeeding guests.

We lowered the coffin into the first of the four foot deep holes. British Leader Hammet read Church of England burial services. When he had finished he reached down, picked up a handful of red soil and tossed it onto the coffin, saying,

"Remember, man, that thou art dust and unto dust thou shalt return."

Following suit, we each stooped, picked up some earth and cast it. It struck the wood with a rattling, hollow sound. The Japanese guards saluted. We filled the hole. Hammet shoved the end of a wooden cross into the soft dirt. Painted in black letters on the cross were Flash's name and the date. Because the new commandant had not continued Peanut's custom of providing flowers for funerals, we broke a few leafy stems from shrubs which grew along the cemetery edge, laid them on the grave and departed.

Back in jail I lay down to rest. Voices from the ward next door indicated Doc West was making his late rounds. My eyes closed and my ears followed him from patient to patient, anticipating his arrival beside old De Groot, a pensioned colonial soldier and, at 73, the oldest man in prison. De Groot was one of the few men who spoke Malay so slowly and clearly I could understand every word. He enunciated deliberately, as if he were afraid he might be misunderstood. Since Doc could speak no Dutch and De Groot no English, they conversed in Malay.

I heard Doc greet De Groot, and De Groot's reply. Calmly the old man announced that his days were ended and that he was about to die. Only persons who know Malay will appreciate the drama of what De Groot said in his simple, colloquial Malay of the market place. For those few, here are De Groot's words.

"Selamat, tuan Doktor. Suda habis. Saya orang mati. Terima kasi banyak."

Translated literally:

"Greetings, Mister Doctor. It is finished. I am a dead man. Thank you very much."

He was grateful for the Doc's attention and he was finished. By morning his voice had risen in the beri-beri song. Then went the engineer whose chopsticks had not missed a beat; and most of those who had watched so apprehensively as Maurice, Bunny, The Gow and Flash were carried out. Day after day, through June, July, August and September, the song continued. Then it ceased as abruptly as it had begun. Men still died of beri-beri but more quietly, more conveniently. During November the song resumed again for a cycle of perhaps ten deaths. After that it was not heard again.

18

Building for the Payoff

THE tomb-like quiet of Muntok Prison yard during the last quarter of 1944 was broken only by bells signaling roll call, food, funerals or work and by the shuffling footsteps of men answering those summonses. The only other sound was an undertone of discord that, as a deceptive bed of ashes erupts to release buried flames and gases, sporadically burst into bitter, violent internecine quarrels.

The petty hates of Barracks Camp were distilled in Muntok Prison until they attained proportions of open warfare. Morale was cracking. As a community we were disintegrating. We had forgotten how to play or study or relax. Worst of all, we had forgotten how to laugh. In the struggle for self-preservation too many men adopted the attitude of survival at any cost and the devil or the grave take the hindmost.

Palembang Jail and Barracks Camp had bustled with activities. When men were not working or studying or playing cards or chess they were out sunning themselves. The sun had been a friend in those days. Now it was an enemy to be avoided, to be hidden from in gloomy cells. And, as more and more men stayed in their cells around the clock, busy only with their thoughts, they became morbid, lost hope, sank into staring apathy.

For such as they, years passed between one meal and the next, and months were centuries. I often wondered why so

214

few of them lost their minds. Maybe they adopted the technique of a life termer I interviewed once in an American penitentiary. He said that while in solitary confinement he kept his sanity by learning how to make his mind a blank. My own technique for bridging the abyss between meals and forgetting the calendar was keeping busy. It worked successfully. Also, my hopes of escaping never abated. They sound so fantastic now, those schemes and plans and dreams of escape, that I prefer not to record them. Readers might think I was either balmy or an opium smoker. Fantastic as they were, however, they helped keep up my spirits. I always figured it was going to be a long war and that prisoner mortality rates would be astronomical but I also always reckoned I would be neither among the dead nor among those living skeletons present when liberation came. I banked on either being repatriated among newspaper men and others exchanged between Japan and the United States, or on escaping to India or New Guinea. Louhenapessie, the smuggler, brought me down to earth one day when we were discussing how best to reach New Guinea.

"You're too thin now," he said. "You must get fatter. You're not strong enough to escape."

Bitter truth. The time to escape is in the beginning when muscles are still pliable and responsive to extraordinary calls upon them. The jungle and the sea are not for weaklings. And daily I was growing weaker. But, somehow, I felt sure, I would regain my strength.

I think there is in the world only one thing as buoyant as love; and that is hope. Between keeping busy and hoping, time flew.

My little world of sores and bandages, scissoring and hot baths, kept me so occupied I seldom walked the corridor from hospital to prison yard. When I did, it was like visiting a ghost camp. Except when a bell rang the yard was deserted. Gravel crunched with startling loudness under foot. The air of desolation was transformed somewhat on walking from the yard into a cell full of men. That was like stepping into a meeting of conspirators. Usually they were plotting how to overthrow the Camp Committee or certain members of it. And, if a sudden silence greeted me as I entered, it meant they had been talking about the hospital and what a graft hospital workers had. But the talkers themselves would not volunteer to nurse the sick. They only talked and bellyached. They simply would not labor in the septic and dysentery wards where there was danger of infection and nursing tasks frequently were stomach turning. Arguments that "you may be next and have no one to nurse you" were of no avail. They would volunteer for two jobs only: the diet kitchen and quartermaster department where Doc West had put men of integrity. No one grew fat in the hospital diet kitchen or in the quartermaster department.

Other prison institutions besides the hospital were under fire. An oil power-play in March had squeezed Beissel from the kitchen as chief cook. Just as Van der Vliet had been ousted from leadership in Barracks Camp ostensibly, but not really, because of a quarrel over dogs, so Beissel's removal was attributed to a reason equally as inane. He was accused of allowing kitchen workers to drink too much coffee.

The same group of men tried a squeeze play on the hospital, claiming that if they got control they would staff it adequately. However, when asked to guarantee they would man the septic and dysentery wards they hedged. West and his staff fought back. Bishop Mekkelholt stepped into the breach with a concrete offer of help: fifteen priests and brothers to man the septic and dysentery wards. He made one stipulation, that his missionaries do the whole job and not just alternate shifts. West gladly accepted. It cost the clergy heavily in sickness but when one dropped out another took his place. The opposition failed to gain control. The first severe storm had been weathered. When the next came, unfortunately, Doc West was not at the helm to pilot us through.

The Japanese took Doc West from us in September and sent him to a military camp in Palembang. Hospital conditions became chaotic after he had gone and even his enemies realized that West had been more than a medical practitioner. He had been a leader and power for good. He had the knack of cheering patients and giving them courage even though he could not give them medicine. And he was impartial. All patients got equal treatment. Brusque he had been and high handed, but there was no doubt in any one's mind what he represented. He kept the hospital from becoming a political football or a factional monopoly. His sharp tongue and blunt manner made enemies but after he left most of them wished he was back.

In our travail we needed leaders who could command the confidence of men of diverse blood, social strata and nationalities; leaders who could rise above factional rivalries of government, oil and business, with their differing ideas of who should be in control and how. Leaders who could be trusted by both the Haves and Have Nots, as well as by European and Eurasian.

Although the hospital fight was settled temporarily, its ramifications were felt in an election which put Oosten into leadership of the camp. Oranje retired from chairmanship of the Camp Committee and Oosten took his place. His tenure was a stormy one. Trouble multiplied from the day he took office. Again the hospital was at the core of it.

Although they deprived us of Doc West, the Japanese brought us three more doctors, making six in prison, all Dutch. One of the newcomers, P. E. Lentze, was named head of the hospital because in pre-war days he had been chief surgeon of the Bangka Tin, in whose bailiwick we now lived. Lentze was a dark skinned Indo-European of ability and integrity and every inch a doctor and a gentleman, but he was unable to cope with the kind of dogfight in which he found himself from the first day he entered Muntok Prison.

I was scouting around the prison one afternoon trying to find a man to join the hospital dressing staff. A Shell engineer named E. E. de Bruyn told me humorously.

"If only we had enough healthy internees so that we could fire from camp jobs all but two types of men, there would be peace around here."

"Proceed," I said, "I'm listening."

"There are four kinds of men," began De Bruyn. "Number one is bright and active, number two is bright and lazy, number three is dumb and active and number four is dumb and lazy.

"The bright and active man must be fired from any smooth running organization because he is too bright and too active for harmony. The dumb and active man also must be fired because he causes too much trouble. Those active men also are hard to live with. The bright one is frustrated by the world's inertia and the dumb one is always in hot water.

"The men to keep in the organization are the lazy ones, both bright and stupid—the bright and lazy because the little he does he does well, and the stupid and lazy because he does only what he is told. And the lazy men are easy to live with, the bright one because he has a sense of humor and no desire to reform the world, and the stupid one because, ignorance being bliss, he is happy."

Grinning, I returned to work, having forgotten for a little while how tough life was getting. I was among those wearing out. The dressing job daily grew more arduous. I had a staff of five assistants including my American partner Eric and Mike Treurniet, who had killed the duck for my New Year's dinner; but seldom were all five on their feet simultaneously. Nearly every patient in the hospital needed dressing of some kind and the number of severe cases was appalling. Night calls were increasingly frequent as more and more beri-beri blisters erupted on swollen legs. The pace was getting me. Day and night there was a tight, dull pain in my back. Dizzy spells and sudden, cold sweats were increasing in frequency.

One ray of help illumined our black horizon in October 1944. The 7th of October was one of the happiest days in our prison camp history. American Red Cross supplies arrived. They were pitifully small but they raised our hopes.

"Now they know we are here," we told each other. "More will come."

More never did come but luckily we could not read the future as we divided what was left after our guards first took their portion. How much they took we never learned. We only knew they smoked American cigarets for days and that Van Asbeck reported an ever growing pile of American butter and powdered milk tins behind Seki's house.

Suspicious of hidden messages, the guards opened all paper wrapped packages, such as cigarets, and burned the paper. They checked tinned goods by opening every can of a certain brand of meat paste and removing the contents. The paste was turned over to the kitchen and served as "Sauce American." The tinned butter and powdered milk that did reach us we reserved for the sick and rationed at the rate of one spoon of powder and one spoon of butter per patient per day while the supply lasted.

General camp distribution to each individual totaled: eighteen cigarets, four ounces of tinned meat—three men would divide a twelve ounce tin—one tiny slice of cheese and one cup of weak coffee.

Late in October we received from the Red Cross 12,470 guilders, in Japanese invasion currency, and another 6,000 guilders from the Vatican.

Chairman Oosten invited me, as a representative of America, to a meeting of the Camp Committee and made a little speech of thanks for the Red Cross goods.

In the food queue that day Controleur de Raat, who was

a food server, gave Eric and me a concrete expression of gratitude.

"This is a token of appreciation to America," he said, and put an extra spoonful of boiled cucumbers on each of our plates.

On November 1, 1944, De Raat called at the hospital to acknowledge he had lost his fifty-guilder bet with me that the war would be over by that date.

"But you'll have to wait until after the war to collect," he said, "I'm broke."

Even if he could have paid there was no satisfaction for me in winning the bet. Joyfully would I have lost. Four funerals a day were not uncommon in November. Nor were we able any longer to carry the coffins on our shoulders. A cart was constructed for the purpose.

As a killer malaria was forging ahead of beri-beri, dysentery and sepsis. My diary for November 17th reads:

"Malaria is replacing beri-beri as the prison scourge. It kills more quickly and frequently. Weakened by malnutrition and exhausted by chronic malaria, men are dying like flies. There is no quinine. Yesterday the Japanese gave us 24 pills—24 quinine pills for 300 malaria-ridden men. They are collapsing in their cells, are carried in here and die a few hours later. Fear is paralyzing internees. Fear that 'I may be next.'

"Our survival is a race against time—the time of freedom. Another six months of this and more than half of us will have died. God send us deliverance soon."

My own health was slipping rapidly. My back gave out from bending too long over too many benches. Dressing hours were from breakfast until dark, with an intermission for midday tiffin. That was the only way we could attend our 120 or 140 patients daily, some requiring up to an hour's work apiece. By mid-November the prison daily sick roster fluctuated between 400 and 500 names. Our total population was dwindling toward 700. Only the most seriously ill of the sick roster were in hospital; others lay in cell blocks waiting for admittance as death created vacancies on hospital benches.

Each day I found it more difficult to bend over the benches or straighten up afterwards. Exhaustion dragged at me. Dr. Lentze stopped me one day to investigate. He listened with his stethoscope, thumped here and there, twisted my neck and came up with two long names that spelled B-A-D.

"Your lungs are bad and you probably have an inflammation of the spine," he said. "No more dressing. Light work only."

I wasn't surprised. I had been kidding myself too long that the ache would wear off. Oosten heard of Lentze's verdict and went into a huddle with him. Then Oosten made a solo decision for which I always will be grateful but which plunged him into more controversy. Without consulting the Camp Committee he requisitioned two one-pound tins of powdered milk from the Red Cross supplies and gave them to Lentze for me.

Quartermaster Thomson had the job of mixing and issuing powdered milk for hospital patients. Lentze told him to give me two cups a day while the tins lasted.

One of the other doctors blew a fuse when he learned Oosten had requisitioned the milk for me and descended on the Camp Committee with demands for an investigation.

Oosten defended his action, saying, "The milk came from the American Red Cross. The least we can do is give some to a sick American."

Small as was the amount of milk it worked wonders, keeping me on my feet.

About that time the Japanese showed a sudden statistical interest in prisoner deaths. They required typewritten death certificates, in triplicate, and a daily roster of sick with names of ailments. I did the typing as one of my light duties.

Seki's interpreter banned use of the words "hunger oedema" and "dysentery" in describing causes of death.

"Internees do not die of hunger," he said, "they are merely sick."

For dysentery he insisted on substituting the word "intestines."

"John Doe died of intestines."

Doctors then began using as death causes the terms "inanition," which means exhaustion from lack or non-assimilation of food; and "marasmus," which means progressive emaciation. "Inanition" and "marasmus" were not in the interpreter's dictionary.

A second storm burst over the hospital in November and Dr. Lentze resigned. He was succeeded as hospital chief by Dr. H. P. Kramer, a tall, pompous Hollander, who with Dr. W. Kampschuur, third of the new doctors, had been on the medical staff of another tin mining company on the island of Billiton. Kramer had been in office only a short while when, backed by Dr. Hollweg and Guy Fawkes, he crossed swords with the Camp Committee and the hospital staff. A long drawn, bitter fight ensued during which both the committee and the doctors appealed to the camp for justification of their respective stands. Quartermaster Thomson, Engineer Harrison and I became deeply involved in the controversy, opposing Kramer and Hollweg on one hand and Oosten's formulas for settlement on the other.

Who was right or wrong I will not attempt to say, because the other side would have no chance of replying. Each of us passionately believed his side was right and the other man's was wrong. Let it remain thus. A blow by blow description of the battle would make an interesting documentary on human nature but I think Bishop Mekkelholt was right when he said, in the thick of the fray,

"I hope you don't write all this some day."

"Why not?" I asked.

"It would only fan old animosities which are better

buried," said the Bishop, "and it might seriously damage the reputations of men who after the war will look back on these times and feel ashamed of their actions. Don't forget, all of us in here are a little abnormal."

He was correct. I wonder how I would look if a talking picture of myself then were played back for me now?

I never heard the Bishop say a mean or petty thing about any man, not even about men who counted themselves his enemies.

The following page, then, will represent a veil drawn over a long, shameful episode in the history of our internment. I hope the hatreds which flared during that human dog-fight and poisoned our relations throughout the remainder of the war have since been extinguished.

19

How Men Die

THEY say Beauty is in the eye of the beholder; and so it is with Death. If a man sees in Death the beginning of Eternal Life, then for him Death holds no terrors except the physical agonies of passing; but if he sees in Death only a dark mirror reflecting his own forebodings, then Death is fearful no matter how painless the crossing.

Death was nothing new to me whose days as a reporter frequently had been concerned with violence: catastrophe and homicide, blood and tears. The persons involved, however, usually had been strangers. In prison camp they were men whom I knew well, whose wounds I had dressed, whom I had nursed, waited beside, laid out, encoffined and helped bury. Having myself nearly slipped through Life's trap door, I felt acquainted with what they were experiencing in their extremity. Always in my mind was the thought, "There, but for the grace of God, go I." And I watched them to see how they faced their final and greatest question.

In Muntok Prison alone, 259 men learned the answer and now lie beneath the pepper trees. Some went trembling with fear, despair or remorse; others bravely, with faith and hope. Some died because they did not have the courage to live while others went down fighting. Greed and personal folly were as responsible in certain instances as were hunger and disease. There were men who cringed and whimpered at the end and others who died almost gaily. Some wel-

225

comed Death as a release from suffering; others, as the door to paradise. Extremely few were conscious to the last. Most entered comas hours before slipping out of life. Even upon those who were waiting and expecting him, Death usually stole like a thief, whisking them off minutes or hours or days before they really knew their visitor was on the threshhold.

Having watched many men die I am convinced that true inner happiness has nothing to do with bodily ills. Men can be in agony yet spiritually serene if they have faith in God. Conversely, if they are wracked with doubts and the Beyond is only a black question mark, their forebodings can be worse than any physical pain.

There are men of no religion who die bravely, too—but with a kind of defiance, an attitude of "whatever comes, I'll face it and be damned to it."

Whenever I saw a man dying defiantly I thought of an execution in the Utah State Prison in 1938. Utah gives a condemned man his choice of being shot or hung. John Deering, murderer, chose shooting. His was a widely heralded execution. Within minutes after his death his eyes were scheduled to be removed, packed in ice and flown to San Francisco to be used for corneal graft operations in restoring sight to three blind persons. The actions of his heart during those awful seconds of suspense before the bullets struck, and afterwards until the final beat, were to be revealed by an electrocardiograph attached to Deering during the execution. It was the first time in medical history a condemned man's last moments were to be so blueprinted.

I was one of five men who sat with Deering through his last night alive, while he awaited dawn and the firing squad. Outwardly, he was the calmest man in death row as we talked the night away and discussed, among other things, God and the hereafter.

"If God exists," said Deering, "and I'm not saying He

either does or does not, but if He does then He knows everything and that I'm getting exactly what I deserve for what I've done. I'm paying and I figure that will balance the books.

"Who knows?" he added facetiously, "Maybe when old Charon ferries me across the River Styx there'll be two beautiful houris waiting to greet me with a jug of wine. What I'd better do is take up a collection to pay Charon his ferrying fee."

Deering held out his hand.

"Give," he said, laughing.

I dropped a fifty cent piece in his open palm.

At 4:00 A.M. when he had only two more hours to live, Deering said he was tired and wanted to sleep. He lay down on his bunk and slept. At five minutes to six he was awakened, the death warrant read to him and he walked down three flights of stairs into the prison yard where the firing squad waited. He was strapped into a chair, a target placed over his heart, the copper bands of the electrocardiograph were fastened to his wrists. He made a brief speech and finished by saying,

"I'm ready. Let 'er go!"

The rifles cracked. After his body had been removed from the chair and laid on a stretcher I placed the fifty cent piece—"Charon's fare"—which he had given back to me when the death march started, on the bloody target over his heart. The firing squad's marksmanship had been excellent. The coin just covered the four bullet holes.

Apparently he had been icy calm to the last second. But the electrocardiograph record showed he was not. The heart specialists who studied the record said Deering was terrified. His iron will had enabled him to hide his fear beneath a defiant exterior. He had been on fire inside but he put on a bold front and staged a dramatic show.

"His heart was beating so fast while he was making his speech just before the bullets struck," said Dr. Stephen H.

Beesley, prison physician, "that if they had not struck and his heart maintained that pace only a little longer he would have collapsed and died of heart failure."

Deering was an example, in my opinion, of how successfully a man can masquerade. Bold fronts no longer impress me but a quiet heart does and I think the latter can be detected. There is something about a peaceful heart that communicates itself to others. At the end of a man's life, possession of such peace is reward beyond measure for whatever it cost him. And nothing can compensate for its absence.

All of which is by way of introducing the stories of some of the men who died in Muntok Prison hospital.

If Old Pop, down-on-his-luck rubber planter who was our first ward "matron" in Palembang Jail, could have known it, he would have considered it some sort of omen when the rope broke as we lowered his coffin into a grave in Muntok cemetery. But he was inside and so knew nothing of being dropped instead of lowered respectfully and gently into the hole as we intended.

Luckily, the fragile, bulging box did not burst and spill its contents of beri-beri swollen flesh. There was only a bump, a crunch of wood and a sodden noise as Pop's bulk jolted roughly to rest.

"Remember man, that thou art dust . . ." intoned Hammet, throwing a handful of earth into the grave. Other little showers of earth rattled on the box as we each tossed our parting tribute. Then, rubbing sore shoulders on which the coffin had rested during the mile-long, weary march from jail to cemetery, we retraced our steps.

There was little conversation. Pop's passing had touched us more than most. It seemed only yesterday instead of two and a half years ago that he had joined us in Palembang Jail and become an institution of bedpans and prophecy. The two were inseparable in Pop's case as he ran the dysentery ward and read his Bible, drawing therefrom prophecies concerning us and the war.

Quoting scriptural passages he forecast when the first American planes would roar overhead, when the war would end and when we would be released. Our good-natured jeers did not in the least perturb him when the dates arrived without fulfillment of his predictions.

"I see where I made my mistake," Pop would admit. "I misread that passage in Revelations by six months. But I'm sure of my interpretation now; we'll be out of here in another six months."

Then he would quote the passage and explain his interpretation. Another six months would pass and we would remind Pop of his prophecy.

"How do we know the war hasn't ended?" he would say. "Fighting could be over months before we'd learn about it in this backwater. Besides, it says in Revelations . . ."

And he would be off again on his favorite theme. All his dates came and went eventlessly but Pop was never discouraged, nor his faith in his prophetical ability shaken. We wished, as we buried him, that he still was around to prophesy. He was a good fellow, rotund, merry, fuss-budget Pop, matron of the Palembang Jail dysentery ward, prophet and perpetual optimist.

Pop's only belongings when I met him were a small suitcase—empty—a Bible, a cheap watch, a knitted green shawl and the shirt and shorts he wore. When he died, the only additions to his possessions were a few tins and coconut shells. Almost all prisoners acquired belongings during their internment but not Pop. He wanted nothing but to rule his domain of bedpans. He ran it, until sickness relieved him of the job, like a fussy old hen mothering a brood of scabby chicks.

Although as ward matron Pop could have enjoyed the prerogative of a wooden door for a bed, he preferred throwing a rice sack on the cement floor and lying on it. Always barefoot, he never wore sandals despite frequently infected feet. Another idiosyncrasy was a pretense of fasting one day a week. He drew his food on that day ostensibly to give a sick friend. While we ate he busied himself with hospital tasks and all day reminded us he had not eaten. At night, when he thought no one could see him, he ate. Next day he would tell us how fit he felt despite twenty-four hours without food.

Pop chattered incessantly. We got so the only times we heard him were when he was suddenly silent; then, startled, we would look around. Two things were possible. Either he had fallen asleep or was studying his Bible for another prophecy.

Pop actually worked only the first nine months of captivity. The rest of the time he was a patient. But he had become a tradition, a part of our surroundings, a sort of gossipy, flesh and blood family skeleton.

On his birthday in October 1943, I gave him a cigar for which I had searched the prison. Beissel finally got it for me from a guard. It was a rank, native-made cheroot but it was the first one Pop had smoked in eight months and he always said he preferred a cigar to a meal. The old boy was as tickled by the fact some one remembered his birthday as by the cheroot.

"Mac," he said, "this cigar is so good I'll let you in on a secret. I've been lying here re-interpreting the scriptures and I have figured out exactly when the war will end. This is an unqualified prophecy. You can write it down. Germany will collapse between October 20th and November 7th. Japan will surrender just before Germany does."

"You mean this year or next year?" I asked. "Tomorrow is October 20th."

"This year of 1943," Pop emphasized. "This very week. At this very minute Germany may be seeking an armistice."

He picked up his Bible.

"It says right here in the Book of Daniel, 'Blessed is he that waiteth and cometh to the thirteen hundred and thirty-fifth day.' Now their calendar in those days was just a little off. Adjusting their calculations to what we know now . . ."

"Wait a minute, Pop. What's the Bible counting from? Thirteen hundred and thirty-five days from what?"

"Munich, of course."

"Munich? Is Munich in the Bible?"

"It says in the thirteenth chapter of Revelations: 'And power was given him to continue forty and two months.' Now, my interpretation is that 'him' means England. Hitler is the beast referred to earlier in the chapter and Japan is the second beast. In other words, England at Munich gave Hitler, the beast, power to continue for thirteen hundred and thirty-five days."

"Hold on, pal. Let me get this straight. Do you mean that tomorrow, October 20th, 1943, is the thirteen hundred and thirty-fifth day since Munich?"

"Not exactly, but you see, we have to make certain adjustments for the differences between the calendars of the Old Testament and now. According to my calculations, this week is the time meant. This very week! Of course, it will take a few more weeks for the Allies to find us here and release us. You wait and see, Mac. We'll be free in a couple weeks."

The weeks passed and the months, nine of them. Pop became so heavy with liquid it required two men to lift him so we could change the dripping mats beneath him and put them in the sun to dry.

"You know, Mac," he said in July 1944, "my calculations were off on that thirteen hundred and thirty-fifth day. I've been thinking it over and I'm positive it will come in October this year. But I probably won't see it. I won't live that long. When your American friends come here in October to liberate the camp, say hello to them for me and remember that I predicted the date."

"I sure will, Pop, but you'll be here when they come."

"Don't talk nonsense. Of course I won't. I know how sick I am. And I'm quite ready to go."

He died, in August 1944, just one year short of V-J Day. Had his bulk been solid it would not have gone in the narrow coffin, but, like a massive sponge, it could be squeezed here and expanded there to fit. Pallbearers included his fellow workers, Kendall, who succeeded him as matron, Doc West, Harrison, Thomson, Drysdale and myself. Because the weight was so heavy we changed frequently with our alternates during the march. The day was hot; sweat poured from us so freely we hardly noticed that some of the moisture which soaked our shoulders was not perspiration but leaked from the coffin. Beri-beri sweat did not stop even in death. We were glad to reach the cemetery.

The last will and testament of handle-bar-moustached cockney Herbert Smallwood, who had been my steadiest monkey-pox customer, was among those "probated" in 1944. I had drawn it up for him in 1942, when he waddled into the clinic on a Sunday morning and expressed concern lest "something happens to my estate if I croak in here."

"Draft me something fancy," he said, "so they'll know it's a genuine will."

So, mustering my stock of legal phrases, I drew up a will containing an impressive number of whereases, wherefores and to-wits. Smallwood had no relatives. He directed that his estate go to a man in Canada who had befriended him during his lumberjack days. In case the man could not be found, the estate should go to a lady friend in England.

"My friend in Canada has a youngster," Smallwood said

in his hoarse tenor. "This money may help put the kid through school."

Smallwood's entire "estate" consisted of ten English pounds in a Liverpool bank and whatever wages would accrue to him from the Canadian Pacific Railroad Steamship Line during the war. Small as the amount may sound it was large to the ex-sailor-lumberjack-grocery-boy-roustabout.

Often on moonlight nights we sat in the yard while he smoked my tobacco, told me tall tales of his roistering life, and speculated what he would do if he did not "croak" but returned to England after the war.

On July 4, 1943, Smallwood wheezed into the Barracks Camp clinic, saluted and began to sing with a voice similar to a leaky barrel organ:

"Oh, say can you see, by the dawn's early light, what so proudly we hailed at the . . . . at the . . . . ta, ta, ta, ta, ta . . . ."

"Sorry," he said breathlessly, "I've forgotten what's next."

He laughed until his eyes watered, his face purpled and the spiked points of his moustache quivered as if in a high wind.

When he had subsided enough to talk he explained further,

"A cutie in Panama taught me the words and I thought I'd never forget them. What a girl!"

He paused in appreciative memory, then continued,

"What I want to say is, Happy July the Fourth! And here is something to remember me by."

He handed me a sample-size cake of an American soap.

The following November Smallwood suffered a heart attack in his block. Doc said he was too ill to be moved so we left him in his bunk, where he had been stricken, until he should either die or recover sufficiently to be brought into hospital. After the initial spasm had passed he sent for me. He was in great pain, shaking violently and could speak only with difficulty. He sounded as though he were talking about wool socks but that made no sense. Finally it was clear he did mean wool socks. His neighbors said he had a pair. They might be outside drying. I found them and brought them in. Smallwood motioned me to get beside him on the bench. I stepped up. He seized my hands and the socks, squeezed one of my hands over the top of one of the socks. In the fabric I felt a ring.

"Yours," he gasped. "Keep . . . . yours . . . . thanks."

He had devised a clever hiding place for the ring, a small plain gold band. The thick top of the socks had been un-ravelled in one spot and reknitted with the ring inside. Smallwood did not die as he feared he was going to. When he recovered I returned the ring, despite his protestations that I keep it.

Smallwood lived until March 29, 1944, when a funeral cortege of thirty men followed his coffin to the cemetery. We told the Japanese it was such a heavy load we needed that many men to take turns carrying it.

Van Hutten's death in 1942 while trying to escape was one of the most bizarre of our internment. Although it oc-curred in Palembang Jail, I tell it here because it was so spectacular.

About two o'clock in the morning of December 24, 1942, wild screams awakened me. The blood chilling sounds, high and continuous, were like the cries of an in-jured dog but worse because they were human. My first thought was that someone had gone berserk and was killing a fellow prisoner.

Throwing aside my mosquito net I jumped up and ran into the yard to see in the starlight a Malay guard running around in circles holding his head and screaming. Men poured from their cells to converge on the front gates which were being clanged shut by frantic guards.

Shouts sounded from the street outside. Someone had escaped.

The screaming guard was quieted and brought into the clinic. He had a deep gash in his scalp. Doc West took several stitches in the wound and we got the story.

Several days previously two Indo-European oil workers from the Shell refinery at Pladjoe had been brought into the jail and kept under constant surveillance in the guard room between the inner and outer gates. Guards frequently left open the outer gate. One of the prisoners, named Van Hutten, asked to be taken to the lavatory which was in the jail yard. A guard escorted him and left open the inner gate. That meant both gates were open, although other guards lounged on chairs between them. In the lavatory Van Hutten jerked the bayonet from the scabbard at the guard's waist, felled him with a blow on the head, dashed across the yard, through the inner gate, passed two startled guards and charged through the outer gate to freedom.

From there on Van Hutten's course was less clear to us and confused by conflicting reports. We heard that on the street he cut down two Japanese soldiers, knocked a third soldier off a bicycle, mounted the cycle himself, pedaled to the Moesi river and, under a fusillade of shots from guards on the river bank, jumped into the stream. He was not captured. Ten days later his fellow prisoner, named Buchanan, was taken from the jail and shown the decomposed body of a man found in the river. He identified it as Van Hutten.

The will to live was vital to survival. Given an even break and a few extras, sick men who had courage and determination might fight their way back to health. Conversely, men who lacked fighting spirit succumbed no matter what help they obtained. Age had little or nothing to do with a man's will. The odds were heavily against elderly men surviving, yet many did while young men died.

During our early months in Palembang Jail an Englishman with dysentery, who had a better than even chance of recovering, said he did not want to recover; he wanted to die.

"I've lost everything," he said, "the Japs cleaned me out. It isn't worth the struggle to start over."

He practically willed himself into the grave by refusing to try.

A British planter, as soon as he entered Muntok prison hospital with malaria, made up his mind he was doomed.

"My doctor told me to avoid all serious illnesses because of my heart," said the planter. "This is a serious illness."

"A headache is serious if you're in that state of mind," he was told. "Snap out of it and eat your dinner."

But he had no more spirit than a lump of clay. His mind was set on dying, not because he wanted to but because he thought it was inevitable, and so he died.

Deaths due to greed and folly were not uncommon. During the beri-beri scourge Doc West was informed that a patient critically ill with beri-beri was selling Vitamin B tablets. Vitamin B was what the sick man needed more than anything else to save his life. Why was he selling the tablets? Because he wanted money.

With commendable acumen the man had purchased his store of Vitamin B before he was interned. He had saved the tablets for an emergency but they commanded such fabulous prices he decided instead to sell. Meanwhile, his friends, who were giving him all the extra food they could scrape up, also were buying back the tablets for him on the black market, not knowing their source.

"Have you lost your mind?" Doc asked the greedy one. "You are selling your life."

"I didn't realize I was that sick," said the patient. "Besides, I need the money."

Doc took charge of the tablets and saw to it that the sick

man swallowed the required number each day. But it was too late. After his death a search of his clothing and mattress disclosed an astonishing sum in hoarded guilders. He died at the age of 29, victim of his own avarice.

Usurers who loaned money for repayment after the war at fantastic interest rates did a thriving business. One of the most enterprising and successful tradesmen and usurers had a Robin Hood streak in him. He was satisfied with a small profit on a trade with a comparatively poor man. By indefatigable buying and selling on narrow profit margins, he gradually cornered a large share of the market in negotiable goods. Then he branched into food buying. Destitute prisoners would sell meals in order to get cash for tobacco, a piece of black market fish or a vitamin tablet. The meal would be resold to a rich man at a fat profit. The food trader's business became so big that he was able, for a monthly retainer's fee, to guarantee a certain number of extra meals of rice per month to men willing to pay the price. Having accumulated capital he became a big-time money lender. His interest rates were as high as 1,000 per cent on small loans and 500 per cent on big loans—repayment after the war.

He amassed a small fortune in cash, goods and promissory notes. He was well nourished and had every prospect of surviving to enjoy his earnings. But he did not. Cerebral malaria killed him. Money could not protect him against mosquitoes or buy quinine when there was none for sale.

Sometimes a gay or gallant death is sadder than a quiet, ordinary one.

Malaria, beri-beri and exhaustion were finishing a Dutch seafaring man I'll call The Trouper. Dr. Lentze gave The Trouper a hypodermic injection and tried to cheer the dying man. The injection had an exhilarating effect. The Trouper suddenly sat up and laughed.

"Don't look so solemn," he said to Dr Lentze and nearby patients. "I know I'm going to die, but it doesn't matter. Cheer up. Let's sing and laugh. Let's smoke cigarets, lots of cigarets. And let's have a drink. By all means let's have a drink."

He raised a bottle of cold tea to his lips and drank.

"We can pretend that's gin."

He lit a cigaret.

"We don't have to pretend that's a cigaret."

He passed nipa leaves and tobacco to men on either side of him. They, too, lit up and smoked.

"Now," he said, "let's sing."

He sang rollicking Dutch tunes. His mind and voice were clear as bells, clear and high pitched.

He sent for a friend. When the friend arrived The Trouper told him:

"Please go to my wife and children after the war. Tell them how happily I died. Tell them that I did not suffer and that I laughed and sang and thought of them at the end."

The friend promised.

"Let's have another cigaret," said The Trouper.

The exertions had drained his strength. He lay back on the mat but he continued to sing for nearly half an hour, until, steadily sinking, he lapsed into a coma, his final sleep.

About eleven o'clock one night Attendant George Bryant informed me a patient I'll call Hals had asked for the doctor, saying,

"I am dying."

I notified Dr. Kramer, then went to the dysentery ward. Stepping up on the bench I felt Hals' pulse. No pulse. No heart beat. No indication of breathing or other animation. The eyes were open, staring, lifeless. Bryant stepped up on the bench beside me, looked, said,

"My gosh, he's gone already."

"Yes," I agreed, looking intently into Hals' blank eyes, "he's dead."

Then a chill ran through me. The dead man's head rolled ever so slightly, in nearly imperceptible but distinct and emphatic denial. His pulse was indistinguishable, he was blind and mute, but he could hear and think!

"Do you want water?" I asked.

His head moved in negation.

Dr. Kramer arrived, examined Hals perfunctorily and departed, saying,

"I can do nothing for him."

Hals' head moved. I had a feeling he wanted something if I could only guess what. Speaking into his ear I said,

"I'll ask questions. You nod yes or no."

"Water?"

No.

"Position changed?"

No.

"Priest?"

Yes.

I walked across the concrete pendopo to the Tin Winning's other wing and awakened Father Van Thiel who had given Hals Extreme Unction two days previously. He squatted beside the dying man.

"This is Father Van Thiel. Can you hear me?"

A nod.

"I will pray aloud. You say the words after me in your mind."

About an hour later Hals' pulse was perceptible. He managed a wraith of a smile and spoke two words.

"Water . . . . finger."

I dipped my finger in cold tea and moistened his lips and tongue. A better idea occurred. I soaked a cloth in the tea and squeezed drops into his mouth. He managed to swallow. He was rallying but ever so slightly. I asked if he wanted me to put the cloth in his mouth so he could suck it. He nodded yes. Later his eyes closed and he appeared to sleep. I went to bed.

When the attendant on the following shift came on duty Bryant warned him of our experience with Hals. Next morning the attendant told us another episode in the macabre drama. About three A.M. he carefully examined Hals and, certain the man was dead beyond all doubt, folded his arms over his breast, pulled a blanket over his face and called the doctor.

The doctor came, found Hals still alive—and conscious! Hals really died, according to the doctor's stethoscope, at four o'clock in the afternoon. But we did not bury him for another twenty-four hours, just to make sure. I wonder what were his thoughts when he heard me pronounce him dead?

A few weeks later the same thing happened to another patient in the dysentery ward. One of the priests was presumed dead by two fellow priests who were ward attendants. They were looping a rag around his head to hold his jaw shut, preparatory to encoffining him, when the "dead man" blinked his eyes to signal he was still alive.

My observations convinced me that most men who are aware death is approaching, desire to be at peace with God. However, some do not want their friends to know it. Why? Because their neighbors might think them weaklings, or sentimental or afraid. A man I will call Crumpet was one of these. He had been in and out of hospital for two years. While I was dressing him one morning he asked, sotto voce,

"Do you know some prayers? It looks like I might not make it and I'd like to say a few."

"Sure. Do you remember the Lord's Prayer?"

"Vaguely."

I said the Lord's Prayer slowly, sentence by sentence,

and he repeated it after me. Soon he knew it again as well as when he had learned it in childhood. As I left him to continue my dressing rounds, he said,

"Don't tell any one, will you?"

"Of course not."

"Can you come back and see me after roll call?"

"Sure."

That night, in undertones, we discussed religion and man's obligations to his Creator. Crumpet talked freely because he was confident no one but me could hear him. He lay on one end of the bench, next to the wall. The two men nearest him on the other side were in comas. Therefore, he felt secure in talking unheard. He admonished me again to say nothing.

"They would think it was queer if they knew," he explained. "And it's none of their business."

"They" was a vague reference to his friends. I suggested that he talk either to one of the Protestant laymen who led English church services—Anglican minister Wardle had died—or to one of the Catholic priests who would be more qualified than I to counsel him.

"No," said Crumpet. "People might think I was getting soft. But you might ask the fathers to pray for me."

I tried to fathom his reluctance to disclose he believed in God and was worried about the hereafter. What did his neighbors' thoughts matter to him, a dying man? His reasons reduced to the concern he felt for what his friends would think if, after a lifetime of ignoring religion, he suddenly should start to pray. The friends about whom Crumpet was so anxious were so little concerned about him that they did not even attend his funeral.

Wembley-Smythe was brought into hospital, for the last time, exhausted from hunger and malaria. Obviously, he was doomed. Just as obviously he didn't realize it. He was surrounded by the same conspiracy of silence that surrounds most dying men—unless they expressly desire to know for religious or other reasons.

The conspiracy of silence is based on the theory that informing him he is dying could only frighten or panic a man. I think it panics only those who have little faith. As far as I could tell by observation, the knowledge they were dying did not frighten those who were informed of it so they could receive the last sacraments of their Church or who, like Old Pop, knew instinctively their condition and accepted it.

Contrary to frightening them, Extreme Unction appeared to give dying men spiritual ammunition that brightened their eyes and in many cases gave them new physical strength. More than a few who were anointed recovered instead of dying.

Wembley-Smythe, like many another, once remarked he hoped that when his time came it would come so quickly he would know nothing about it. His wish was partially fulfilled in that he had no idea how sick he was. He drifted into a coma the second morning after his arrival. That night about ten o'clock I crouched beside him on the bench and, as I counted his waning pulse, he died.

The Hollander lying next to him began to cry. He and Wembley-Smythe and I had been good friends. To him, as to me, Wembley-Smythe's story was the story of most of the British community. Shipwrecked, penniless, inept at caring for himself, with never a cent except occasional infinitesimal loans, uncomplaining, cheerful, cultured, tolerant, and a strange mixture of agnosticism and Sunday church going.

His body was so emaciated the ward attendant and I had no difficulty lifting it onto a stretcher and carrying it to the mortuary. There were several coffins waiting. We opened one but it already was occupied.

The occupant gazed blankly up at us, his cold eyes reflecting the light of the kerosene lamp. We replaced the lid and opened another box. It, too, was occupied.

"Damn," we exploded simultaneously. "The empties are on the bottom."

Four coffins were in the mortuary, stacked in twos, and the attendants who carried out the previous two bodies had not switched the bottom empties to the top. We carried Wembley-Smythe back outside, got additional help to lift the full boxes off the empties and finally put him into one.

As we encoffined him I thought of the discussion Wembley-Smythe and I had the night of a moonlit thunderstorm in Barracks Camp. He had expressed doubt there was a hereafter for the souls of men and jokingly remarked how dreadfully boring it would be if eternity were one long black-out and he was compelled to be aware of it.

I bade Wembley-Smythe a silent goodbye as I closed the lid and wondered if, wherever his spirit might be, he was bored.

When all the chips are in and the showdown is against him, a man has only his spiritual reservoir on which to draw. If that treasury of the soul is empty he has only one companion—that most dreadful of enemies: Despair. Spiritual bankruptcy affects men in different ways. It causes some to seek Death because they fear Life. It causes others to fear Death with a fear that is stark and terrible.

A man I will call Hamilcar was one of those who in his old age could not face new hazards and so sought Death. Another man I will call The Cynic was one of those for whom Death meant terror immeasurable.

Hamilcar's passing I call the Death of the Wild Goat because he was more than the family black sheep. He had been a wild, black goat if even half the stories told of him were true. He was a magnificent old boy who barehanded would fight a wild cat, but who could not live with himself.

Tall, slender, white-haired, hawk-nosed and 70, he first

aroused my interest in the garden of Charitas hospital where I saw him catching sparrows.

"Keeps me from going crazy," he explained, "and besides, I need the meat."

His technique was simple but called for adroitness and a patience he could command only for short, intense periods while stalking prey. He held one end of a long string. The other end was a running loop lying on the ground and filled with grains of rice. When a bird hopped into the loop he jerked the string, lassoing it by the leg.

All his life Hamilcar had successfully stalked things, adventure, battle, roistering fun, fortune. He ran away to sea when a boy, prospected for gold and tin and fished for pearls in the tropics and sub-tropics. He fought in the Boer War and in World War I, winning decorations for gallantry in action and distinguished service as a commanding officer. Returning after the wars to the tropics he struck it rich in tin mining, rapidly won and lost two fortunes and was in the midst of accumulating and spending his third and largest when the Japanese interrupted.

Hamilcar's idiosyncrasies were notorious. While in town from his mines, men who knew him well told me, he visited as many clubs and bars as possible in one evening, using a different ricksha for each journey but not paying off any of the pullers. However, the pullers did not mind. They knew Hamilcar and what was coming. The evening's climax occurred when he returned to his hotel with a dozen rickshas trailing behind. Dismissing his last puller Hamilcar would mount the hotel steps, pause at the top, throw handfuls of currency into the air and howl with laughter at the ensuing scramble.

Hamilcar never notified his cook in advance of dinner guests until the guests arrived, whereupon he would point a loaded revolver skyward and pull the trigger. One shot for each guest. The listening cook prepared accordingly.

Bird catching and other activities occupied Hamilcar's

daylight hours in Charitas but when everyone else had gone to sleep his private hell began. He could not sleep. There was no one with whom he might talk. He could not walk around in the garden, nor could he lie still in bed. He had to be moving. So he would go into a bathroom, lock the door and pace up and down its twelve foot length. He paced, not by striding but by placing one foot exactly in front of the other, heel to toe, like a man measuring distance with his feet.

"That's how I keep from going crazy at night," he explained.

Confinement was his nemesis. He lived in dread of being returned to jail. He said he would kill himself if he had to go back. Because of his age and ailments he remained in Charitas until it was closed, then he had to return. Soon after arriving in Muntok Prison he tried to make good his threat. Matron Kendall caught Hamilcar trying to hang himself. After that we watched him but one night he fooled the watcher. He rose from his mat on the hospital bench and stood up. His six feet of lean frame towered in the flickering light from the oil lamp. The attendant thought Hamilcar was standing at the foot of the bench preparatory to stepping down. But he was not. He dove head first onto the concrete floor.

The impact did not kill him as he hoped, nor even knock him out. But it sliced his scalp and was such a severe shock he was finished physically. He lay for three days begging for a shot of dope to quiet his nerves. Death finally quieted them.

Suicide attempts were rare throughout internment. Only two besides Hamilcar came close to success. One man slashed his wrist as he lay in bed. He planned to bleed to death quietly but neighbors noticed the blood and a tourniquet saved him.

Another man stabbed himself in the chest, but instead of

piercing his heart inflicted only a minor flesh wound. However, he nearly died of shock. Doc West had a few ampules of adrenalin. They brought the man out of his shock after a nip and tuck period of thirty minutes.

Threats of a would-be suicide caused us to guard another internee day and night for months. Finally a watcher, tiring of his vigil, said:

"I'm going to bed and I hope you kill yourself while I'm gone because you're nothing but a damn nuisance."

Next morning the nuisance complained to the Camp Committee that he was being improperly guarded. No one guarded him after his bluff was called; but, like the man who stabbed himself, he died later of "natural" causes at the age of 38.

The Cynic displayed abject terror at its worst. I call him The Cynic because he had been an habitual scoffer. But when Death looked him in the eye The Cynic collapsed in a heap of howls and tears. He was in strong voice when he was carried into hospital and the voice continued strong until the end, two days later. Such fear I have never seen.

Over and over he cried out:

"I'm dying. I'm dying. Don't let me go. Hold on to me. Don't let me go. Hold my hands."

He screamed for Dr. Hollweg and when Hollweg arrived cried,

"Pull me back. I'm sinking down the long tunnel. Pull me back. Stay here. You are going farther away. You are fading away. Save me. Save me. Don't let me die. Hold on to me. Pull me back."

The Cynic clung to Hollweg with a grip of frenzy. For a man who was dying he had uncommon strength. His mind was clear. He talked and answered questions rationally. There was no question of delirium or insanity. It was sheer terror. The be-all and the end-all of The Cynic's life had been his own egotism. But it would not succor him when he was about to embark on a voyage into the unknown. So he screamed for his friends to pull him back from the edge of the abyss. For him life had been completely material and now at the end material assistance was all he could understand. To ask God's help in his travail did not occur to him. He could only ask Hollweg, "Hang on to me. Don't let me go!"

Finally, for the sake of other patients and our own frayed nerves, it was necessary to quiet him with an ampule of the rapidly dwindling and precious stock of morphine Doc West reserved only for men suffering intense pain. The Cynic was moved into my "Bedroom & Morgue" where an attendant remained constantly beside him. During his last twenty-four hours of life The Cynic repeated endlessly, over and over again, like a broken phonograph record, a strange monologue. In Dutch the words had a certain rhyme and cadence. The nearest English translation is:

> *There is a village.*
> *There is a woman in the village.*
> *The sun comes up over the woman in the village.*
> *The sun goes down over the village.*
> *God goes down over the village.*
> *The woman leaves the village.*
> *The village is gone.*
> *Goodbye village.*
> *Goodbye woman.*
> *Goodbye sun.*
> *Goodbye God.*

Hour after hour The Cynic's deep voice repeated those words. The only variation was in volume. As he weakened his voice weakened, faded to a mutter, then to a snore. Finally it ceased with The Cynic's heart.

The Cynic's opposite number for gameness was a jovial salesman, likeable, big hearted and courageous. Hard luck had dogged him from his first day in Palembang Jail. He had been one of my early "Palembang Bottom" customers.

Monkey-pox, boils, hernia, a lame knee, fever, dysentery and finally beri-beri had plagued him. He smiled through them all. The flesh of his legs was unbelievably distended, taut as a drum skin and excruciatingly painful. Wet compresses brought a little relief so I kept his legs wrapped in damp rags. While I changed the rags one morning as the salesman hovered on the border of semi-consciousness, his mind came alive. His lips writhed in the too-familiar, open mouthed, ghastly beri-beri smile. He grasped my hand and startled me by saying,

"Oh Mac, what a fool I've been."

And died.

The difference spiritual reserves make was illustrated by two men who lay side by side in the dysentery ward. One was an oil technician in the prime of life. His friends lavished their resources on him. The other was a 60-year-old tin miner whose friends had nothing. But the miner had a courage and shining faith which the technician completely lacked.

Hiccuping was a nearly infallible symptom that a dysentery patient was dying. Although his heart might be strong he usually was doomed once he began to hiccup.

The miner got hiccups and was in great distress but he was game. He knew he was doomed but he insisted on helping himself as much as possible and he even managed a smile or joke between hiccups.

Buoyed by extra nourishment and the encouragement of his friends, the technician put up a good fight until his first hiccup. Then he quit and begged for an injection to end his life.

"Put me to sleep," he whined. "Let me die. What have I done to deserve this?"

The will is like a dam holding back the waters of Lethe.

When the will is gone, the flood sweeps in, drowning the life too tired to fight. Forty-eight hours after his abject surrender the technician died, whining to the last.

The miner had no prosperous friends but he had a well of inner strength on which he drew and with which he fought to the last. He received the last rites of his faith and died serenely.

The technician, with no spiritual reserves, lacked the most essential thing of all.

Vincent Mitbo, 59, a Norwegian and, until jailed, the director of the Salvation Army leprosarium near Palembang, died November 19, 1944, ending a lifetime of service for his fellow man.

Only one other man in prison knew the Salvation Army funeral ritual: Oom Piet (Uncle Peter) Rolffs, who had been director of an orphanage in a south Sumatra Indo-European colony and once a Salvation Army man himself. Oom Piet was seriously ill in the septic ward. He had not walked for weeks but, summoning a strength which was not there until his will created it, he rose from his bench and, supported by two friends, walked down the long flight of steps to the pendopo where Mitbo's coffin rested on two sawhorses.

Oom Piet leaned against the coffin, bracing himself with his hands, and recited what prayers he could remember of the formal service. Then, still leaning on the coffin, he sang the Dutch version of "Onward Christian Soldiers." His voice was little more than a high, quavering rasp. He had to pause for breath between bars. To me the words were in an unfamiliar tongue but he sang them unforgettably. It was the first time "Onward Christian Soldiers" had meant anything more to me than a street corner band and a woman in blue passing a tambourine.

Oom Piet finished and was helped back to the septic ward. He was exhausted, trembling with feverish warnings that his exertions had brought on another attack of the re-current erysipelas which plagued him. But he was happy in the knowledge that he had made possible a proper funeral for his friend who had been a real soldier of the Lord.

Of the dead Mitbo, keeper of lepers, and the dying Oom Piet, keeper of orphans, I thought could be written those words spoken some nineteen hundred years ago:

" 'Amen I say to you, as long as you did it for one of these, the least of my brethren, you did it for me.' "

On December 4, 1944, Father Bakker was assisted from his sick bed to lead the choir in a special song at the funeral of Oom Piet.

Like other men of deep faith, whether lay or clerical, a New Zealand tin miner named Enright and a Dutch brother named Richardus, of the Order of Our Lady of Lourdes, accepted death with a quiet smile. They were secure in the belief that beyond the grave eternal life awaited them.

Enright, who attended Mass every morning before falling sick, told me while I was dressing his beri-beri leg,

"Mac, be sure and give me ample warning if ever I'm in danger of death. I want to know."

I told Doc West of Enright's wishes. A few days later Doc said,

"You can tell him now. He won't last much longer."

So I told him.

"Very well," said Enright, as matter-of-factly as if he were discussing the weather. "Ask Father Elling to come and give me Extreme Unction. I'm quite ready to go."

Father Elling came. Later in the day I asked Enright if he wished any ointment for his itch. Ointment was scarce, as Enright knew.

"No thanks," he whispered, "give it to some one else."

He managed another whisper and a smile.

"I have only a little longer to itch."

He died that night.

Brother Richardus died with a quiet joke in the dysentery ward which stank indescribably because we were short-handed and in the midst of an epidemic. He had received Extreme Unction days before and cheerfully was waiting for death to relieve him of his suffering.

It happened to be the durian season when those heavy fruits ripened and dropped from the tall spreading trees which bore them. Durians are as large as coconuts and have a similar protective husk. The edible fruit inside is a creamy substance delicious in flavor but stronger in odor than overripe limburger. Because of its fetid scent the durian is sometimes called civet fruit.

As was my custom after dressing the patients who obviously needed it, I asked other patients, by turn, if I could do anything for them.

A grin creased the death's head that was Brother Richardus' face. His voice was a hoarse whisper but it could still make a joke.

"What will you do for me?"

"Anything I can, Brother."

"Then bring me a durian so I can smell its perfume."

"Okay," I said, "if you'll only smell it and let me eat it."

"We will divide it," said Brother Richardus, laughing soundlessly, "so I can tell St. Peter how good it tastes. I think he never ate a durian."

Half an hour later Brother Richardus was in St. Peter's realm.

20

Christmas Comes Again

THIS is where we came in, nineteen chapters ago when this story began with old Brinker dying in Muntok Prison hospital the night of December 24, 1944 as the choir sang Christmas carols.

After encoffining Brinker I returned to the staff room where Eric gave me a Christmas present, an American cigaret he had saved from the Red Cross issue in October. I smoked it and occupied the time until sleep came thinking that the events of this Christmas of 1944 furnished a key to the whole story of our prison life and its struggles which were trying the souls of men.

Old Brinker had lost the battle for his life but, as he remarked to Father Bakker several days before, he wasn't worrying because he believed he had saved his soul. In these surroundings, at this time and place, Brinker's passing had been somber, yes, but not a tragedy. Rather, it had been a happy passage. He was ready to go; he had returned to his faith after thirty years away and his heart was at peace. That was why he could crack his last joke when I told him the choir would sing in time for him to hear them.

"Good," he had said, "then I'll be able to compare them with the angels."

Perhaps Death had been a welcome Christmas visitor to old Brinker.

Thinking those thoughts I fell asleep. When I awakened Christmas morning I remembered how I had opened my eyes just one year before, in 1943, from the long blackout of cerebral malaria, to see Father Elling looking down at me and hear him saying, "Merry Christmas."

"Now to reverse the proceedings," I said to myself.

Rising, I slipped my toes into a pair of terompaks and clumped into the fever ward where Father Elling lay recuperating from a siege of malaria and dysentery which had nearly finished him. He had been one of the fifteen clergymen who volunteered to man the dysentery and septic wards. Three of them were now dead—of dysentery—and eleven were sick. Father Elling had fooled us by throwing off the dysentery but chronic malaria still slowed his recovery. I stepped up on the bench, looked down at him and said,

"Merry Christmas, pal. The tables are now turned."

He laughed weakly, shook hands and said, "Completely turned, and the same to you."

Then I walked across the pendopo to the Pangkal Pinang block where Father Bakker lived. Last night he had been too wracked with fever to lead his beloved choir. This morning the fever had subsided and he was dragging himself around getting ready to say Mass.

"Merry Christmas, Mac," he said. "Next year I hope you will be at home for Christmas."

After Mass I stood at the front gate with a host of others seeing Bishop Mekkelholt off to visit the Women's Camp. It was the first and the last time any internee from Muntok Prison was permitted to visit the women and every man rejoiced that now, after a year and three months, we would learn something of their condition.

Bishop Mekkelholt, wearing his episcopal robes as he waited for the gate to be opened, was a strange contrast to the everyday Bishop Mekkelholt we were accustomed to seeing, wearing a pair of shorts and a pajama jacket and squatting over a tiny fireplace cooking kachang ijau soup for his sick priests.

He returned in two hours with cheering news. Although not permitted to converse with the women he was allowed to preach a sermon. His eyes had been busy and the nuns who sang the responses to the High Mass he celebrated had managed to convey him some information too.

He said the women looked in better health than we men. Their camp, of seven wooden barracks and a hall open on the sides, was set on a hill about 300 feet above sea level, in a healthier location than our miasmic one. He believed their mortality rate would be lower than ours. Seki give him a few statistics. In the Women's Camp that Christmas day were 696 persons, of whom 160 were children and 83 were nuns. Approximately 350 attended Mass, many in tears. Their choir, the same one that had serenaded our working party from afar Christmas Day, 1942, sang carols.

Old Brinker and another man were buried Christmas afternoon. The double funeral did not dampen our limited celebration. Funerals were too commonplace to affect our morale. Already it was about as low as it could go. But our spirits were raised temporarily by 100 grams ($3\frac{1}{2}$ ounces) of pork sauce on our rice and three cups of coffee, one in the morning, one at noon and one at night. The pork was from our own pig. We had been raising pigs—feeding them ourselves—ever since arriving in Muntok but this was the first time Seki had allowed us to kill one. Not even news could help morale like pork sauce and coffee.

The food situation was becoming grimmer. Rations had shrunk another 15 per cent. Although there had been no announcement of reduction, a shrinkage was evident. Our kitchen staff could estimate to an ounce.

A dog somehow got into the Tin Winning yard the night of December 28th. Dr. Kampschuur and a friend were the closest. They seized and killed it in a trice and soon were cooking canine stew.

Although rations diminished, Seki's attitude toward us

improved. On January 1, 1945, he gave us our third pleasant surprise in a month. The first had been allowing Dr. Lentze to be taken to a Japanese hospital on the other side of Bangka Island for an emergency appendectomy. The second had been allowing Bishop Mekkelholt to visit the Women's Camp. The third, New Year's day, was a general distribution of Japanese cigarets and the gift of two wild pigs, caught by natives and bought by Seki. The pigs together weighed 200 kilograms (440 pounds). We divided the meat equally and asked Seki to take half to the Women's Camp, which he did.

Seki surprised us still further by unexpectedly taking an interest in a hospital patient, G. J. Geursens, former manager of the Bangka Tin Company, who lay critically ill in the dysentery ward. Daily for two weeks Seki sent three eggs, three bananas and a cup of kachang ijau soup to Geursens. A patient alongside Geursens died cursing Seki for not bringing food for other sick men too.

Seki's interest in Geursens was at the request of the Japanese doctor Hasegawa who operated on Dr. Lentze and brought him back from Muntok. Hasegawa said he acted at behest of Japanese officials who were trying to operate the tin company. Geursens disappointed them by dying.

On January 9th Seki allowed a few boys under sixteen to go to the Women's Camp and talk for five minutes with their mothers.

A few days later Seki furnished the hospital with large mosquito nets which he said would accommodate "eight Japanese soldiers or twelve internees."

January 11, 1945, Eric and I received our first mail from home. Some British mail had been received previously. Letters from our mothers disclosed they had received at Christmas time, 1943, the cards we wrote in March 1943. We hoped they knew we still were alive. We hoped, too, that atrocity stories concerning prisoners of war were not being published in America and adding to their worries. (After the war I learned atrocity stories had been widely published because they stimulated war bond drives.)

A clue to Seki's changing attitude was furnished by the Chinese food contractor who, for the first time since he had done business with us, opened his mouth on other than business matters and muttered to a worker unloading rations,

"War soon finished."

That was in January, 1945. The war couldn't finish too soon. Blackwater fever, a complication of chronic malaria, had appeared among us. My own health, which had been buoyed in November by the powdered milk and change of jobs to lighter duties, was slipping again. My knees were too shaky for even lighter duties and intestinal troubles were plaguing me. Lentze ordered me to bed, and onto the dreaded diet of all intestinal patients—soft rice porridge. It was a necessary cure but contained little nourishment except starch. If prolonged, the diet inevitably resulted in beri-beri.

Wrapped around some bean curd cakes delivered to the hospital by the contractor were several Malay newspapers. They disclosed that American forces had landed in the Philippines the previous October and that Germany was crumbling. One of the newspapers said that the battle for Leyte would decide the fate of the Pacific war but that there was no question who would win it: Nippon. Enroute to the cemetery next day pallbearers saw a public notice posted in the street. It exhorted natives to help the Japanese defend Indonesia against white invaders.

Piet van der Bergh, a kitchen worker, rushed to the staff room where I lay to tell me the news. Joyously I offered to bet twenty-five guilders—for repayment after the war because I was flat broke—that we would be free by June. Piet was more pessimistic and took the bet, saying,

"That's too soon."

January 17th Oosten resigned from the Camp Committee because of ill health.

January 29th died New Zealander Burt, who had been the guinea pig for our Palembang Bottom experiments. Physically, he had been one of the toughest internees. He had studied Spanish and learned to play the guitar so he could surprise his wife when he got home.

Just before fleeing Singapore he had been notified of his decoration with the Order of the British Empire for his services with the engineering corps.

"They'll probably send it to my wife to keep for me," he said. "Boy, won't that be a great day when I get home!"

February 4th died our poet laureate Curran-Sharp who had composed the Ode to Phoebus and had entertained at early concerts with verses concerning Palembang Jail personalities. Curran-Sharp lost interest in life when he was notified by the Japanese that his wife had died in the Women's Camp. She had been the woman caught smuggling letters into Charitas Hospital. However, there was no connection between that episode and her death. When or how she died he did not know. Only that she was dead. From that day he began to fade.

Curran-Sharp left a sealed will to be opened after the war. In 1947 his friends Doc West and Oosten received small cash legacies from Curran-Sharp's estate "in gratitude for your help and friendship during internment and to buy some small memento of me."

February 5th Dr. Lentze diagnosed my latest troubles as intestinal malaria.

February 7th Direct Action Drysdale finally won an election, defeating Hammet and becoming British Leader. Van Asbeck succeeded Oosten as chairman of the Camp Committee.

February 10th Lentze said my insides were getting worse.

February 11th occurred our second death from that stalking horse of malaria, blackwater fever. The victim was only 21 years old.

February 12th I awakened to that dreadful symbol of starvation: swollen feet.

Lentze redoubled his efforts to save me from the toboggan slide into the dysentery or beri-beri wards. He had returned from the Japanese hospital with a bottle of cod liver oil malt to use for his own convalescence. He gave me what remained in the bottle. He found a man willing to sell a bottle of a native herb called *seri awan*, a specific against dysentery. The seller wanted fifteen guilders. I was broke. Bishop Mekkelholt loaned me the guilders.

February 13th Seki announced we would be moved from Muntok Prison back to Sumatra. Patients in danger of death enroute could remain behind with a doctor and a few ward attendants until they either died or recovered sufficiently to join us. Among those who were left behind and who died was the nephew of Boris Karloff, D. F. Pratt, who had been master of ceremonies at many jail shows.

February 19th Doctors Kramer and Kampschuur, who with Hollweg had headed the opposition in the November hospital fight, returned to power and notified seven hospital staff members including myself that, on the grounds of physical unfitness, we were through as hospital workers.

February 26th moving began. Prisoners were divided into three groups for transportation purposes. I went in the second group, March 5th.

Dr. Lentze elected to remain with the patients too sick to be transported. He chose Engineer Harrison and a few Dutch ward attendants who also had volunteered, to remain and help him.

Just before my group left I walked into the fever ward to say goodbye to my old friend Colijn, who was among those too sick to be moved. He had been in the lifeboat which picked me out of the Indian Ocean. Later, with his three daughters, we had hiked along the Sumatra coast looking for a boat in which to escape again.

"How much longer will it be, Mac?" he asked, meaning the war.

I said my bets were on June.

"That will be too long for my strength, I'm afraid," he said.

It was the first time I had ever heard him admit discouragement. But his next words were more cheerful.

"We will have some big dinners together in America after the war," he said, managing a smile.

"We sure will," I replied, knowing we never would. He knew it too.

Tired as he was he reached out to shake hands.

"We've been through a lot together, Mac."

I remembered well. In my mind's eye I saw him again, taking a turn at the lifeboat tiller and later, hiking along the beach and through the jungle, outwalking a boastful native guide who had tried to exhaust him. I thought of his escape from the Japanese after he and his wife were captured at Tarakan and of the dreams we both had shared for escaping again. Now it was the end of the trail.

"Goodbye, Mac," he said.

"Goodbye, Mr. Colijn."

We shook hands. I turned and walked out of the ward.

21

Belalau

SOMEWHERE enroute to our new prison camp I became the party of the second part to a new lease on life. Doing everything I should not have done cured me. Under no circumstances was I supposed to eat anything except soft rice. But soft rice was not available. I ate whatever came to hand. I was not to walk but I walked and toted a heavy knapsack. When our destination was reached my intestinal troubles had disappeared. Thanks to efforts of Doc Lentze and other friends I was apparently on the road to recovery and needed only one final push to effect a cure. The trip did it. From then on rice porridge was only a bad dream. I could eat anything and did, even the heart of a banana tree. I was rarin' for action. It came.

The journey from Muntok Prison verged on the nightmarish. My group numbered 250 men of whom twenty-five were stretcher cases and many more walking cadavers. Midafternoon of March 5th we were stuffed, baggage and all, into the holds of a small ship and the hatches were closed. Except for the stretcher patients we stood or crouched or sprawled on top of each other and our luggage.

In the packed, suffocating darkness I understood what the Black Hole of Calcutta must have been like. The ship lay in harbor all night. In small groups and for brief periods we were permitted on deck, then herded below again. Fortunately the voyage was short. We docked that night at Palembang and were loaded into a waiting train of four coaches and a freight car. Windows and doors were sealed and blinds drawn so we could neither see outside nor be seen. The wooden seats were hard, the floors harder, the darkness hot and airless, but it was better than the ship's hold. Next morning the train chugged from the yards and halted at the end of the line twelve hours later. Instead of being detrained we spent another night in the cars and at dawn were unloaded and herded into a fenced enclosure near the railroad depot.

End of the line was a little town named Loeboek Linggau in the jungle-clad foothills of Sumatra's west coast mountains. Across the mountain range, on the sea side, I had been captured three years before, in April 1942. In pre-war days Loeboek Linggau had been one of the debarkation points for thousands of Javanese farmer colonists, brought from their homes in over-populated Java to clear jungles and establish settlements in under-populated Sumatra.

For Resident Oranje our arrival in Loeboek Linggau was particularly ironic. At exactly the same spot and in circumstances strikingly similar but in reverse, he, as a representative of the Dutch Government of Sumatra, often had greeted trainloads of Javanese colonists.

"They arrived here just as we," Oranje told me, "crowded into third-class coaches; tired, dirty and loaded with tacky baggage."

Now Oranje himself was one of a group of ragged, dirty, tired, heavy-laden men debarking from jam-packed railroad cars to be greeted by Sumatra's new guardians, the Japanese.

"Mac," said Oranje with a doleful smile, "the Japs are treating us worse than if we were Javanese coolies!"

I think he missed the full irony of his words.

A convoy of trucks carried us over a winding gravel road from Loeboek Linggau. The road was little more than a swath between jungle and rubber trees. Occasionally the jungle fell away at a clearing and mountain peaks were visible in the distance. The clearings were areas where trees had been felled and burned by Javanese farmer colonists and the land planted with maize, rice, beans, papaya, banana and the ubiquitous ubi kayu. The other side of the road was a solid phalanx of rubber trees, tall, slender, standing in silent ranks that stretched into the perpetual twilight of the rubber forest. Undergrowth choked their feet.

About twelve kilometers (7½ miles) from Loeboek Linggau the trucks turned into the rubber, followed a winding trail through the trees for perhaps another four or five kilometers, emerged into sunshine at a large clearing and stopped.

In the clearing were a few low wooden buildings with galvanized iron roofs. The inevitable barbed wire fence encircled the area and a stream flowed through it, the fence spanning the stream. At the fence gate was a guardroom and up a small hill above the road and outside the fence was a building containing Seki's headquarters. The fence was the only new thing about the place. The buildings had been accommodations for estate laborers and their families and were known as coolie lines.

The coolie lines became our new camp, named after the rubber estate, Belalau. Doctors warned us not to walk barefoot because the area was infested with hookworm. At first we observed the warning but mud tore terompaks from our feet so frequently we were involuntarily barefoot much of the time.

Our water came from the dirty creek and a well sunk beside it and had to be boiled. The stream also was our only bathing facility. There was not enough fuel for lamps except those burning in hospital. A few men, hungry for light at night, made firefly lamps by catching and imprisoning the insects in bottles. Others tapped rubber trees for latex and burned the substance but it made more smoke than flame and soon was abandoned.

The women followed us to the rubber estate in April and were installed in similar coolie lines about two or three kilometers from our camp. As in Muntok there was no communication between us and it was not until after the war we heard the horrors of their trip.

Like us they were moved in three groups and packed in the ship's hold. A severe storm increased their misery. Antoinette Colijn, who occupied a stretcher herself, said nuns had to lie across the stretcher patients to keep them from being thrown out of their crude beds. Five women patients died in her freight car on the train trip from Palembang to Loeboek Linggau.

The women could have left their most critically ill behind to be nursed by a woman doctor—they had four—and volunteers, as we did, but, mistrusting the Japanese, they chose to take all their sick.

Life in Belalau was like camping out. The buildings were so vermin-ridden and hot we spent most of our time outdoors, prowling for things to eat and wood to cook them. We were able to supplement our Japanese issued rations with an astonishing variety of self-gathered food. Undergrowth teeming with edible leaves, vines and berries choked the clearing. The banana trees were barren, having produced their one and only yield. We felled the trees, stripped off outer bark and laid bare the heart, a soft, sweet, fibrous, white stalk, that can be eaten when diced and boiled. It contains no nourishment but is filling.

Banana leaves are not edible but have an astonishing variety of uses. They serve as umbrellas in a rain storm and as wrappers for packages. They make excellent food containers and also can be used to line cooking vessels. Dried and cut up they become cigaret papers and shredded they can be mixed with tobacco to stretch it out. Ribs of the leaves can be used as makeshift spoons or woven into baskets.

In a few weeks, of course, our camp was stripped bare of its edible foliage. Gardens then were dug and planted with ubi, maize, chili peppers and quick growing, leafy plants. Next source of food was the creek but it was soon fished, then seined, then scraped empty of stream life.

The health of nearly all prisoners, except those too far gone for saving, improved almost magically. Men were cheerful and optimistic in contrast with their former gloom and pessimism. Part of the uplift was psychological. No longer were we behind walls. Around us were green trees and unparalleled opportunity for black marketing with Haihos at night along the fence. Their prices were fantastic but, pirates though they were, they brought rice, maize and beans to trade for our clothing, jewelry, watches or fountain pens.

After three years of imprisonment it was surprising that men had anything left to trade. Many who had been wearing rags and walking barefoot produced brand new shirts and trousers that had never been worn.

The Japanese paid no attention to what we did inside the barricades. The camp was dotted with private fireplaces cooking black market or self-gathered food. Had Seki cared to, he could have uncovered any amount of evidence of smuggling from the outside but during the first month of internment he did nothing.

My American partner Eric and I lived with British internees in a building next to the creek. As in previous camps, men lay shoulder to shoulder on long platforms. Vermin life was worse and hospital facilities more primitive than any previous place. Although Eric and I no longer were members of the hospital staff, having been fired, I resumed one chore by request of the Camp Committee: compiling the daily sick roster. The job was welcome because it furnished an opportunity to steal Japanese newspapers.

Seki's medical orderly, Sergeant Tani, was a harried little man buried under a mountain of paper work. One of his tasks was to keep a daily report on each internee, as to whether he was well enough to work or sick, and if sick, how sick. He had two voluminous books for the purpose.

The pages of each book were divided into five spaces, one space for each sick man. Those spaces in turn were subdivided into tiny squares, one square for each day of the month. Every day one square had to be filled with a Japanese character denoting the man's condition, whether he had gotten well, was a little sick, very sick, in hospital, or dying. My job was to fill each of those little squares, using as a guide daily master sheets prepared in camp. The job was impossibly long until Tani procured some rubber stamps and I did not have to write the characters. After that it could be done in an hour or two.

Seki received Japanese newspapers and mimeographed army bulletins at irregular intervals. After he read them they were passed around his office to the interpreter and clerks and then came to the adjoining office occupied by Tani, a clerk and the quartermaster. After each had read the newspapers they were placed in a bound file beside Seki's desk. Tani occasionally left one lying on his desk. That was my opportunity.

My nineteen master sheets, containing the name of each internee and his state of health, were slightly larger in dimension than the tabloid sized Japanese newspaper. Tani's desk was big enough for four persons to work at, two on each side facing each other. I sat on the side opposite Tani and directly across from his clerk. Beside me sat the quartermaster. Seki's interpreter was a suspicious soldier who frequently stepped into Tani's office and looked over my shoulder. If for any reason Tani, his clerk and the quartermaster were out of the office simultaneously, the interpreter sent another soldier in to sit beside me. I was never alone except when the interpreter happened to be away; then everyone in the office relaxed and Tani would bring me a cup of coffee from the kitchen. I always scattered my sheets around my quarter of the table, where Tani laid the newspaper when he finished with it. If he forgot about the newspaper and did not look for it under the sheets all was well.

At the end of my morning's work I would gather the sheets, shuffling the newspaper into them, and leave.

The first time I did it I was as nervous as a burglar on his first job. However, I was never caught and apparently they never connected me with their missing newspapers. One harrowing morning, just as I had gathered up my sheets with a newspaper in them, the interpreter came to the desk looking for it. While I stood there holding the master sheets and two books of medical reports, Tani, the interpreter and two clerks ransacked the desk and then the entire office. Why not even the suspicious interpreter connected me with the loss was strange but apparently they decided one of the gate guards had taken it for they sent a clerk to the guardhouse and I left. Father Van Gisbergen translated the newspaper as he did others which followed.

The tone of Japanese press reports in 1945 was an interesting contrast to that of 1942, '43 and '44. During the first two years newspapers sang paeans of victory even when the stories themselves betrayed continuous defeats. The Japanese fleet kept sinking the American fleet closer and closer to Japan. Japanese soldiers kept annihilating American soldiers on various Pacific islands, also closer and closer to Japan. But, said Japanese propaganda, these battles were being fought in an ever narrowing radius to the homeland, merely for the purpose of luring foolish Americans into traps so they could be wiped out more easily.

However, in 1945 Japanese propaganda took another turn, changing to wails of despair. Already we had seen, in Muntok, posters exhorting Indonesians to assist Nippon in repelling expected invaders. Then had come the surprising story declaring, "The battle of Leyte will decide the fate of Nippon's holy war in the Pacific."

A newspaper I stole in May, 1945, said "America is cruelly and bloodily attacking Nippon whose only motive in this holy war is to make Asia a land of peace and co-prosperity."

But surprise of surprises was a picture magazine I found

on Tani's desk when I sat down to work one morning. The magazine lay open at a double spread in color of a mighty fleet steaming to victory. Plowing the waves straight off the page into the reader's eye was a head-on view of a battleship flanked by cruisers and destroyers and followed by aircraft carriers. Overhead the sky was black with warplanes. Wing markings of the planes were symbols of the American air force and the battleship was flying the Stars and Stripes!

The fleet Japan had been sinking with such monotonous regularity now was steaming in full battle array straight for Tokyo Bay and a Japanese magazine was telling its readers all about it.

I made no pretense of not seeing the magazine, as I usually did the newspapers. I studied the picture, wishing fervently I could read the caption. Then I thumbed through the magazine. A full page was devoted to a drawing and story of an American four-motored airplane, the biggest thing I had ever seen. It was labeled B-29.

"I've got to get this article," I said to myself. "I've got to."

I closed the magazine, pushed it aside and looked up into the eyes of Tani's clerk. His face was expressionless. I glanced at Tani. He, too, was watching me. He turned his eyes away, back to his work. We busied ourselves with our respective tasks. Presently the clerk left the room. Tani rose from his desk, walked around the table and stood beside me. He asked a question about the number of sick. I showed him the figures. He picked up the magazine, turned the pages to the battle fleet picture and laid the magazine down, open. Then he said in Malay two words.

"Big ship."

"Yes," I replied, also in Malay, "big ship."

"American," he said.

"Yes, American."

"America big country. Yes?"

"Yes, America big country."

He hissed, with a long intake of breath, and said,

"America very strong, yes?"

"Yes, very strong."

He walked back around the desk, stood for a moment looking out the window, and said,

"Nippon very brave, but so small."

Tani turned from the window and poked among some bottles on a shelf behind him. Selecting a jar marked "Vit.B" he turned to the table, poured powder from the jar into a small piece of paper. Carefully he folded the paper around the powder and handed it to me.

"Eat," he said. "Good for you."

His clerk returned to the office bearing a tray on which were three glasses. He placed one in front of me. Tani handed me a Japanese cigaret and a match. I lit the cigaret. The glass contained hot coffee with an inch of sugar on the bottom. The interpreter and Seki were away.

Tani and his clerk had always been cordial but today they were more so. Plainly they had wanted me to see the magazine. And just as plainly I could not steal it because they would spot its absence the moment it was gone. But I could do one thing if given half a chance. Tear out the story of the B-29. The chance came when the clerk returned the glasses and Tani also left the room. In the other office was another clerk but my back was toward him. I took a knife from my pocket and cut the page so there would be no tearing noise.

Father Van Gisbergen translated the article. It described in detail the new American super-plane that was "cruelly and wantonly raining fire on Japanese women and children, thereby violating all the rules of humanity and Christianity which Americans so loudly profess."

It described the plane's fire power, bomb capacity, cruising range and invincibility.

Japanese propaganda was preparing the people for defeat. America was too big, too strong and too cruel to be conquered.

Compiling the sick roster had another advantage than stealing newspapers. Back in 1939 as I was leaving my home in Salt Lake City to start my journey to the Orient, I suddenly remembered I had lost my fountain pen. Lying on my father's desk was a dollar pen he had purchased and discarded. I picked it up, carried it to Japan, China, India, the Indies, and when I was fished out of the sea into a lifeboat it was still safely clipped in my shirt pocket. I still had it in Belalau and used it occasionally as bait in Tani's office. Haihos wanted fountain pens and I supposed the Japanese did too and would pay more, if no one was looking.

Seki's clerk, on a morning he was the only Japanese in the office, made an offer. I rejected it. After several weeks of furtive haggling he paid what I wanted: two beer bottles filled with coconut oil, a bottle of palm oil and thirty guilders—for my dollar fountain pen. Oil was the most precious foodstuff obtainable, next to meat.

My oil driller friend, Nick Koot, who had made the containers in which I buried Camp News, was a partner in a neat trick on the Japanese. Koot's camp job was to keep in repair the ramshackle truck that brought our daily rations. The garage was adjacent to Seki's office. Food supplies for Seki's staff were kept in a locked storeroom next to the garage. Among the supplies was a 200 liter (52.8 gallons) drum of palm oil.

Koot determined to tap the oil drum. He requested and obtained an assistant named Roel de Jong for the truck repairing job. Koot and De Jong spent two weeks preparing for the palm oil burglary. Vital to the project was a duplicate key to the storeroom. Dangling from his belt on the end of a chain Sesuki, the Japanese quartermaster, carried the only key. De Jong engaged Sesuki in conversation while Koot surreptitiously fingered the key and made an impression on a small piece of soap. Using the impression as a model they made a duplicate key. Next, while one stood watch, the other oiled the lock and tried the key to make sure both worked silently. Third step was fashioning a wrench to fit the drum lid. Finally, they dug two holes, the size of water buckets, in the private garden outside their block. There the oil would be buried until any possibility of a camp search had passed.

Choosing a torrential night rain storm to cover sight and sound of their movements they crawled on their bellies through the fence gate, directly in front of the guard room, reached the storeroom, unlocked the door, slipped through, closed it behind them and went to work.

From an adjoining room came voices of two guards, shouting to make themselves heard by each other above the violent drumming of the rain. The palm oil drum was tipped on its side, the lid unscrewed and the two water buckets filled. Working only by their sense of touch in the pitch darkness of the storeroom, Koot and De Jong accomplished the entire job without clanging metal against metal. Also, they wiped the floor with rags to obliterate mud and any spilled oil. Still protected by the rain storm they returned to camp and buried their oil.

Doctors Kampschuur and Kramer distinguished themselves in Belalau; Kampschuur by his hunting prowess and Kramer by a daring and successful operation.

Kampschuur talked Seki into allowing him to hunt wild pigs, with gun and flashlight, one night a week accompanied by a guard. Pigs come out of the jungle at night to feed on rubber tree nuts and ubi kayu. The Japanese benefited by a cut of the meat and we benefited by pork sauce on our rice whenever Kampschuur was successful. Seki furnished the gun and ammunition.

Kramer performed a successful major abdominal operation on a 62-year-old Dutchman named J. A. M. van der Vossen, whom Kramer diagnosed as having an intestinal obstruction. The chances of surviving such an operation in our primitive circumstances were overwhelmingly negative.

On the other hand, death was certain if the obstruction was not removed. Van der Vossen chose to gamble.

I did not witness the operation but Kramer said he used a table knife and spoon. His scalpel was made from the table knife. The spoon's use I don't know. He made clips from fence wire to hold the intestines. Everything was boiled for two hours. Morphine was the only anesthetic. The operation was performed in the open air, on a bamboo table. Van der Vossen was walking around within two weeks.

The hospital in Belalau was a bamboo shed with a palm roof, dirt floor and space on its benches for only forty patients; hence only critical cases could be admitted. Blackwater fever, which derives its name from excessive bleeding through the kidneys, increased. Once chronic malaria changed into blackwater fever, death usually followed quickly, the crisis coming within forty-eight hours of the fever's onset. Doctors said a victim had only a ten per cent chance of survival without blood transfusions. Internees were not physically able to donate blood.

Librarian Harold Lawson was one of two men who survived blackwater fever. However, the sickness left him with a revulsion for food. He would not eat. Several friends, myself included, took turns feeding him. It was no mere mechanical process of spooning rice into his mouth, but of making him swallow it by pleading, cajolery or threats.

"Open your mouth, Harold, and take this spoonful."

He was so weak his voice was scarcely audible.

"I can't."

"You've got to. If you don't eat you won't recover."

"I can't."

"Please, Harold, just one swallow."

"Only one?"

"That's all."

He opened his mouth. The spoon went in. He held the

rice in his mouth a time, trying to chew. His jaws moved feebly, then he swallowed. I filled the spoon again, brought it to his mouth."

"No."

"Yes."

"You said only one."

"I know, but it wasn't a whole spoon. I put only a little in it so you could swallow easier."

"I can't."

"Say, are you throwing in the sponge? Show some guts and eat this."

He opened his mouth. Swallowed. Closed his eyes.

I waited while he rested from the effort, then filled another spoon.

"Harold. Wake up."

His eyes opened.

"Open your mouth."

"No."

"Listen. I've got other things to do besides sitting here and playing nursemaid. If you can't reciprocate a courtesy, the hell with you."

He opened his mouth. Swallowed and fell asleep. Poor guy. He couldn't help it but unless he was forced to eat he would die like those who had no friends to bully them into eating. I joggled his shoulder.

"Wake up, Harold."

He awakened.

"Open your mouth."

"I can't."

"Eat this, damn you, or I'll shove it down your throat."

He opened his mouth and swallowed.

After a week of that kind of feeding Lawson's body was strong enough to awaken his will. Once the will took hold the battle was nearly won. Lawson's feeding was by no means unique. Other men were saved similarly.

Black-bearded W. Probyn Allen, who had helped me

edit Camp News and each Christmas had read the English words of the gospel story sung by Father Bakker's choir, was stricken with blackwater fever and carried into hospital March 22nd. He had weighed around 240 pounds when we first met in Palembang Jail. Now he weighed less than half of that.

In 1942 we had gone partnerships in buying an old Dutch atlas. While I was visiting him in hospital the day after he was stricken he suddenly remembered the atlas. He told me where it was concealed next to his bunk.

"We located a lot of places in that old atlas," he said, "didn't we?"

"We sure did."

"Best investment we made in camp."

I agreed it was and asked if he wanted anything done.

"Nothing, thanks, except bring me some news when you get it."

He was in pain but he did not betray it by word or action. He knew exactly how deadly was blackwater and that he had it but if any fears were in his mind he did not show them.

I asked Hollweg, his doctor, about giving Allen a blood transfusion.

"Where will we get the blood?" he asked.

"How about mine?"

"You haven't enough for yourself," said Hollweg, "nor has anyone else."

Saturday morning I told Allen I would have some news for him the following day because a Japanese newspaper was being translated.

"That's fine, Mac, I'll be expecting you tomorrow."

When "tomorrow" came it was Palm Sunday, March 25th. I was walking into the hospital when an attendant told me Allen had just died. That was my first real shock of internment. I thought he was going to pull through. He was only 34.

I sat down on the edge of the hospital bench, at the

place where Allen had lain and which now was vacant. Through memory tumbled the words of the poem he had written to his wife and published in Camp News at Christmas, 1942, more than three years before in Palembang Jail. The opening lines were:

It needs no festal time to bring you to my mind,
For every sunrise, every close of day, I find
Your image by me, smiling, bidding me good cheer,
Whispering our private nonsenses I love to hear. . . .

Often he had talked of their country cottage in England and of the reunion they would have there when the war ended. Well, God had willed otherwise. The sixteen-line poem, I thought, would be an imperishable thing of Allen for his wife to treasure and in which to find comfort. It ended:

Have faith, my love, although the night is dark, the day
Will break, and peace and good will come to men at last.
God bless you and keep you always.

I walked back to my bunk and wrote a letter to his wife enclosing the poem. It was delivered after the war.

The working party was enlarging our cemetery space in the rubber trees two hundred meters from camp and did not finish in time to dig more graves Sunday. By Monday another man had died, necessitating a double funeral.

Friends of the two men lined up beside the coffins and Hammet read Church of England services. Then, flanked by guards, we struck out through the rubber trees.

"It doesn't seem possible that he has gone," said Oosten. "He had so much life. I can still hear his voice. How it rang when he laughed."

I could still hear it too, as the coffins were lowered into

a double grave in the clearing. The trees were very high all around us but enough had been felled in this one spot so that a patch of sky was visible above us and sunlight streamed through to illuminate the reddish mounds of earth in the vast dimness of the rubber forest.

22

Let's Go Smuggling

A NEW kind of hunger ravished our vitals in Bela-lau. In contrast to the sick gnawing of Muntok Jail the hunger was a healthy, ravenous, never satisfied appetite.

In Muntok our stomach capacities had shrunk until they could not hold a full meal even when such a phenomenon occurred as it had on the birthday of Queen Wilhelmina, August 31, 1944. The kitchen, by careful husbanding and special appeals to the Chinese contractor, had amassed enough supplies to give every internee a full meal. Most of us were unable to eat it at one sitting.

In Belalau our new lease on life expanded both our appetites and our stomachs. But we could never get enough to satisfy them. Ironically, although Belalau was in a land of plenty, our rations increased only slightly. The region abounded in rice, maize, vegetables, fruit, tobacco and coffee. Its streams were full of fish, its jungles teemed with game. However, we could get none of its bounty through the Japanese. There was no alternative but to get it ourselves. Three methods were possible: trading through guards, smuggling, or ubi raiding.

All three enterprises were included under the general designation of black marketing; however, in prison camp that word did not have the connotation it has in ordinary society. For the most part black marketing was a highly honorable—and vitally necessary—profession. It saved more lives than doctors or medicine.

Inflation and acute goods shortages were disrupting the Japanese occupation economy. Chinese merchants in Loeboek Linggau were turning paper money into goods. They would pay fantastic paper prices for cloth, watches, jewelry or silver money. Javanese and Malay farmers, unable for three years to obtain cloth, were in rags and anxious to trade farm produce for our clothing.

Our Haiho guards, eager for money whether silver or paper, were ready-made middle men between us and the merchants or natives. The squeeze they exacted, however, was so high that a handful of daring men began slipping through the fence at night, with or without connivance of bribed Haihos, and traveling to native huts about three hours distant, to do their own bartering. These men were the smugglers.

Ubi raiders were those who sneaked out at night to a nearby cultivated area known as a *ladang* and dug up ubi kayu.

There was a flurry of trading, smuggling and ubi raiding within two weeks of our arrival at Belalau. Then Seki cracked down on the Haihos who, in turn, laid for the smugglers. Four were caught the first night. One of them, a big Indo-European named Bolle, was tied to a tree for sixteen hours and beaten at intervals by the same Haihos who had been trading with us. Then all four smugglers were turned over to the Kempeitai, who took them to jail in Loeboek Linggau where Bolle died. His three companions, hollow eyed and weak, returned to camp after fifty days.

The Kempeitai assigned Malay field police to watch the native kampongs. Seki increased the guard and instructed them to shoot on sight. Seki's real *coup d'état* on smuggling was not the increased guards or shooting orders but a barricade of felled trees around the camp. Crossing it without making a noise was ticklish and difficult.

Our food situation once more became acute and some men reverted to catching rats.

Despite Seki's efforts, certain Haihos still traded with internees and a few prisoners found ways of getting out. Smuggling gangs were organized by men experienced in jungle work and willing to run any risk for food. Leaders of the most successful smuggling rings were a Dutchman named Anton Breet, the Ambonese Louhenapessie, the Indo-European policeman Max Breuer, and a husky native of the Celebes islands, named Mandang. I decided to become a smuggler myself. Mandang took me under his wing.

*　　*　　*　　*

Let's go on my first smuggling trip:

Mandang's inside men have spotted the position of each guard. The sergeant in charge of the night shift has just left the guardhouse, walked across the plank bridge over the creek and now is inspecting guard posts along the fence. Mandang has chosen to leave camp by wading up the creek, slipping under the fence, which spans it, then under the guards' bridge, and climbing the opposite bank. In that way we avoid the tree barricade. We run the risk of a Haiho or Japanese leaving the guardhouse unexpectedly and spotting us in the water below the bridge but the odds are in our favor. Mandang knows by heart the guard routine.

Four of us have been sitting by the creek waiting for the sergeant to cross the bridge. The four are Mandang, an Ambonese named Sitanala, the Indo-European Tempelers, who scaled the Muntok Jail wall, and myself. I am a tenderfoot, the others jungle veterans. The sergeant clumps across the bridge and walks along the fence. Now is the time. Mandang steps into the creek and wades up it, keeping close to the bank. He ducks under the barbed wire. Sitanala follows, then me, and lastly, Tempelers. We are to keep this order throughout the trip.

The time is shortly after 7 P.M. The moon has not yet risen and thunderclouds are beginning to blanket the heavens; however, the quality of darkness still permits us vision of shapes and obstacles.

We move slowly, feeling with our bare toes for firm footing. To fall or splash would arouse Haihos in the guardhouse. I'm under the fence now and, straightening, see Sitanala going under the bridge. He waits for me in its darker shadow. When I arrive he crosses the creek in the shadow of the bridge. I follow. He snakes up the bank and disappears into bushes. I belly after him, wishing I could move with his silent suppleness. We rise to hands and knees, moving very slowly and parting the bushes with our hands until we are in the rubber trees, then we stand erect.

No words are spoken. Sitanala directs me with his hands to hold onto the knapsack on his back. Behind me I feel Tempelers holding onto mine. Night is Stygian in the rubber forest. I am blind. So is our leader Mandang but he does not need to see. His toes are his eyes. They explore the ground, tell him where to step. He inches forward; we follow in lock step, placing our feet where his have been, striving to move without breaking twigs or dead branches. Every sound we make is magnified by our straining ears and sends little waves of alarm along tingling nerves. Over and over I repeat to myself,

"Quiet. Quiet. The Japs will hear."

Because of the location of Japanese occupied buildings, the undergrowth choked terrain of the rubber estate and surrounding jungle, and certain geographical bottlenecks caused by swamps, deep streams and steep hillsides, there are only three possible routes to our destination. The one we are using tonight is the shortest because for approximately two kilometers it utilizes the road to the Women's Camp instead of jungle or rubber tree trail. A path extends from the guard's footbridge to the road on this side of the creek but it is too likely to be patrolled this time of night so we cross it, go farther into the rubber, then travel parallel to the path until we reach the road. Although the distance is short it takes an hour of painfully slow progress to cover it because we are still within earshot of Japanese quarters.

We reach the road. Sitanala's hands tell me to wait. He and Mandang explore along the road in opposite directions, stopping every few feet to listen. They return. All clear. We sit down and put on our rubber shoes. Mine are a pair I bought just before being captured and have preserved by wearing only on special occasions, like funerals or tonight. The road is stony. Mandang whispers,

"Are you ready, Mac?"

"Yes."

"We start. Walk fast. We lost much time."

They walk so fast I find it difficult to keep up. We no longer cling to each other. I follow by ear, listening to the scuffling pad, pad of their feet. Occasionally one of us accidentally kicks a stone. It cracks sharply against other stones. Mandang halts, commands more caution and resumes his breakneck pace.

We leave the road and follow a steep, slippery trail. I go up, using my hands to keep from sliding back. At the top we again intersect the road. The trail is a shortcut.

Lightning abruptly rips the night. Thunder claps and, while I'm reswallowing my heart, rain hits us as though thrown from a bucket. Ten minutes later it stops. Mandang has slowed to a crawl. He is feeling along the road edge. He halts, whispers my name, cups his mouth to my ear and says,

"A sentry post is just ahead. We are near the Women's Camp. Now we leave the road and go around the camp."

Now comes another hazardous leg of the journey. We must circle the Women's Camp by clambering up a tree covered hillside to a long unused trail above the camp. Mandang leads us off the road and we start climbing, again clinging to each other's knapsacks. We reach the old trail. My legs feel knee high grass or weeds. We halt. Sitanala puts his lips to my ear.

"Straight below is the Women's Camp, close enough for guards to hear. We must climb over a fallen tree. I will guide your feet. Take care."

Below us, as in a black void, I see pinpoints of light marking the Women's Camp.

Sitanala maneuvers his way across the tree. My exploring hands, following Sitanala's passage, feel a waist high tree trunk. Lower down, my feet touch branches and above is another branch, as if the tree forks near me. I wriggle between the two. Sitanala's hands guide one of my feet and place it on a branch which gives me a step up and over another tree trunk. Then I am across.

I inch forward a few paces to make room for Tempelers behind me. My face bangs against another tree. Constellations of pain blaze in my eyes. My nose feels smashed flat. Mandang, hearing the thud, seizes my arm and pulls me down to my knees. We duck under a tree that lies across the trail at head height.

Slowly the night becomes lighter. Objects distinguish themselves as darker masses in the darkness. Mandang orders a halt. We listen. While we stand, straining our ears, the moon comes out. In the trees we can not see it but the gloom lessens. We start forward, negotiate another fallen tree, pick up speed for a time but gradually slow to a crawl. Somewhere close, Mandang knows, is a wooden footbridge over a little stream. Planks are missing from the approach on this side so that we must take a long, almost leaping, stride, from earth to bridge. His sense of timing tells him the bridge should be near but his toes cannot find the jumping off place. We keep going forward, first one foot feeling, then the other . . .

Suddenly Mandang starts stamping and muttering curses. Sitanala jumps as though shot and slaps at his legs. I lose my balance, fall forward and the next second my hands and arms are stung with electric fire. Ants. Myriads of vicious, biting, stinging, flesh piercing ants. We have walked into a bed of them. Mandang's bare feet—he removed his shoes when we left the road—felt them first; Sitanala, not until they swarmed over his shoe tops, while I reached them first with my hands. Tempelers, amply warned, jumps back to safety. Retreating likewise I beat, slap and rub the ants from my hands and arms. Mandang reverses our course. There had been no ant bed on the trail when he last traveled it. We have taken a wrong fork. Backtracking, he finds the correct fork and continues along it to the foot bridge. We each take a long, blind stride, to clear the missing plank, then step cautiously, feeling for loose planks or holes.

The trail swings sharply left, dips downhill. I hear running water and see a patch of moonlight ahead. We emerge from the gloom of the trees onto a bridge which has not been used for a long time. Missing planks leave treacherous holes. Mandang speaks aloud for the first time since leaving camp.

"Sit down. Let us smoke."

Tempelers laughs loudly.

"Now we can talk. We are past danger."

"We are far from the Women's Camp," says Mandang. "No one can hear us here."

In the moonlight we examine each other for leeches which infest the trail, lying in wait on foliage for passing prey. Dark smears on our legs, arms or necks disclose where the repulsive, carnivorous worms have embedded themselves to suck our blood. Removing them with thumb and fore-finger is not easy. Pulled from the skin they stick to fingers. We flip them off, crushing them on the wood of the bridge.

Uneasily I keep looking around. Sensing my thoughts, Mandang says,

"No Japanese come this far at night. They are afraid of tigers and wild pigs."

"Are there tigers here?"

"I am not sure but the Japanese and Haihos think so. There are many pigs. Perhaps we will see some. I would rather meet a tiger than a mother pig with young. The tiger will run away but the pig might charge."

We roll nipa leaf cigarets and smoke. The moon rides just above the tree tops, bathing the bridge with light and silvering the stream on either side. We are relaxed and feel an exuberant thrill of freedom. Around us are no fences or walls or guards. Our companions are trees, a running stream, forest noises and insects which glow suddenly in the gloom and sometimes startle me because they look so much like distant flashlights.

My skin crawls momentarily as I look across the stream into two gleaming eyes, or what I think are eyes. They disappear. I relax again.

Our cigarets smoked, we leave the bridge and step once more into darkness. The trail dips into a gully. Trees and bushes close over our heads and we are once more blind, holding onto each other's sacks, moving slowly.

"We are coming to a narrow bridge," says Mandang.

I can hear his feet tapping the ground, feeling, then a hollow thump. I move closer to Sitanala so that our bodies are practically one as I try to follow the movement of his feet. Tempelers similarly is glued to me. I feel wood, hear a hollow sound. Then Mandang falls heavily, plunging through a rotten board. Such falls can break a leg. His breath hisses in pain as he drags his leg out of the hole. We wait while he recovers, then continue on.

I slip and land flat on my back. Tempelers, like a cat, jumps over me but loses his balance and thuds to the ground.

Mandang halts, takes a torch of resinous wood from his knapsack and lights it with three matches struck simultaneously. The matches I have saved since buying them in 1942. The torch flares, lighting a trail slimy underfoot, crisscrossed with fallen limbs and overhung with giant ferns.

"Here it is safe for lights," says Mandang. He walks, fanning the torch by waving it vigorously so it will stay alight. We can see enough to walk rapidly.

We emerge from the gully onto a flat, hard, grassless surface. Instead of vines or weeds the undergrowth on either side of what appears once to have been a road is sparse bushes, like individual saplings without branches. Mandang extinguishes the torch.

"Now we must be careful, Mac. Here is danger. Ahead is the main road. If anything happens stand still. Don't move."

We creep along, moving slightly uphill. Far ahead my straining eyes discern a greyness through the trees. The edge of the rubber.

Crash! My heart flipflops. Moving figures smash through the brush at us. We're caught! Smart Japanese have been lying at the rubber edge waiting. Run! But Mandang's orders were to stand still. I freeze. Why don't they flash lights on us? Other sounds become audible in the uproar of trampling brush. Grunts. More grunts. Sitanala speaks.

"Pigs. Not Japs. Wild pigs."

The relief is comic. We can hear each other's breathing. Wordlessly we sit down while pounding pulses quiet. After a while Mandang rises and we creep toward the grey light. Soon we are at the edge of the rubber, but ahead are bushes, thick and higher than our heads. Mandang tells us to wait. He wriggles through the bushes silently as a Red Indian of fiction. After a long time a faint whistle sounds.

Tempelers now leads. We follow him through the bushes but not with Mandang's stealth. I struggle with embracing tendrils. Sometimes it seems I'm hopelessly tangled. Finally we are through into clear moonlight. Directly in front of us is the road. Almost invisible at our feet is a deep, narrow, grass-concealed ditch. A long step takes me across. Mandang hisses,

"Back! Into the ditch!"

Tempelers and Sitanala throw themselves into the weeds,

roll into the ditch. I likewise. And Mandang. As I roll into the ditch I find myself on the shoulders of Sitanala. That saves me from a rough tumble because the ditch is shoulder high.

"Listen," says Mandang.

A rumbling sounds. Unmistakably a motor vehicle. Mandang's keen ears detected the noise before any of us. Another moment and headlights flood the road. We crouch too low to see anything. Sounds like a truck. It passes with a rumble and rattle. We raise our heads only to duck again. Another truck. And another. Mandang tears handfuls of long grass, holds it above his head and peers over the ditch top. A truck convoy.

We wait a considerable time before crawling from the ditch. Mandang leads. Instead of scuttling across the road, however, he walks leisurely along it. We follow in single file. He turns, points to a board spanning a deep ditch on the other side of the road, balances himself across the board while we follow one by one and walk along a footpath to a steeply roofed building. It is the first house in the Javanese settlement known as Petanahan. We walk around it and continue deeper into the cultivated area. Scattered, one-story houses stand out sharply on the moon-bathed land. We slide down one side of a deep ravine, scramble up the other and find ourselves in a patch of ubi kayu, the stalks higher than our heads.

"Wait," says Mandang.

He and Tempelers disappear.

Presently a whistle sounds beyond the ubi kayu. We follow it, emerge beside a house. Mandang and Tempelers are talking to a small Javanese man in white shorts and dark jacket. Beside him is an even smaller woman, clad in a sarong. The little man leads us away from the house into a field of maize. We pick our way between the rows until we come to a small clearing in the middle of the field where grow a few papaya trees. This is our trading rendezvous. It is safer than the house because police sometimes pay surprise night calls at Petanahan.

The farmer leaves us there, squatting on the soft earth so our heads are below the maize tops, and soon reappears with a second man. They are carrying straw mats which they spread on the ground. Mandang introduces me. The first man is named Barto and the second is his son, Radi. Mandang tells them I am an American.

"Selamat, Tuan American," they greet me.

"Selamat," I reply.

We all sit, cross-legged, on the mats. Linguist Mandang converses with them in their native Javanese. Radi lays a small, flat tin on the mat in front of me. Tobacco and nipa leaves. I roll a long, fat cigaret and light it with a match to astound Radi and Barto. It does. Matches they have not seen since the war began.

Radi asks me, in Malay, how far it is to America.

My guess is 15,000 kilometers.*

His mind can not grasp such a distance. I translate it into days of travel by steamboat. Thirty days. He murmurs incredulously.

Sitanala whispers to me occasional translated tidbits from Barto's words to Mandang. Barto says the head man of Petanahan, a man named Mangoen, was informed by the Japanese, when they came to confiscate more rice, that the war would end this year for certain. The price of rice in Loeboek Linggau now is 400 guilders a *kaling*. A kaling is the standard of bulk measurement among colonists. It is the amount contained in a kerosene tin, between 15 and 16 kilograms (33 to 35.2 pounds).** Tobacco prices also are sky high—five guilders a lempeng, an amount about the size of a shredded wheat biscuit, and weighing about forty grams. Petanahan is full of fever and there is no quinine. Have we any quinine? Radi's friend Ali has a wife with a

* 1 kilometer = .62 of a mile. 1 mile = 1.6 kilometer.
** 1 kilogram = 2.2 pounds.

sore leg. Have we medicine? I promise to bring medicine next time.

Barto's wife appears bearing food. Hot rice, small fried fish and ubi chips and two vegetables I do not recognize. Radi says it is the first fish they have had in moons.

Rice is ladled from the central dish onto banana leaves and passed to us. I take an ubi chip with my left hand and convey it to my mouth. Radi speaks sharply.

I have committed a crude *faux pas*. Eating with the left hand is unclean. Only the right hand can convey food to the mouth. Mandang, Tempelers and Sitanala make voluble excuses for my barbarity, explain that Americans are ignorant of table manners. I am pardoned.

By mistake I take too much hot pepper sauce. My mouth catches fire, my eyes and nose run and I sneeze and hiccup. Tempelers laughs uproariously. Barto and Radi grin. Mrs. Barto comes with hot coffee. Barto pours it into china cups. We light cigarets and the business of trading begins.

"Show him your goods," Mandang tells me.

From my homemade knapsack of rice sacking I draw precious clothing Eric and I have acquired and saved. Two pairs of good shorts, a shirt and one of the ties I found in Palembang Jail. I brought the tie on a hunch. Radi seizes it for his own, not permitting it to be placed with the shorts and shirt for which Barto will bargain.

Mandang, Barto and Radi haggle politely in Javanese. While they talk the round moon drifts across the sky from one side of the papaya trees to the other. At last Mandang tells me,

"Barto will give you a kaling of red rice for your things. Radi will give two kilograms for the tie. He wants the tie as a waist sash for his sarong. Do you agree?"

I agree. It is a good bargain.

Trading resumes as Mandang and Tempelers dispose of their own goods. Barto's wife leaves to find Radi's friend Ali. Ali comes and the three men carry kalings of rice and maize from their hiding places to us. My knapsack holds just one kaling of rice.

When trading is finished, the goods exchanged and paid for, I remind Radi he still owes me two kilograms for the tie. Radi says he will pay me next trip. We have traded them out of all their rice. In fact he would like to borrow back a kilogram of rice for his meal next day. Mandang says Radi evidently is telling the truth and for the sake of future good will I should lend him the kilogram. With a coconut shell we measure the amount, give it back to Radi. Now he owes me three kilograms. I have an irritating hunch he'll never pay.

We help each other to shoulder our loads. Mine is the lightest, 15 kilograms (33 pounds). I volunteer to carry more because Mandang is bent under 35 kilograms (77 pounds) but he advises me to walk for an hour and then decide whether my load shall be increased. Sitanala and Tempelers have around 25 kilograms each. We have not walked a kilometer before I am thankful my 15 kilograms is not more. I begin to realize how much strength I have lost.

Down the ravine we slide and crawl up the other side on hands and knees. Successfully I negotiate the first roadside ditch but disaster overtakes me on the second. I take the necessary long stride but it is not long enough. The load shortens my step and down I tumble. My chest strikes the opposite side and the 15 kilograms on my back combines with the blow to punch every breath of air from my lungs. Stunned and gasping I lie wedged in the bottom of the ditch. My companions drop their loads to extricate me, shove me into the bushes and crawl in themselves. Now we are safely off the road.

Every place that had given us difficulty enroute to Petanahan is tougher returning, loaded. I dread falling, not only because of the noise, but because of the effort to rise again with a dead weight on my back.

We ignite the torch and its smoky flare helps us up the long, tunnel-like gully. At the top we extinguish the torch. Moonlight helps us across the crucial fallen trees above the Women's Camp. We strike the road. This is the last lap. We hurry to make up for lost time. Sweat soaks me and stings my eyes.

The moon is too high for us to chance slipping into camp via the creek behind the guardhouse. Behind the hospital is a break in the tree barrier through which coffins are carried to the cemetery. A sentry box is there but the sentry has a habit of leaving it shortly before he is to be relieved. Instead of waiting for his relief to arrive at the box he walks along the fence to meet him, thus gaining a few minutes on quitting time. The guards will change at 5 A.M. Mandang's watch says 4:15.

To reach the barrier break we must pass directly behind Seki's house where he and his officers are sleeping. Once at the barrier we must lie and listen for the sentry to stir in his box and walk away toward the main gate. After that we will have about three minutes to slip through the opening, reach the fence, get through it with our loads and out of sight.

We leave the road and start through the trees around Seki's house. We make or break from here in. Either we get through, or get caught and face the music. To my nervous ears our footsteps sound like men with iron feet walking on broken glass. Seki must be drugged to sleep through such noise. And if he's drugged the Haiho sentry must be dead. Any second now there should be a yell and a shot and running footsteps.

We are crouching outside the barrier, waiting, waiting, waiting. After an interminable time we hear a scuffle of feet in the sentry box. The guard clears his throat and spits, rattles his rifle, hums a few bars of a Malay tune, steps from the box and begins his illicit stroll to the front gate, seventy-five feet away.

This is the payoff. Mandang rises. We rise. Mandang heads for the fence. We follow. I'm so nervous my stomach is turning somersaults, my heart is doing the high hurdles and the hair of my neck is sending off sparks. How can the guard not hear us?

We're at the fence. Moonlight floods it like a giant searchlight. How can the guard not see us? This is how a convict must feel when he's going over the wall. Only we're going in not out. Mandang shucks his knapsack like a lizard shedding its skin, seizes a strand of barbed wire and raises it, depresses another strand with his foot. Sitanala is through. I'm through. Mandang and Tempelers hoist their loads over the top, drop them into our arms. We set them on the ground, spread the barbed wire strands for Mandang and Tempelers. They're through. We pick up our loads and run across the moonlit expanse for the hospital doorway, duck into its shadow and stop, panting. Seconds later a scuffling in the box announces the five o'clock sentry has arrived.

A curious attendant looks us over. He chuckles,

"Ten per cent commission for using hospital hiding facilities."

We separate and go to our respective blocks.

Eric had been up for an hour keeping a can of tea warm on a tiny fire.

"I was beginning to worry," he said. "It's awfully close to roll call."

I drank the tea. It was warm and stimulating.

"Better get out of those clothes," Eric said. "You look a mess."

I was daubed with mud. Stripping, I waded into the creek to wash and pull off leeches. Even after removing them blood continued to well, for a while, in a little trickle marking where each leech had clung.

When I returned Eric had the rice emptied into small sacks and stowed away in our rat-proof tin trunk, another treasure from Palembang Jail. We smoked Radi's tobacco and talked. I was still keyed up by the nervous tension of the trip and its success. After roll call I lay down and tried to sleep. Too much noise. I got up.

"Let's have some rice," I suggested to Eric.

"Right."

We borrowed a *kuali,* a heavy iron cooking vessel reminiscent of a gold pan, and measured into it 400 grams of rice. We gloated over the beauty of the red, hill rice. Unlike the white, polished rice of camp rations the red rice was only partially husked and had a nutty flavor. We decided to cook 400 grams a day. Fifteen kilograms would last 37 days. That would do much toward rebuilding our strength. Meanwhile, we would acquire goods for another smuggling trip.

As our rice stocks dwindled we cast around camp for goods to barter on a percentage basis. That required estimating the value of any article to within a kilogram. Smuggling was pure gamble. My first trip had been a success but the next might not be. Clothing owners were reluctant to share risks with a smuggler—splitting the profits if his trip succeeded and losing if he was caught or otherwise failed. They preferred to sell outright for a standard price—three to five kilograms on the spot for a pair of shorts—and let the smuggler take all the risks—both on his investment and on his neck. I decided to get a customer who would trust me and be willing to lose if I lost.

"Get cloth, thread and silver guilders," I told Bishop Mekkelholt, "and we'll do business on a fifty-fifty basis. If the trip is successful we split. If not, we both lose."

"Agreed," said the Bishop.

He put a Brother to work cutting up white cassocks and sewing them into shorts of a correct size for small statured Javanese. Another Brother laboriously unraveled socks and sweaters for thread and yarn to sell to Javanese women.

Handing me a wide red satin sash, such as bishops wear with their cassocks, he commented,

"One of the Javanese wives might like this."

On my second trip I accompanied another smuggling king, former policeman Max Breuer and his three men. There was no moon. We slipped through the fence behind the kitchen, where wood cutters had made a passage through the tree barrier. On striking the road we sat down in the darkness and donned our shoes.

At Petanahan we went to the house of Ali, for whose wife I had brought medicine and a bandage for her ulcerated leg.

A wick burning in a dish of palm oil was the only illumination in Ali's hut. We palavered in Malay. Ali and his wife wanted goods but they had no rice or maize to trade. They said the Japanese had taken everything. Ali's house was of bamboo slats chinked with mud. It had a thatched roof and dirt floor. We sat on wooden stools around the table in the light of the palm oil lamp.

Bishop Mekkelholt had asked me to get a few eggs for one of his sick priests.

"Even if they are very expensive, get them," Bishop Mekkelholt had said, "because he is dying."

Mrs. Ali said she would sell two eggs for one silver guilder —fifty cents an egg. Fantastic as was the price I bought two, reflecting that Mrs. Ali was not very grateful for the medicine I had brought her.

We moved to the house of Karman. He was prosperous and had been expecting Breuer. Karman's house was two stories high. A ladder led to the upper floor where we ate and bargained in whispers. Mrs. Karman and several other women appeared. I reached in the knapsack for the crimson sash of Bishop Mekkelholt. That would widen their eyes! The sash wasn't there. I turned the sack inside out. Still no sash. The horrid truth chilled me. It had fallen out when I took my shoes from the sack when we reached the road outside camp.

Breuer traded Karman out of all his rice and maize, about

fifty kilos. There was none left for me and my goods, except a bottle of palm oil Mrs. Karman gave me for a ball of thread.

I packed the bottle and the two eggs into twelve kilograms of rice I agreed to pack back for Breuer. Before entering camp we searched in vain for the sash. For me the trip was a failure. I had lost the sash, worth many kilograms, and gotten only two eggs and a small bottle of palm oil.

Next morning a native bullock herder found the sash, brought it to Seki's office. Seki knew it had come from our camp but could prove nothing. However, the find disclosed our exit and it was bottled up. Smuggling became more difficult.

My third trip was with Mandang again.

"We must fix a Haiho," Mandang decreed, "it is too dangerous otherwise."

My share of the "fix" was one towel and a bar of soap, costing me five kilograms of rice to purchase in camp. Haihos worked around the clock in twelve hour shifts, alternating hours off and on sentry post duty. For example the Haiho going on fence guard duty at 6 P.M. would be relieved at 7 P.M., spend the next hour in the guardhouse and go back to the sentry post at 8 o'clock. And so on through the night until 6 A.M. The Haiho we bribed agreed not to be at a certain spot on the fence at 6:30 P.M. and again at 4:30 A.M. Roll calls were at 6 P.M. and 6 A.M.

At 6:30 P.M., just after roll call and before dark, we wriggled through the fence, gingerly picked our way across the barrier of fallen trees and ducked into the rubber. We took a different route. Although longer, it avoided places we feared might be watched not only by Seki's men but by other Haihos who would demand a cut and "capture" us if we refused. We struggled through a knee deep morass, gained a trail and headed for the main road.

A heavy rainstorm drenched us. We plodded on, slipping, falling, miserable. We reached the main road after dark, at a point about four kilometers from Petanahan. Mandang depended on his keen ears to warn us of approaching traffic in time to jump off the road. None came. The rain stung our flesh like hail. We spied some banana trees, cut off leaves and held them over our heads as shields. At Petanahan we went directly to the house of Mangoen, the head man.

Mangoen's house was more a hall with back room and upper story for living quarters. The hall was a gathering place for his people. Seventy Javanese farmers and their families were scattered over the colony of Petanahan. Mangoen refined palm oil and cured tobacco, in addition to farming.

My trading goods totaled three pairs of shorts, one undershirt, one white polo shirt, one ball of black wool yarn (made from a sweater), two rolls of white thread (made from the Bishop's socks), two silver guilders and two pieces of white muslin cloth each eighteen feet long and one foot wide. Mrs. Mangoen took the thread and cloth and three of Mangoen's friends took the shorts. For my goods I received seventeen kilograms of maize, two kilograms of rice, two beer bottles of palm oil and two live chickens. If kampong chickens are carried by their feet, head down, they do not squawk.

The return trip was easier because my legs and back were stronger. My nerves never got any stronger though. I was always scared going through the fence. Mandang never betrayed fear of anything. He had nerves of steel.

We had started the return trip too late. Although we walked at top speed, without a single stop for rest, dawn was lighting the world when we reached the barrier. It was after 5 A.M., too late for our fixed Haiho. Another guard would be on duty. We would have to risk getting in on our own.

Mandang shed his load and told us to wait while he explored. He crept along the barricade, peeking through and listening. Dawn rapidly became full daylight. We heard the bell clang for 5:30 A.M. tea. That was when we filled our drinking bottles for the day. More time passed. No Mandang. A single clang of the bell warned that roll call was about to ring.

Holy Mackerel! We would have to ditch our loads—and my chickens—and make a break for it.

Mandang suddenly materialized. He seized his sack, threw it over his shoulder and started along the barrier at a dog trot. At a certain place he turned and started across. We followed, over tree trunks and big limbs. Strangely, there were no small dead branches to break and pop and crackle underfoot. We crossed, ran for the fence. On the other side were three of Mandang's friends. They held the wire strands apart and grabbed our loads. Then we went through.

The roll call bell clanged. I ran to my block, jumped up onto my mat and pulled a blanket over my muddy clothing. The block leader changed his roster to include me as a sick man. For roll call, well men lined up outside the block and sick men lay in their beds. Japanese guards counted inside and outside simultaneously so there could be no switching for cover up purposes. I was safe.

Eric came in after roll call. He said,

"Don't give me heart failure like that again."

"My heart's still out there on the fence," I said.

Eric roasted some ubi he had brought back from a raid while I was at Petanahan. I did the trading with natives because I knew some Malay, while Eric, who was huskier and could carry bigger loads, sneaked out to a nearby cultivated area and dug ubi, which was harder to carry.

Seven kilograms of maize were required to pay my share of our debts and the new fix required to get in that morning. Mandang's inside pals had been watching the fence. When they spotted him on the other side of the barrier they went to work. The guard was bribed to stand where he was and talk to them while two others found the best place for us to come through. Mandang then had done a quick but thorough job of removing small dead branches to lessen the noise of our passage at the selected place.

Later that morning I delivered Bishop Mekkelholt his share, including one of the chickens. The other chicken Eric and I planned to fatten and eat on the Fourth of July.

"You'd better say a few prayers of thanksgiving that we got in," I told the Bishop. "We nearly didn't make it."

He laughed.

"I already have," he said. "In fact I offered Mass this morning for the success of your black market expedition."

That established a custom. Whenever we went out smuggling or ubi raiding Bishop Mekkelholt offered a Mass for our safe return.

We named our chicken Oscar and assiduously went about the business of fattening him for a feast July 4th and guarding him from the hazards of camp life. We fed him raw and cooked maize and rice, acquired in our smuggling deals, and grubs we unearthed ourselves around camp. Nothing was too good or too much trouble for Oscar. We guarded him zealously by day and at night staked him under our sleeping bench. We determined to make the Fourth of July, 1945, in Belalau as memorable an event as had been the Fourth of July, 1942, in Palembang Jail. Every year, and this was our fourth Independence Day in captivity, Eric and I had managed to stage some kind of celebration.

The first one, July 4, 1942, in Palembang Jail had been a red letter day to which our Dutch and British friends contributed. Beissel had cooked the dinner for ten. Around the table had been the two honored American guests, Eric and I; my two shipwreck mates Oosten and Colijn, my Camp News partner Allen, Doc West, Van der Vliet who was then Camp Leader, Dr. Hollweg who amazed us by producing a fifth of gin, Camp Poet Curran-Sharp and Beissel himself.

Standing solemnly with upraised tin cups containing Independence Day gin rickeys we had drunk a toast proposed by Allen:

"Gentlemen, I give you the President of the United States of America, Queen Wilhelmina and King George of England."

Three years later, on July 4, 1945, in Belalau, Eric and I raised two tin cups filled with coffee, waved them over Oscar, who lay beautifully fried in an iron skillet, and toasted our good luck in being alive. We said:

"Here's how."

And drank.

Allen, Colijn and Curran-Sharp were dead. West was gone, taken away by the Japanese. We hoped he was still alive. Van der Vliet and Beissel were mere private citizens of the camp, having long since been succeeded as Leader and Chief Cook respectively. With Hollweg we rarely spoke. Beissel and Oosten remembered the day and brought us a present of tobacco.

I wished that Herbert Smallwood of the handlebar moustache was still around to trumpet the Star Spangled Banner as he did on July 4, 1943. I wondered why Christmas and Independence Day meant so much more to me in captivity.

Oscar was our first and last chicken dinner of internment. During ensuing months smuggling became more difficult and dangerous. Frequently we returned empty handed. Let's go on the trip that finished Petanahan:

Again Mandang, Sitanala, Tempelers and I have taken the shortest but most dangerous route, the same one we took on my first trip. As on previous journeys we hurry along the road, circle the Women's Camp, negotiate the fallen trees and rest for awhile on the bridge to smoke and pull leeches from our hides. Tonight there is no moon, the sky is overcast and, except for the road, progress has been painfully slow.

Tempelers suggests we light the torches. Mandang demurs, explaining,

"I don't feel good."

That's his way of saying he has a hunch there is danger ahead. We respect his hunches.

"Mac," says Mandang, "change places with Sitanala and hang onto me. No falling in the gully. We must go slow and quiet. And no lights."

Never have I gone down the steep gully without slipping and falling at least once. Mandang removes his shoes. We do likewise.

"Okay," says Mandang, starting.

"Okay," we echo and begin moving.

I try to follow Mandang's feet with my feet. He takes short, solid steps. At every step his foot seems to become rooted to the ground. Only once has he ever fallen when I was along and that was when a bridge plank broke beneath his weight. My eyes ache from trying to see where sight is impossible. I close them. The quality of darkness is not changed whether my eyes are open or closed. It is like the time my lamp went out in a lead-silver mine where I worked summers while going to college. I had to feel my way for 1200 feet back to a pumping station where I had left my can of fresh carbide fuel for the lamp. The gully's darkness is like that, only more treacherous.

Tempelers, bringing up the rear, slips, thuds down striking Sitanala, who is knocked down and bangs into me. Down I go, striking Mandang, but he stands like a rock. Struggling to my feet I slip and fall into a water filled hole beside the trail. Tempelers is swearing in a shrill whisper and saying his ankle must be broken.

"Take it easy," Mandang says. "Be quiet. We will wait."

We untangle ourselves, continue. My right hip feels as though a sledge hammer had struck it.

After a century or two we are out of the gully and onto the flat, near the main road. We halt, listen and listen and listen. Then listen some more. If ears could stretch, mine would be sweeping the air in all directions like the antennæ of a sightless bug.

This is where the wild pigs frightened us before. The trail we are on is broad and slippery and ends at the road a few hundred feet away. Across the road is Petanahan. We inch forward, feeling with our bare toes before putting down our weight, avoiding twigs and branches. Mandang moves off the trail into the bushes—we following—and halts. At that instant it happens.

The trail is a blaze of light. We freeze at the edge of the trees. The lights do not move to sweep the terrain but remain stationary, pointing along the trail. The sudden growl of an engine starter and roar of a motor indicate that the lights are headlights of a truck parked on the trail where it intersects the road. It is backing onto the road. As it turns the headlights sweep us but our motionless figures probably blend with the trees, for nothing happens. The truck moves only a short distance along the road and halts. Voices sound, sharp staccato Japanese voices. Flashlights dart hither and thither, occasionally flashing in our direction but it is apparent they are not looking for us and do not suspect our presence.

Mandang's hunch had been correct. Had we come down that gully waving a torch, or been even seconds slower leaving the trail, we would have been pinioned in those headlights.

What's going on? A raid on Petanahan?

Another pair of headlights flash on. Another motor sounds. More voices, a rattle as of bayonets being sheathed or unsheathed. The vehicles grind into gear and move, gather speed, disappear.

We remain motionless until my legs go numb from the cramp of holding them rigid. Finally Mandang sits down. We too. Time drags. At last Mandang and Tempelers creep to the road. Another long time, then a whistle. Sitanala and I go. Mandang and Tempelers are in the ditch. They climb out. We leap the ditch, hurry across the road and the other ditch, strike across the fields to the ravine near Barto's. We wait while Mandang calls on Barto. He returns to say Mrs. Barto told him to go away, the Japanese have been there. Did they take her husband? She does not know. He was not home when they called.

We visit house after house, find only women. The Japanese raided Petanahan, searched houses. Wherever they found European clothing the men were arrested. A Javanese farmer had sold some of our clothing in Loeboek Linggau. It had been traced.

The women are anxious to get rid of us. Mandang asks Ali's wife to find Mangoen and bring him to us. She says she will if I doctor her sore leg. Okay. We go into her house. The palm oil lamp is flickering. The sore on her leg is nearly healed. I rebandage it and tell her to leave it alone for a week. Meanwhile, a girl arrives, limping badly. Around her foot is a filthy rag. I remove it. An ulcer. I tell Ali's wife to heat water and soak the girl's foot. While it is soaking Ali's wife goes for Mangoen and we go out and hide in a nearby ubi patch.

Mangoen comes after a long time. He says fifteen men were arrested. He is afraid the Japanese will return. Please, won't we go? He has no more rice or maize and will not trade clothing for palm oil or chickens. I tell him I have thread for his wife and silver guilders for him. I want oil and chickens.

Mangoen owes Mandang thirty kilograms of maize and rice and me five kilograms from a previous deal. Mandang insists on receiving something. We know we can not return. Mangoen finally agrees to pay each of us half of what he owes. He also will buy my thread and silver guilders. We pay him for permission to dig ubi from his patch so we will have full loads. He leaves to get the maize, oil and chickens. While we are digging a man comes running.

"Nippon! Nippon!"

We seize the sacks, drag them far back into the ubi patch and lie down. My heart thumps mightily. Perhaps an hour passes. Nippon does not come. Mangoen appears, says it was a false alarm. He has two bottles of oil and a chicken. Another farmer carries a kaling of maize for Mandang. That is all we can get.

Mangoen leads us over an unfamiliar route winding through Petanahan's rolling fields, hills and ravines. We balance across logs spanning ditches. On one I sit down, ignominiously, and worm across on my backside. The sack of ubi is like a bag of rocks.

Finally we emerge on the road. Mangoen says that directly across the road begins a trail that will take us eventually to a point behind the guardhouse. Mandang leading, we strike the trail. He snails along, frequently testing the ground with his hands. Later he explains that the rubber plantation has different kinds of earth and he can tell approximately where he is by feeling the earth. We come out behind the guardhouse.

I have been carrying the chicken by its feet, head down, and it has been silent for three hours, all the way. But at this moment, directly behind the guardhouse, the chicken flaps its wings and squawks. I fall on it to smother its noise.

"Knife," hisses Mandang.

I have a knife in my hip pocket. Quick as a flash Mandang reaches beneath me, seizes the chicken's neck, throttles it with one hand and grasps it around the body with the other. I whip out the knife, open it, slice the chicken's throat. When not a quiver is left in the bird I roll off it.

We lie for a long time in the bushes beside the creek, behind the guardhouse, listening for the Haihos to walk across the bridge at guard change time. Finally they do. As soon as their footsteps die away, and before the men coming off duty approach, we slip into the creek, duck under the bridge, under the fence and come up inside camp.

After roll call I take the dead chicken to my friends, Quartermaster Thomson and Hospital Bookkeeper Hilling. I had promised them one a long time ago. They wanted to fatten it as Eric and I did ours for the Fourth of July. Now they will have to eat it immediately, skinny as it is.

"Sorry fellows," I say, "but the damn thing just wouldn't cooperate."

I'm too tired to explain further. I go to my bunk and stretch out. My nerves and muscles twitch and jump. I'm afraid that's the last trip to Petanahan.

The following night two smugglers named Smit and Stegeman left for Petanahan. Mandang warned them not to risk it but they ignored him. They did not return.

Two or three friendly Haihos told us not to smuggle any more. They said the rubber estate was being patrolled by Malay field police known as *Jehos*, under direction of Kempeitai officers. It was the job of the Jehos not only to watch for internees but also to keep the Haihos from reaching the native kampongs when off duty and thus bartering goods for grain to resell in our camp. Thus the Haihos also became prisoners in a sense. The Japanese learned they could no longer trust them even to guard us.

Cut off from smuggling we concentrated on ubi raiding.

23

Ubi Raiding

CAMP BELALAU was near one edge of the rubber estate, on the side opposite the hill tract and settlement known as Petanahan. Not far from the camp was another ladang, or cultivated tract, several square miles in area, that had been abandoned except for a small part used by the Japanese. The ladang was bounded on one side by the rubber estate and on three sides by jungle. It was a wild area in which one easily could become lost at night. Patches of ubi kayu, scattered over its hillsides, were targets for our ubi raiders.

Men caught visiting the ladang were not punished as severely as were smugglers who dealt with natives. The Japanese regarded dealing with natives as dangerous to their occupation. Instead of being beaten and turned over to the Kempeitai as were smugglers, the ubi raiders were beaten and imprisoned for thirty days on half rations in a dark room in Seki's quarters.

There was a constant, brisk demand for ubi kayu. It was cheaper—only three to six guilders a kilogram compared with thirty to seventy guilders a kilogram for maize, rice, and beans. Also it had more bulk than the grains. Because of the demand and the lesser risks involved, more men engaged in ubi raiding although comparatively few did it regularly for a living. Eric and I became members of a small circle of men who smuggled ubi regularly on a cash basis. Eventually we were nicknamed the Ubi Kings. We had narrow escapes but were never caught. Many others were less fortunate.

Routes to the ladang, like routes to Petanahan, were limited by geographical as well as by Japanese factors. The shortest route was handicapped by an initial hazard of two fences, the outer fence being about fifty feet beyond the inner one.

A gate used by Japanese to reach their garden in the ladang was in the outer fence. A sentry box was at the gate. When a bribable Haiho was on duty at the gate it was a matter of timing our exits and entrances to a brief period he agreed not to be at the gate. For that purpose a time-piece was necessary. Since I had no watch of my own I usually borrowed a small alarm clock from Hospital Book-keeper Hilling or rented, for a kilogram of ubi, a watch from Direct Action Drysdale, who resigned as British leader five months after his hard won election. If the wrong Haiho was at the gate, or the guards were unexpectedly changed, we had to spend an hour or more circling the camp and coming in elsewhere at our own risk. Haihos, also, some-times betrayed us.

Let's go ubi raiding:

Successfully Eric and I have left camp and now are entering the ladang—a rolling wilderness of tall grass and weeds, scattered trees, swampy ground and bushes which resemble scrub oak and are just as impenetrable. The horizon is a distant black arc where sky meets trees, either rubber or jungle.

A well defined trail continues into the ladang from where we leave the rubber but the trail is deceptive because at a point several hundred meters into the ladang it branches like a river on reaching a swampy delta by the sea. The in-experienced ubi raider is apt to take a false trail that dis-appears in undergrowth. A huge tree towering above its fellows near the ladang edge is the only landmark near the trail. Even that vanishes as we go deeper into the area. A ground mist diffuses the moon's rays, casting an eerie half-light over everything. The Japanese do not know of the ubi patch on this end of the ladang. They guard the other end.

We watch the ground carefully so as not to lose the twisting trail. It guides us to our second landmark, a clump of barren banana trees in the middle of an open space. Up a hill from the trees are the ubi. We reach the ubi and go to work. This patch contains the biggest roots I have ever seen. Some are as large as a man's leg.

The technique of ubi picking is to seize a plant at the base of its thick, brittle stem and, by exerting a steady pull so as not to break off the stalk with a loud pop, uproot it. Two men are required to uproot large ubi, the stems of which are sometimes fifteen to twenty feet high with crooked, leafy branches. Pulling is easier when rain has softened the earth. Once the plant is loosened we feel along the roots, following their underground meanderings, digging with our hands so as not to miss a single tuber.

Crackling noises nearby startle us. We halt. Grunts tell us that other ubi fanciers—wild pigs—also are rooting for dinner. We resume our labors. Each expedition requires a longer time to fill our sacks because the patch is being culled to extinction. Tonight we work our way up to the crest of a little hill and down the other side. Finally our sacks are filled. My carrying capacity now is between twenty and twenty-five kilograms. Eric can pack up to thirty-five.

On a previous trip I learned the foolishness of trying to carry a bigger load than I could lift onto my own back without assistance. The lesson was a hard one:

On that occasion I had taken burly Peter de Groot, Nick Koot's partner in the Bottom Bath business, on his first ubi raid. We had wandered far in our picking and were late starting back. My load was so heavy I couldn't lift it by myself. Peter had to help me. I staggered forward, back bent, chin buried on my chest. We had walked a much longer time than necessary to reach the trail before I realized I had missed it. I began circling to regain my bearings. Peter followed unquestioningly. Finally I had to tell him we were lost. I dropped my load and told him to stay where he was and act as a beacon for me by whistling every two or three minutes while I cast about in ever widening circles to find the trail. It took me nearly an hour and the night was running out.

After we had followed the trail until it became well enough defined so Peter could not lose it, I told him,

"Go ahead of me. You can walk faster with your load and make it in time. I'll keep plugging along and, if necessary, I'll ditch my load and come back for it tonight."

Peter went around me. He was probably fifty feet ahead when a light flashed on him. Caught! I moved off the trail, sank to the ground and rolled over so my sack would not drop with a thud. I was sure they had not yet seen me.

But Peter had not been caught. The light was Mandang returning from a smuggling trip. He had found a new place to trade. The route lay partly through the ladang. He also had found a flashlight that operated, not on batteries, but on a tiny dynamo powered by alternately squeezing and releasing a pistol-like handle. The light blinked on and off as the handle was squeezed and released.

Together we resumed our hike to camp. My load grew heavier at every step. I would stumble and find it impossible to rise. Mandang or Peter would have to help me up. My knees were giving out under the overload. Finally, near the gate, I dropped the sack and began removing part of its contents.

"What's the matter?" asked Mandang.

"I'll never get this through the fence if I don't unload part of it."

"Don't do that," he said, and seizing the sack, swung it onto his own powerful shoulders on top of the knapsack he already was carrying.

"Go on," he said, "we're late."
After that I never carried a load I couldn't lift by myself.

Tonight, when our sacks are filled, Eric and I shoulder them and start for camp. However, instead of climbing back up the hill and going down the other side to the trail, we circle the hill to save time. The moon is still up but a mist has settled at knee height so that the ground is invisible, and our legs disappear from the knees down. It is like wading through water without pressure or wetness. Presently we are on mushy ground, then swampy, then a morass. Another painful lesson. There is no shortcut over unfamiliar ground. We work back to the hill, climb it, sight our banana trees and strike out for the trail.

When we reach the rubber trees we readjust our loads, preparatory to tackling the last stretch to the gate. We find the gate ajar and the sentry box empty. The Haiho has been well bribed. We close the gate, hurry to the inner fence, slip through, wade the creek and are safely home.

One of Mandang's men is waiting for us.

"You're in luck again," he says. "Did you hear the shots?"

"No."

"The Japs caught a bunch coming in from the ladang and beat hell out of them. They are in the guardhouse now."

Eric built a fire while I peeled and washed half a dozen small ubi. Private cooking fires during the night did not excite Japanese curiosity. I think they did not want to know what we were doing.

The Japanese could have kept us in camp by various methods, such as a ring of Japanese guards—because Malay Haihos were too susceptible to bribery—or by building a solid wall around us, or by summarily executing any prisoner caught outside the fence. They had neither the manpower for so many Japanese guards, nor materials for a wall.

Executions would have stopped us but Seki apparently did not wish to indulge in firing squads.

The crime of ubi raiding obviously was not so much in the raiding as in getting caught. It was a kind of grim game we played with the Japanese. The losers paid in beatings and acute starvation for thirty days. The winners ate ubi kayu undisturbed.

Eric and I roasted the ubi, split them lengthwise, removed the tough center fiber and spread palm oil exactly as if we were buttering a roast potato. Ubi kayu hot and roasted was delicious.

When morning came word got around that the American Ubi Kings had made another successful trip. Customers arrived, buying in lots from 250 grams upwards. Our sale price that day was four guilders a kilogram (1000 grams). We sold two-thirds of our load and kept the other third for our own use. When we ran out we would go on another raid.

We brought a kilogram to the Bishop, along with our standing joke.

"Here is a Mass stipend. We made another safe trip."

Eric played a leading role in one of the wildest and most disastrous nights for ubi raiders. We had planned a trip together that night but, when I heard sixteen other internees also were planning to go out and wanted experienced men to lead them, I declined. Crowds were too risky.

Eric agreed to lead a party of four. When the trip began he discovered eight were waiting. He decided to take a chance anyway and got them all through the first fence. Just as he reached the second fence lights flashed. Ambushed! Japanese converged from both sides. Fences were behind and in front. However, the gate already had been partially opened by the bribed Haiho. Eric hurled himself at the opening and was through as rifles cracked and bullets whistled over his head. He leaped off the trail into a tangle of bushes and lay still. Two guards pounded past, running up the trail toward the ladang where they thought he had gone.

The other ubi raiders were trapped inside the fences, caught and taken to the guardhouse. In the confusion the gate was left open. Eric had to get back inside camp before a roll call was held to discover his identity. The open gate was the quickest way. If the bribed Haiho was still in the sentry box he might allow Eric to pass. Eric snaked up to the sentry box on his belly, maneuvered silently so as to get a look at the guard's profile against the sky and thus ascertain if he was the right Haiho. Such an angle view meant that Eric's head was only a few feet from the side of the sentry box. Eric lined up the Haiho's profile with the sky and at that instant the Haiho raised his rifle and fired, not at Eric but through the roof of the box.

Eric leaped up and ran back into the rubber. Japanese and more Haihos came running. A game of blindman's buff ensued with Eric and his pursuers trying to locate each other by sound. Flashlights stabbed the night but he kept out of their range. The interruption had delayed roll call. While Japanese and Haihos beat the bushes and trees at the lower end of camp Eric clawed his way through undergrowth to the upper end, scrambled across the barricade and got through the fence. He was so winded and exhausted when he reached our block he could not speak.

Meanwhile, day shift guards had been called out to supplement the night shift crew. Japanese and Haihos held sack at the fence all night, nabbing other ubi raiders who had left before Eric's gang and were returning unaware of what had happened.

Although Eric got in safely and in time for roll call his identity was revealed by some of his companions who betrayed him in order to escape a beating. Next morning Eric and three other internees were summoned to Seki's office. The other three had not been out but had intended to go and were stopped by the commotion. Eric's betrayers knew of their intentions and told the Japanese they also had been out but, like Eric, must have managed to get back in undetected.

Evidently Seki despised traitors even while he used them. He lectured Eric and the other three on how fortunate they were not to have been shot during the chase, warned them they would be shot next time and told them to go back to camp. The informers he sentenced to the customary thirty days on half rations in the total darkness of the detention room.

Later he told Camp Leader Van Asbeck:

"If you let only experts go to the ladang they will not get caught. Amateurs are bunglers."

What about internees who could neither trade nor smuggle nor raid and who were too poor to buy even ubi?

If they did not have friends to help them and lived solely on the Japanese rations they died, even among the comparative plenty of Belalau. Many men were doomed by beri-beri or chronic malaria or dysentery before they reached Belalau. Extra food could not save them. Others seemed unable to help themselves in any way, either because they feared the risks or simply were constitutionally helpless. Even during the most prosperous smuggling periods there was never enough coming in to supply the demands of all.

Like other smugglers Eric and I had sick friends we helped gratis but our supplies were never enough to go far and our own bellies frequently were empty.

24

By Eastern Windows

"And not by eastern windows only
When daylight comes, comes in the light;
In front the sun climbs slow, how slowly!
But westward look, the land is bright!"
Arthur Hugh Clough, 1819–1861

PRIME MINISTER WINSTON CHURCHILL quoted that stanza, from the poem "Say Not the Struggle Naught Availeth," during a memorable speech to Parliament in gloomy 1941. Churchill's fighting words and the golden hope expressed in the poem echoed around the world to Bangka Island and lodged in the heart of an obscure missionary priest, Father Benedictus Bakker. They helped give Father Bakker courage when the Japanese overran his parish, disrupted his work of a lifetime, destroyed his beloved music and threw him into prison. They so inspired him during dark days of imprisonment that, in gratitude, he set the poem to music, dedicated the composition to Churchill and taught it to the choir in Palembang Jail.

I wondered how Father Bakker could compose in the babel of the jail. Perhaps it was because the songs in his heart drowned out the noises of men.

He was such a small man that friends made him a podium on which to stand while directing his singers. One of his happiest moments was the night he used it during a jail concert and conducted the choir in singing for the first time the poem he had set to music:

> *Say not the struggle naught availeth,*
>   *The labour and the wounds are vain,*
> *The enemy faints not, nor faileth,*
>   *And as things have been they remain.*
>
> *If hopes were dupes, fears may be liars;*
>   *It may be, in yon smoke conceal'd,*
> *Your comrades chase e'en now the fliers,*
>   *And, but for you, possess the field.*
>
> *For while the tired waves, vainly breaking,*
>   *Seem here no painful inch to gain,*
> *Far back, through creeks and inlets making,*
>   *Comes silent, flooding in, the main.*
>
> *And not by eastern windows only,*
>   *When daylight comes, comes in the light;*
> *In front the sun climbs slow, how slowly!*
>   *But westward look, the land is bright!*

Besides his God, his church, his mission, his music and Mr. Churchill, Father Bakker had another love: Queen Wilhelmina. So for her he also composed and dedicated a song. The choir sang it first on her birthday, August 31, 1942.

Father Bakker had intended to send his compositions to Churchill and Wilhelmina after the war. He asked me one day, while we were exchanging language lessons, if I would send the manuscripts to the Prime Minister and the Queen should anything happen to him. I promised.

"Whenever I am worried," said Father Bakker, "I think of how Mr. Churchill and our Queen are beset by world shaking problems; then my own troubles seem small."

Just as Churchill and Wilhelmina inspired Father Bakker, so that little priest's zeal, devotion and music inspired us, his fellow prisoners. The choir was more than pleasant entertainment. Amid the dirt, suffering and concentrated meannesses of men in prison, the choir was a symbol both of man's better nature and of achievement. It not only cheered us at concerts but lent a needed warmth and solemnity to funerals, the last gestures we could make for departed friends.

Death and disease reduced the choir's ranks until it ceased to function. Christmas, 1944, was its last appearance. The beginning of the end for Father Bakker himself had been when his twenty-nine fellow Bangka missionaries entered Muntok Prison from Pangkal Pinang and he worked himself to exhaustion trying to save them. Death took seventeen of them, including Monsignor Bouma who died in Belalau April 19, 1945.

As Father Bakker's own strength began to fail he drove himself to complete a project to which he had dedicated his talents: a composition in a new style of music for a complete Mass. He had a premonition his time was short so he worked on the manuscript each day as long as there was light to see. Finally, he collapsed and was taken into hospital.

The soup Eric and I brought could only cheer his spirits, it was too late to help his body. On an afternoon in June, 1945, I had something besides soup to cheer him. A new internee had arrived in camp with authentic news of American victories in the Pacific. He was an Indo-European radio technician who had been forced to work for the Japanese keeping in repair military transmitters and receivers in Palembang. He said American broadcasts had made much of the capture of an island named Iwo Jima, describing it as the first real Japanese soil conquered by American forces. Now Tokyo could be bombed at will.

I had lost my twenty-five guilder bet that the war would

end by June 1st but I made another wager with Doc Lentze that we would be free by September 1st. The loser was to give the winner a chicken.

Dr. Lentze, Harrison and others, who had remained in Muntok with fifteen patients too sick to be transported, had rejoined us in Belalau after eleven patients died and four improved sufficiently to travel.

Father Bakker smiled weakly when I told him of the chicken bet. But his eyes lighted at the news of Iwo Jima. He needed something more than Churchill's words to cheer him now. His life was draining away. "Intestines," as the Japanese would say. His black Vandyke beard failed to hide drawn lips and sunken cheeks. The pinched look of death was in his face. His arms lay limply beside him. He fingered a rosary with one hand as we talked.

"It can't be long now, Father," I said. "The radio says Iwo Jima is only about seven hundred miles from Japan. In a couple of months we'll walk out of here together."

"I am afraid not, Mac," he said. "I am exhausted and now I have the dysentery."

He paused to gather breath for more words.

"I am trying but I have no strength."

He rested awhile, then,

"Maybe you will see Iwo Jima after the war."

"Perhaps I will."

"If you do, say a prayer for me when you get there, and say one also for the Japanese. Don't hate them."

He gathered his breath for more words.

"Don't forget the manuscripts, will you, Mac?"

"I won't forget. I promise you they will be delivered." *

Father Bakker died June 14, 1945, at Belalau. His grave is the sixty-eighth in the clearing among the rubber trees.

* Representatives of United Press delivered the manuscripts early in 1946. Mr. Churchill, through the British Consul in Miami, Florida, where he was visiting at the time; and Queen Wilhelmina, through her secretary, wrote me, acknowledging receipt of the songs. I hope that in their busy lives they found time to have them played.

"Say a prayer for the Japanese. Don't hate them."

Father Bakker had asked that in behalf of those responsible for his death. His heart had been too big for hate. That was my second object lesson in charity in Belalau. The first had been shortly after our arrival in March, 1945.

Bishop Mekkelholt was in hospital with dysentery. He sent word he would like to see me. He was lying on the end of a row. I squatted down beside the bench. He did not waste words.

Naming a man I despised and who was no friend of the Bishop's, he said,

"An emergency appeal has been made for quinine hydrochloride to give him."

Pills containing the compound quinine hydrochloride could be dissolved into liquid for hypodermic injection in cases of severe malaria. One pill was sufficient for one injection. Other types of quinine could not be used for injection but had to be taken by mouth.

I knew what was coming. I had a few pills of quinine hydrochloride. Bishop Mekkelholt wanted me to give them up.

Just before leaving Muntok, Harrison handed me the pills saying,

"Doc West gave me these in case you got another bad attack of malaria. Now that we're being separated you had better take them."

Already I had given away some of the pills. They had helped save a priest ward attendant who was dying of malaria. That was how Bishop Mekkelholt had learned of them. Now he was asking me to give away some more—not for himself, nor for one of his priests, nor even for a friend, but for a man who, to say the least, was no friend of his and who was an enemy of mine. In my opinion the man had done much harm in camp, from the time he first joined us in Muntok Prison. He had not been with us in

Palembang. I can not say more about him without revealing his identity.

"He isn't worth saving," I said, "and even if he were he doesn't really need them. I saw him this morning and he is not critically ill. He only thinks he is."

Bishop Mekkelholt thought differently, saying,

"Dr. Kampschuur says the man has both dysentery and malaria and is allergic to quinine by mouth. One or two injections now will stop the malaria and enable him to fight off the dysentery."

"No, Bishop. I have only ten pills left and I might need them to save myself or a friend, or some one more valuable to the camp than he."

"Mac," said the Bishop, "he may have done some mischief but he also is capable of doing much good. It is not for you or me to judge the value of a life."

I hesitated.

"Please, Mac," said the Bishop, and he smiled. "I'll pray that you don't get malaria."

I returned to my bunk, got five pills and gave them to the Bishop, saying,

"Give them to the doctor for him but don't say where they came from."

The remaining five pills were used to help save a young Englishman who was critically ill with malaria.

Neither man was ever told the origin of the pills.

Things began occurring in August which encouraged me to believe I might win my bet of a chicken with Dr. Lentze.

On August 18th four-motored planes passed over camp, but they were too high for identification. I believed the Japanese did not have four-motored, land based planes and that the planes therefore were British or American. If they were Allied craft there should have been an air raid alarm. Since no alarm, why?

On August 20th Smit and Stegeman, the smugglers who had disappeared, returned. They said they had been caught by Japanese on the trail to Petanahan, imprisoned, but not beaten.

August 21st several Haihos ran away. Their fellows sent a spokesman into camp at night to ask a Dutch official what fate awaited Haihos when the Japanese surrendered. The official told him that depended on the individual Haiho.

August 23rd a Japanese machine gun company replaced the Haihos. That night two Japanese guards, who had been trading with internees, returned goods they had taken for resale in Loeboek Linggau and paid debts they owed the prisoners.

Simultaneously Seki announced a phenomenal ration increase, quadrupling the amount we had been receiving.

August 24th at 2 P.M. all men who could walk were summoned to gather outside the barbed wire, near Seki's office. That was the first time such a thing had happened. We felt sure the war had ended.

Seki appeared, accompanied by the interpreter, whose face was swollen from an infected tooth. Tani, the medical sergeant, and a Japanese major also were there. Guards remained at their usual posts and did not come near us.

A table had been placed under the rubber trees. Seki and the interpreter mounted it. Seki spoke in Japanese, a few sentences at a time, and the interpreter translated. It was a long speech. I will only paraphrase its substance.

"'Tuans," the interpreter said, and we pricked up our ears. Heretofore the interpreter always had been careful to address us by using a Malay phrase which was considered an insult because it was used only in addressing coolies. Now he spoke to us politely as Tuans.

"By the will of the Emperor," Seki said through the interpreter, "the war is ended. The Emperor has decided to end the war because the Americans are fighting cruelly and using a new type of bomb. It is called atom bomb. The Emperor does not wish to continue such a cruel and inhuman war. Therefore the war is ended. Once more we are friends."

Seki paused. There was no sound from his listeners. Curious to see how men would react to one of the greatest announcements of their lives, I studied the faces around me. Most of them were expressionless. Not a murmur rose from the crowd. There were no displays of emotion.

Seki continued:

"American soldiers, and perhaps also British, will come to occupy Sumatra. [He said something else about American troops but I missed it.] We Japanese soldiers will soon go home. I have been in charge of you since April, 1944, and I have done my best for you. I know it has not been enough but I was powerless to do more.

"Men and women now may visit each other's camps in the daytime. Each internee must remain here until the new occupation forces come. There will be no more roll calls."

So this was my last roll call. I thought of my first in Palembang Jail the morning of April 6, 1942. Standing in line that morning had been well fleshed, shirtless men in various stages of sunburn. Today, August 24, 1945, most survivors of that first roll call were rail thin and uniformly suntanned. Some were shambling skeletons who had severely taxed their strength to stagger out here. Others, like Eric and me, were gaunt but holding their own as a result of smuggled food. A few were fat.

I thought of those missing from this last roll call who were lying now in hospital or their cell blocks, too sick to walk, or in the cemeteries of Palembang, Muntok and Belalau.

Seki's voice and the interpreter's barking brought my thoughts back to the business of learning we were free. Why did they keep talking, repeating over and over the message we had waited so long to hear? Seki went into considerable detail on what we should and should not do until the Allied soldiers came. We were still in his custody and, until he should be relieved of his post, he was responsible for our well-being. Well-being! Ha!

Finally he finished, repeating again:

"Let us be friends once more."

He stepped down from the table, turned and walked back to his office.

I asked a Dutch Indo-European beside me,

"Did you understand exactly what he said about the American troops?"

The man looked as if he were about to burst into tears. His eyes were misty and when he spoke his voice was choked. He said:

"He didn't say anything about our Queen!"

I was so astonished all I could reply was,

"Didn't he?"

"No," sobbed the Indo-European and now he really was crying. "No. He didn't say a word about our Queen."

That was the kind of hold Wilhelmina had on the hearts of her people.

As we walked back into camp a buzz of voices rose. Men smiled and shook hands with each other. There were no shouts. Eric and I sat down by our fireplace. Passers-by, enroute to their own blocks, shook our hands. I felt no exhilaration. We had been expecting the announcement. Seki's words seemed an anti-climax. For three years, four months and nineteen days I had wondered what this moment would be like. Often I had discussed it. However, my imagination had balked at envisaging it. Now it had come, with no particular thrill, and was over. Perhaps the lack of thrill was because we still were so far from freedom. The war had long ago caught us up, spilled us into imprisonment and passed on. Fighting had been distant and unreal, like the new peace.

I rose and walked the length of camp to the hospital to

see how patients were taking the news. They were far more emotional than their healthier fellow prisoners.

Three beri-beri patients were "dancing" in the aisle—strutting grotesquely up and down, performing stiff gyrations on their swollen limbs. Those who could not walk lay in their beds, some laughing, some crying, a few singing.

Andrew Carruthers, 27, radio announcer for the Malayan Broadcasting Corporation, who had been a prime organizer of our pre-Muntok shows, was crying. Tears streamed down his beri-beri swollen face. He said he was crying both from happiness and pain.

"Now I will get well," he said. "Soon the Allied soldiers will be here with medicine to save me. They surely will. I'm so happy."

When I first saw Carruthers, standing in line on my first roll call in Palembang Jail, he had been a slender, gracefully formed chap. Now, the last roll call had sounded and, except for his eyes and voice and shining hope, he was nearly unrecognizable.

Other men were lying there as badly off as Carruthers, but I remember him best because of his shining hope.

"I'll recover in no time," he said, "as soon as the Allies arrive with vitamin injections."

But one day followed another and no Allies came. We were too far from anywhere.

Carruthers' wife came from the Women's Camp to find her husband. She shuddered, halted and closed her eyes when she entered our thatch-roofed hospital. Quickly, however, she recovered herself and walked down the aisle toward her husband's bed on the other end of the ward. She passed the patients who had both beri-beri and dysentery, each one of them a sodden, living stench. Their eyes were slits in swollen, putty-colored faces. Serum oozed through rag bandages, soaked blankets of rice sacking, and dripped through bamboo bed slats to the earthen floor. It was as though their bodies were inexhaustible reservoirs whose contents were being forced by hydraulic pressure through distended skins.

Since February, 1942, Mrs. Carruthers had waited for this moment. Through three years and a half of misery she had anticipated their reunion when the war was over. And her husband too. Now it had come and she was walking to meet him, the last man in a row of beri-beri cases.

Attendants had managed to prop him up a little bit, so he was not lying flat. She reached his bed and smiled and kissed him.

"Don't worry, now," he told her. "I'm going to be all right. Vitamin injections are all I need and the Allies will have those when they come."

Four paratroopers,* three Dutch and one Chinese, dropped to locate prison camps, found us September 6th. They said hostilities had ceased three weeks before on August 15th. They radioed our location to their headquarters across the Indian Ocean in Colombo, Ceylon.

Planes flew up from the Cocos Islands about eight hundred miles away, in the Indian Ocean, and dropped food and medicine. But it was too late to save six men, including Carruthers. He died September 9th, still bright with hope and with his wife beside him.

* The paratroopers, working with British forces, were members of the *Korps Insulinde* of the Royal Netherlands East Indies Army. Their names: Regimental Sergeant-Major Hakkenberg, Corps Officer Wilhelm, Sergeant Van Hasselt, and the Chinese officer, Suet. Twenty paratroopers, flown from Colombo, Ceylon, and dropped at five key points of Sumatra, "occupied" the entire island, sixth largest in the world.

25

New Brews in Old Bottles

"ASIDE from G.I. Joe," said the Dutch paratroopers who found our Belalau Camp, "they say three things won the war: the Dakota, the Jeep and penicillin."

They were talking strange jargon from another world. Who or what was G.I. Joe? And a Jeep? A Dakota and penicillin? They told of other wonders, of such incongruities as radar and jet propulsion and rocket bombs. And of that "inhuman" weapon of which Seki had spoken, the atom bomb.

They confirmed rumors we had heard that Hitler and Mussolini were dead and answered another question that had puzzled us ever since the Japanese themselves informed us President Roosevelt had died. Who was Truman?

"Rip Van Winkle II" the paratroopers dubbed me when I fired questions about things that made them laugh, they were so old to them and new to me.

When the paratroopers walked into camp they found about half the living inmates were walking skeletons, a quarter cast respectable shadows and some even were fat. Statistically our mortality rate was difficult to estimate because the Dutch population had fluctuated radically as we moved from place to place. An over-all figure for Dutch deaths based on the highest number of Hollanders in camp at any one time, would be slightly over 38 percent. The British mortality rate was easy to figure: of 200 originally in

322

Palembang Jail, 109 died, for a score of 54½ percent. Of the 200 men who joined us in Muntok from Pangkal Pinang, the death rate was nearly 60 percent.

The appearance of the Women's Camp appalled us when we reached there but the women, statistically, had survived better than the men. Thirty per cent of British women had died and twenty per cent of the Dutch.

Higher mortality rates for the British in both camps were attributed to the fact that the English had two strikes against them initially. Most had been shipwrecked and come ashore penniless and without belongings to trade for food in prison camp. Also they were not as adept at survival as the Dutch.

Women doctors attributed the generally lower death rates in the Women's Camp to three things: first, nurses to care for the sick; second, slightly better food and treatment, although this item would be highly debatable; and third, mental vitality.

There were numerous stories of women having been slapped by irritated guards, of having been punished for rules infractions by being made to stand at attention in the yard when mosquitoes were thickest in the early evening, or of having been made to cultivate gardens in the hottest part of the day. However, there was not a single instance of women being otherwise molested by the Japanese. The women doctors and the British and Dutch Camp Leaders said the same thing on that score:

"The Japanese officers and guards never made improper advances to us. Only women who wanted to flirt were flirted with."

Leader of the Dutch women was the nun, Mother Laurentia, while the leader of the British women was the only American in camp, Milwaukee-born Mrs. Gertrude B. Hinch, wife of the head master of the Anglo-Chinese school in Singapore.

Neither men nor women had atrocity stories to relate,

unless Japanese utter neglect and indifference in allowing us to starve in a land of plenty could be called an atrocity. When I saw the hunger-stunted children in the Women's Camp I believed it could.

When the paratroopers told us of other prison camps, like the German-run horror holes of Dachau and Belsen, I decided that instead of having suffered hell, as we thought we had, our experience had been only purgatorial.

In the Women's Camp I quickly found the three Colijn girls who, with their father, had shared my shipwreck adventures. Antoinette had fully recovered from her machine gun wounds. Allette was a woman, in contrast to the girl I remembered. Helen, the oldest, was but a shadow of the young woman who had pulled an oar in our lifeboat. She was in the hospital, yellow with jaundice and malaria and suffering skin sores. However, her condition was not critical and she was recovering rapidly as a result of Japanese medicine and food.

Anxious to atone for their neglect, the Japanese flooded both camps with food, medicine and clothing. They sent doctors and "Red Cross" men. One of the "Red Cross" men was recognized by former victims as a Kempeitai officer who had grilled them in Pangkal Pinang.

After September 13th British planes showered us almost daily with parachute packages in metal cylinders. Although several such packages crashed through barrack roofs onto sleeping benches no one was injured. The crew of one plane attached a puckish note telling of elections in England and ending with:

"What do you think of the labour government?"

Thus we learned Churchill and his cabinet had fallen.

Strangest contribution to our ever growing pile of supplies was cloth—bolts and bolts of cloth the Japanese had been hoarding. We promptly traded all the cloth, and most of the Japanese army clothing issued to us, for chickens, ducks and fish. We scoured the countryside in search of meat.

Welcome as were the parachuted tinned goods they were not fresh meat, which we craved more than anything else. We visited our Javanese friends of Petanahan. Many of them had just been liberated from the Kempeitai prison in Loeboek Linggau. They showed us scars from the beatings they suffered when their inquisitors tried to learn names of internees with whom they had traded. Mangoen, the head man, was in bad shape.

I spent half a night sitting in Mangoen's hall talking with Javanese farmers who wanted to hear about America and to know what I thought would happen to them now that the war was over. My Malay was not good enough for a political discussion but one man, whom I had not met before and who spoke a little English, helped bridge the language gap.

While we smoked raw tobacco, drank black coffee, munched fried ubi kayu chips and talked, the others listened intently and occasionally put questions. Their spokesman wanted to know if now the Indonesians would be regarded as equals by Dutch, British and Americans.

My answers were vague. I believed they would find little difference in the attitude of white men toward them but I did not like to say so. On the other hand I also was determined not to tell any lies just to make them happy. So I mumbled about the Atlantic Charter and its four freedoms and guarantees for self determination of peoples.

I felt ashamed when I mentioned the charter because I did not believe its guarantees were worth the paper they had been written on. Apparently the spokesman did not either for he said, in effect,

"If we Indonesians are treated as inferior people after the war the same as before there will be trouble."

One question the colonists of Petanahan asked over and over: "When are the Americans coming?"

"When the Americans come" seemed to be a millenium they expected and eagerly awaited. Maybe that was why they treated me so cordially. They made me feel they liked me. I know I liked them.

About midnight I left Mangoen's house. Radi, waving a blazing torch, led me to Barto's where earlier in the day I had feasted on chicken, rice and coconut pudding. Rain was falling but not hard enough to extinguish the torch. My bed that night was in a recess just below the eaves of Barto's house. It was reached by a ladder from the chicken yard and, although theoretically protected from the elements by the roof and by being on the leeward side of the house, was open to anything which might blow contrary to the prevailing wind. Since my clothing was wet and the bedding consisted only of the straw mat on which I lay, all the breezes felt contrary.

Next morning I spent trading around Petanahan and acquired six chickens. When I started back to camp Radi and his wife begged me to do something for their only child, a malaria withered infant of ten months, but so tiny he looked about two. Each of their previous three children had died in infancy of malaria. Could I not save this one?

"We will take him to the doctors in camp," I said.

A heavy thunder shower drenched us before we had gone half way. The baby was wrapped in a tarpaulin to keep dry. We slipped and slithered along the same trail I had traveled with Mandang on our smuggling trips. Now, however, the fallen trees had been removed. I wondered how we used to make it in the dark.

Japanese sentries stopped us at the front gate. Natives were not allowed inside camp. (A few days later, however, ragged natives entered in droves to trade.)

"Baby dying!" I shouted in Malay, and brushed past the guards.

Radi's wife, who was carrying the infant, was too frightened to follow. She was an undernourished wisp of a thing less than five feet tall and nervously chewing betel nut. The thunder shower had chilled her and now she was beginning to shiver from incipient malaria that broke out on slightest provocation. I seized her arm and dragged her past the sentries. They protested feebly but made no further effort to stop us.

Doctor Kampschuur was as startled as the sentries when I walked into his quarters with the woman and child. However, he gave her special quinine for infants and ordinary quinine for herself.

Eric and I went to Petanahan a week later with more quinine and some cod liver oil. When he gave it to me Kampschuur said,

"I am afraid it is no use because that child has had chronic malaria too long."

He guessed correctly. We arrived at Radi's house to learn the baby had died. We gave presents of cloth and tinned butter, issued by the Japanese, to Radi, Barto, Ali and their wives. It happened to be the first day of the Moslem New Year. In every Javanese hut was open house and on every table were cakes and sweets, coffee and tobacco. They were unbelievably poor, those Javanese farmers, but they were rich in hospitality.

On my last afternoon in camp I paid a farewell call to the cemetery in the rubber trees with its ninety-five graves. There lay Kendall, who had succeeded Old Pop as ward matron; Phillips who had posted the 25,000 guilder wager offer that we would be free by January 1, 1944 (he died July 5, 1945, when freedom was so near); Carruthers of the shining hope; Allen, my first cell mate; Father Bakker and the man he had tried so hard to save, Monsignor Bouma, Vicar Apostolic of Bangka Island.

Unless these graves were constantly tended they soon would be covered by advancing undergrowth. The cemeteries of Muntok and Palembang were better off in that respect. They were in city burial grounds.

That night I said goodbye to my best smuggling customer, Bishop Mekkelholt.

"If you are able," the Bishop asked, "please send us some wheat flour for communion hosts and some altar wine."

Sacramental wine and hosts are necessary for celebration of Mass. The priests had managed to say Mass daily for over three years by rationing their wine supply with an eye dropper and dividing hosts into fractional particles. The supplies and the war ended almost simultaneously. I promised to send wine and wheat flour from the first place they could be found.

Father Elling who, burning with malarial fever, lay nearby in his bedspace on the floor, sat up to wish me luck. He said something about the future of the missions.

"You'd better return to Holland and recover your health and then think about the missions," I said.

"Nonsense," he said. "Now is when the natives need us."

The following afternoon, September 19th, a month and four days after V-J Day, Australian planes flew us back to the world we had left in 1942. We landed in Singapore. In the airport canteen Eric met Lloyd, the other man who escaped from the Japanese executioners on the shore of Bangka Island. The two had met before, when they congratulated each other in Muntok Prison shortly after that macabre beach party in February, 1942. Now they exchanged congratulations on their second identical escape—this time from prison camp.

I found Doc West * in the Raffles Hotel. He was worn from dysentery but on his feet. Conditions in the Palembang military camp, where he was taken from Muntok Prison, had been considerably better than in Muntok, he said, until the last quarter of 1944; after that they deteriorated rapidly. Beginning in May, 1945, the Japanese pursued a deliberate policy of wiping out the military prisoners by starvation. Rations were drastically and systematically

---

* For his services to military prisoners of war and civilian internees in Muntok and Palembang, Dr. West was decorated after the war with the Order of the British Empire.

cut in graduating percentages during May, June, July and August. Survivors were to have been massacred by machine gun in a barbed wire stockade on August 27th, according to a friendly Korean guard who kept prisoners informed of Japanese plans for them. The stockade was built and preparations for the execution were going forward when liberation came.*

More than anything else in Singapore, even more than a glass of fresh milk and a dish of ice cream, I wanted to find the Press Relations Office and start sending cables. When I found it I felt I was back in civilization. At last I could relax. In a cloth belt worn next to my skin I had been carrying the most essential of the notes transcribed after I buried my diaries in 1943. Also in the belt were my passport and press credentials which I managed to save through everything, including swimming in the sea. Feeling secure among friends I removed the belt and put it in a little sack containing my recent diaries and other possessions, then went to work writing cables. Someone, probably a hungry Chinese messenger, took the sack. It was found later in a garbage can minus the belt, notes and credentials. Luckily, however, two diary notebooks still were there.

A few days later two plane loads of American correspondents arrived in Singapore. Among them were several friends of my Tokyo and Shanghai days and Vern Haugland of Associated Press whom I had known at home in Salt Lake City. When I told Vern of my buried diaries in Sumatra and my recently stolen notes he and other correspondents arranged to fly me to Palembang to dig them up.

The plane which brought us there was the first American craft to land in Palembang after V-J Day. It caused quite a stir. The Japanese who, ironically, now were policing

* Japanese officers and non-commissioned officers in charge of military camp in Palembang were tried by a British tribunal in Singapore and were executed. A Dutch War Crimes tribunal in Sumatra tried Japanese in charge of civilian internees and sentenced Seki to fifteen years and the commander of the Women's Camp to six years.

Sumatra under Allied supervision, because there were no Allied troops for that purpose, supplied us automobile transportation into town.

We stopped first at Charitas Hospital which had been opened that day, September 28th, by Mother Alacoque who had survived her term of Kempeitai imprisonment. She said she was alive because one of the Indonesian jailers had smuggled food to her "and by God's grace I did not get dysentery."

The medicines and bandages the nuns had given native friends in Palembang to hide until the war's end were returned and made possible the re-opening.

Bishop Mekkelholt greeted us. He was wearing a glistening white cassock. Around his waist was a crimson sash similar to the one I had lost on a smuggling trip. I handed him a package containing altar wine and wheat flour for communion hosts that had been flown to a Singapore church from Australia. For the first time in our long acquaintance he was at a loss for words. Father van Gisbergen, the newspaper translator, was there, too, grinning like the proverbial Cheshire cat. Father Elling was still in Belalau.

We drove to Palembang's principal hotel. In the airy lobby, from which Japanese officers had been ousted a few days before, sat the oil men, Oosten, De Bruyn and others. While the correspondents visited the Shell and Standard refineries outside Palembang to survey the accuracy of Allied bombing, I went after my diaries.

Oosten and another oil man named Schoorel went along with me. Our bodyguards were Colonel C. A. Coltharp, pilot of the plane that brought me, and Lieutenant V. W. Pennanen. We found Barracks Camp, where the diaries were buried, a shambles. After the men had been transferred to Muntok, in September, 1943, the women had been moved into Barracks Camp. When the women also were taken to Bangka Island, the camp had been turned into a Japanese truck depot. Some barracks had been demolished but the floor of the hospital was still intact. I measured off twenty-seven feet from what had been the bathroom corner, dug under the foundation and found the first bottle.

By this time Japanese soldiers, some of whom had been our former guards, had arrived on the scene. They watched intently but made no move to interfere. The Allies, as personified by Colonel Coltharp and Lieutenant Pennanen, both armed, were masters now.

Three feet beyond the first bottle I dug again and found the second. Another three feet and the cylindrical tin containing Camp News was uncovered. The first layer of tin had rusted through but the second layer was intact. Koot had insulated the container well. It had been buried a month over two years. The bottles were undamaged and the diaries in perfect condition.

Oosten and Schoorel returned to the hotel. Coltharp, Pennanen and I directed the chauffeur to drive to Palembang Jail.

"Open up," we ordered the Japanese jailer.

He swung open the iron gates which had received me the night of Easter Sunday, April 5, 1942. Instinctively I glanced up over the gate, as I had done that first sickening night, and saw the date "A.D. 1883."

The jail had been refurbished. The barbed wire dividing the yard into sections was fresh and taut. The cell doors which we had removed to use as bed frames and for other purposes had been replaced and were closed and locked. Behind them, at rigid attention, stood thin, ragged, dark-skinned prisoners, Malay, Chinese, Ambonese. They were utterly quiet. We stood for a moment stunned by the impact of the place. It was worse than I remembered it.

Coltharp voiced my feelings when he said, "This is horrible."

Just like the Japanese officers who had inspected us as

prisoners in this same jail while we stood at rigid attention, Coltharp, Pennanen and I walked around the jail inspecting the prisoners who now stood where once I had stood. I thought I knew something of what they felt. And I was sick inside. Had they been our recent Japanese captors I might have gloated. But they were not. They were poor, forgotten natives who had been here since heaven knew when and who were still here more than a month after the war ended. I turned to the jailer, who was keeping a respectful distance.

"For what are these men being held?"

"Murder. Theft. Lawbreaking."

"Where are the political prisoners?"

"We have none."

I did not believe him but could prove nothing contrary.

"How long have they been here?"

He shrugged.

I looked over the little hedge into what once had been the clinic where Allen and I had lived, and into the other room where dysentery patients had lain with Old Pop ministering to them. Women were there now, hollow cheeked, staring. The rooms had reverted to their pre-war status as quarters for female prisoners. The clock had spun around four years lacking two months and eleven days since Pearl Harbor and the hands were right back where they had started, as far as Palembang Jail was concerned.

In the rear of the jail we found a dozen emaciated prisoners sitting on mats on the covered walk. I stared at them and then at the jailer.

"Dysentery," he said.

The cycle was complete.

Suddenly one of the human wrecks spoke in English.

"Help me, in the name of God, please help me."

The only help we could give him was to ask his name, which was Li Tai Sun, and give it to the British and Dutch prisoner of war teams now in charge of Palembang. Li Tai

Sun was a Chinese from Penang, Malaya. He said he had been a lorry driver in the British defense corps during 1941–42 fighting in Malaya and had come to Sumatra from Singapore as a "volunteer" in a Japanese sponsored "People's Army" work unit. In Palembang he had deserted. I asked him,

"Will the jailer beat you for having spoken to us?"

"I don't know. Probably."

I warned the jailer,

"Don't harm this man. We are coming back for him."

Actually we could neither come back for him nor take him with us. He was too sick to care for himself and he had no friends to care for him in the city outside. We could not take a dysentery-ridden man in a crowded plane to Singapore. We could only appeal to the compassion of harried Allied officers to investigate this jail and its native prisoners and do something for Li Tai Sun.

"It's getting late," said Coltharp. "We've got to make Singapore before dark."

Pennanen had a camera. He took some pictures and we walked toward the gate.

Strange, I thought, this place now is so grim. In Muntok and Belalau we had looked back on Palembang Jail as our time of prosperity. The present prisoners were less crowded than we had been. Maybe it was their air of silent hopelessness that now made the jail so forbidding; that, and the locked cell doors.

The jailer opened the inner gates for us and closed them while we stood in the corridor. The outer gates were opened; we stepped through and they clanged shut behind us. We walked to the waiting automobile. Two Japanese officers passing by snapped to attention and saluted us. We returned the salute, climbed into the car and were driven to the airport.

I gave Li Tai Sun's name to a Dutch officer who promised to investigate.

The correspondents had returned from inspecting the refineries. They said Allied bombing had done comparatively little damage. Although much of the Standard plant had been destroyed by its American operators prior to Japanese occupation, the Japanese had combined the two plants and claimed to have operated them at about one-third capacity to the end of the war.

We climbed into the bomber. It roared down the runway which had been extended by British and Dutch military prisoners under Japanese direction. The plane rose, circled Palembang, the refineries, followed the course of the Moesi river to the Bangka Straits and headed north for Singapore.

Now I was leaving Sumatra, home of little brown men toiling in ladangs, of the Tuan Besar—literally, Mr. Big—as colonial big shots are called by natives, and of King Kong, monstrous ape of the silent movie era. The things I had seen and done in that land below me now seemed as distant and unreal as the King Kong thrill picture of so many years ago. I had to look at my malaria yellowed hands to make the immediate past seem true.

King Kong, you may remember, was a Hollywood version of the orang-utan, a genuine anthropoid ape that lives in Sumatra's jungles. I wondered what Hollywood would do with another Sumatra denizen, the Tuan Besar.

Had the war changed him? True, the prison camps had shrunk his paunch until it was little more than a series of wrinkles over a bony pelvis. But had his mind shrunk with it or had the experience given new breadth to his thinking and his values? For three and one-half years he had slept cheek by jowl with all manner of men. Now he knew what it was to hunger and live on the ragged edge of poverty. Would the experience influence his dealings with the little brown men who had known poverty for centuries? Or would he try to climb back on his pedestal and expect the little brown men to support him once more in style to which the Tuan Besar for generations had been accustomed? I was afraid many Tuans would try to resume the pedestals, with disastrous consequences to themselves and their colonial world.

There had been exceptions among the Tuans. Some minds and hearts had expanded to such proportions as to transform their owners into enlightened human beings. But I was afraid their voices would not be heard in the clamor for guilders and dollars.

Nor would the fault lie entirely with the colonials. Already there were ominous signs from Indonesian extremists. Correspondents had told me that in Java the newly self-proclaimed Indonesian Republic was holding as hostages the Dutch internees who had spent the war looking forward to Allied liberation. The internees still were prisoners, but of the Indonesians. Having seen the Haihos I shuddered to think what they would do when under no restraint. They had all the makings of first class gangsters.

Already it looked as if the liberation and the forces it had released would only breed more hates.

I was glad I had met some good men, both white and dark, to remember when hate stoked the furnaces of discord.

26

Return

THE road back to life from the peculiar burial that was internment really began in Singapore. There I fattened up for a week at an army mess to which I was brought by Captain Gunnar Larson, the first American I met on arriving from prison camp. Larson was on hand again when I returned from digging up my diaries.

"Come on," he said, grabbing my arm and rushing me to a squat, stripped-down vehicle with the strange name *Jeep*, "we're going to the airport. You've got a plane ride to Calcutta."

My teeth rattled while the rolling box jolted along the airport road. I had been seeing Jeeps for a week but still they looked—and felt—unreal.

Across the Bay of Bengal I flew to India. In Calcutta's Great Eastern Hotel I met, by chance, Lieutenant Colonel B. C. Bowker, public relations officer for the party of John J. McCloy, then United States Assistant Secretary of War and later president of the International Bank for Reconstruction and Development, known as the World Bank. Bowker introduced me to McCloy who was flying around the world inspecting American war theaters. He offered to take me home. Few things could have pleased me more The trip would retrace the journey I had taken in the opposite direction so long ago . . . up through China, over to Japan and across the Pacific . . . and bring me home just six years after my departure.

We left Calcutta, flew over the green hell that is upper Burma, hopped The Hump to Kunming and went on to China's war time capital, Chungking. There I walked into the Press Hostel, rickety haven for correspondents, where I had stayed a few days in 1942 after escaping from Shanghai. Maurice Votaw, doyen of the place, gaped as at a ghost, saying,

"You're dead, at least we thought you were."

Hugh Baillie, president of United Press, was interviewing Chiang Kai-shek at the Generalissimo's residence where the McCloy party stopped overnight.

"We had written you off," said Baillie. "After your folks received a P.O.W. card from you in 1943 we checked Tokyo through the International Red Cross and were informed that your name no longer was on the roster of internees in Sumatra. To us that meant you had died."

"I'll sure enjoy reading my obituary," I said.

Baillie laughed, and said, "You won't have any trouble finding it."

We took off for Shanghai. As the mountains disappeared beneath us and we found ourselves above China's coastal plain, I spotted Lake Tai and the thin lines that were the railroad and highway across which Martin, Lee and I had escaped to Free China in the Christmas-New Year season of 1941–42. In Shanghai I was greeted again as a man from the grave.

"It can't be you," said the priest who had loaned me his Christmas collection to finance our escape. "You were killed in Java."

"It's my ghost," I said, "come to return your loan."

Northward flew McCloy's plane over familiar country which first unrolled beneath my eyes from a passenger plane in 1941. Rivers, lakes and canals glistened in the great delta that is coastal China. In late afternoon we sighted China's northern mountains and soon were over the walled ramparts of majestic Peiping which lies just south of the mountains at the edge of the plain. Instead of landing immediately at Peiping we continued on in order to wing along the Great Wall, following its endless writhings westward over barren, sunbaked mountains which stretch into infinity like burned, brown waves in a boundless sea.

Hardly a better time of day could have been chosen for viewing that ancient Wonder of the World. A lowering sun in a bronze-blue sky etched in bold relief the desolate, windswept mountains that form a natural northern barrier to the China plains. The Wall twists along the very crest of the east-west chain, topping peaks, descending precipitous slopes and ascending cliff-like gradients. At intervals are lonely watch towers from which once might have sped arrows into besieging hordes.

Parts of the wall have crumbled and look as though a man easily could climb over the rubble, but we saw few such places. The wall had been rebuilt and repaired through the centuries. Most of what we saw stands as firmly as when Shih Huang-ti began it 2,100 years ago. Even from our height the wall looked high, wide, massive, formidable. Occasionally, where it crosses the floors of narrow canyons or high defiles, are gates through which pass tortuous ribbons that are caravan trails. Through one gate a truck crowded a string of camels, outward bound.

It has been said that China's Great Wall is the only man-made thing on earth which could be seen from Mars. Only a few days previously, at the southern end of China, we had stood on the terminus of another man-made wonder—the incredible, 2,200 mile oil pipe line from Calcutta to Kunming.

On that occasion the McCloy party had been driven from teeming Kunming to the quiet hillside that once was a Chinese cemetery and now held the tanks and valves marking the end of the mighty line which stretched southward toward the canyons of The Hump and disappeared like an interminable snake wriggling through the hills. As we had gazed on the line, thinking of what it represented, a member of our party, Dr. Douglas S. Freeman, Pulitzer Prize biographer of General Robert E. Lee, remarked,

"This is an historic spot in the logistics of war."

I had wondered how long the line would last and for whom it would be used, if at all, now that the war which caused it was finished.

At opposite ends of China man had wrought wonders with steel and stone. The Great Wall had been another historic landmark in the logistics of war.

When the pipeline has disappeared so completely it no longer even is a footnote in China's history, the Wall will still be there. And when the Wall is gone, consumed by Time, what will remain? The souls of the builders. Thoughts. Words. Only the non-material is permanent. If the Wall could talk would it weep or laugh at men who tried to keep other men behind a wall?

After Peiping, Japan was our next stop. McCloy's itinerary included an examination of Omori Camp on the shores of Yokohama Bay where Allied prisoners had suffered through the war. Now it held high ranking Japanese scheduled for war crimes trials. Here, I thought as we entered, is my chance to inspect row on row of the kind of men who once inspected me. Obviously cleaned and repaired since Allied prisoners vacated, Omori was nearly empty and neat as a pin. Only twenty-four Japanese had been collected in it thus far and they were comfortably ensconced with mats and blankets in wooden barracks. The officer in charge said that the new Japanese prisoners were given exactly the same blankets and food that were given to Allied prisoners.

"The only difference," he said, "is that we keep the place clean."

Seated at a desk, writing, was a man of familiar figure and visage. A member of our party, Marine Corps Colonel Chauncey G. Parker, Jr., startled at meeting face to face the one man whom he had never expected to see, exclaimed,

"Tojo!"

Japan's once supreme war lord and Premier, who vainly had attempted suicide and was now recovered, bowed his head slightly and replied,

"Tojo! Yes!"

General Homma of the Bataan Death March was there; and also General Kenji Doihara, that arch conspirator of North China intrigue.

"How does this compare with your Sumatra camps?" asked Lieutenant Colonel Bowker.

"It is nearly a palace," I told him.

At Eighth Army headquarters I saw my first American soldiers on parade since the Marines left Shanghai in 1941, just before the curtain fell on the white man's era in China. While the band played "The Old Grey Mare," young men in khaki strode by, their arms swinging rhythmically, their feet in solid step, their helmeted heads high, and over them the colors flying. The thrill of pride as I watched was something akin to the stir of patriotism on that Fourth of July, 1942, in Palembang Jail when black-bearded Allen raised his tin cup and said,

"Gentlemen, I give you the President of the United States of America. . . ."

Almost everywhere the plane stopped along the way— Chungking, Shanghai, Peiping—friends who had greeted me as one returned from the dead, in their next breath would tell me of some friend or acquaintance of pre-war days who was dead beyond doubt. It was the same in Tokyo. There I learned for certain that of the six correspondents who had remained in Java to cover the last days of fighting on that beleaguered island in March, 1942, only one survived. Me. The fate of another I already knew because we had looked at death together and he lost. DeWitt Hancock, of Associated Press, went down with the ship on which I was sunk in the Indian Ocean. The other four correspondents, three Englishmen and an Australian, simply disappeared when Java fell.

As McCloy's plane flew from Tokyo to Iwo Jima I thought of those correspondents who were not coming home. They were gone now, every one, along with Allen and Colijn and Father Bakker and all those others lying beneath the pepper trees of Bangka and the rubber trees of Sumatra.

The plane landed at Iwo Jima and in a little while I was standing where the Marines had raised the flag atop Mt. Suribachi, leaning into the stiff Pacific wind which whips eternally over that great pile of dead volcanic spew, and gazing over Iwo Jima's blood soaked desolation. So many others had died here too, thousands of them, American and Japanese. And this was only a little, sulphurous, surf beaten island . . . a cinderous pin point in the war I had come East to cover and missed. I felt empty inside at having missed so much. Yet, with the emptiness there was an indefinable sense of fulfillment. A feeling of loss coupled with one of gain. As though a part of me had died giving birth to another life.

I had been in a different kind of war, a battle of souls and minds instead of bullets and bombs. During the fighting I had explored the heart of my fellow man but, most important of all, I had searched my own soul and found myself. The missing years had not been a total loss.

I felt that the Lord had been with me at various times and places of that circuit of the unfathomable which is Asia—from the day the Japanese occupied Shanghai to this moment standing on Suribachi's summit and wondering how the Marines ever scaled it in the face of fire.

I thought of Father Bakker's request for a special prayer should I ever reach Iwo Jima, so I said it while looking down on the ugliness of East Beach. The prayer was for him and for the Japanese, as he had asked. I added a few thanksgivings too . . . thanksgivings for the indomitable courage that took Marines up Suribachi's sides, and for another kind of courage that shone in such widely different ways as—

The words of the poem quoted by Churchill.

The plea of Bishop Mekkelholt in behalf of a man I despised, "Please give him the quinine, Mac. It is not for you or me to judge the value of a life."

The request of a dying priest to pray for the men who killed him.

As I gazed over battle-scarred Iwo Jima and thought of all it represented in the turbulent affairs of men, I realized what I had learned during the missing years—the only answer to war. Father Bakker and the Bishop had lived the answer, because they had lived the commandments: "Thou shalt love the Lord thy God with thy whole heart and with thy whole soul and with thy whole mind . . . and . . . thy neighbor as thyself."

Conference tables and peace treaties and international covenants mean nothing as long as one man hates another. If I hate the Japanese because of what happened in Sumatra, or if they hate me because my country crushed them, there can be no peace, only a truce.

The first job is to stop hating. But hate does not cease because it is willed to cease. Something else just as solid and powerful has to push out hate and fill the place it occupied. That is the biggest and the hardest job—filling the vacancy with positive action. For the replacement must live and breathe and burn as fiercely for the good of man as does hate for his destruction. What shall we call the replacement? Christ called it love.

If I can get on my knees tonight and, with a full heart, pray,

"God, please help Seki and his interpreter—and have mercy on Tojo, too,"

Then my private battle against hate is half won. The other half will be continuing in this prayer every day. When all the men of all the earth do that for one another there will be no more war. And until they do, war is inevitable.

There is no possible disarmament except in the hearts of men.

INDEX